C-41   CAREER EXAMINATION SERIES

This is your
PASSBOOK for...

Assistant Housing Manager

Test Preparation Study Guide
Questions & Answers

NATIONAL LEARNING CORPORATION®

COPYRIGHT NOTICE

This book is SOLELY intended for, is sold ONLY to, and its use is RESTRICTED to individual, bona fide applicants or candidates who qualify by virtue of having seriously filed applications for appropriate license, certificate, professional and/or promotional advancement, higher school matriculation, scholarship, or other legitimate requirements of education and/or governmental authorities.

This book is NOT intended for use, class instruction, tutoring, training, duplication, copying, reprinting, excerption, or adaptation, etc., by:

1) Other publishers
2) Proprietors and/or Instructors of "Coaching" and/or Preparatory Courses
3) Personnel and/or Training Divisions of commercial, industrial, and governmental organizations
4) Schools, colleges, or universities and/or their departments and staffs, including teachers and other personnel
5) Testing Agencies or Bureaus
6) Study groups which seek by the purchase of a single volume to copy and/or duplicate and/or adapt this material for use by the group as a whole without having purchased individual volumes for each of the members of the group
7) Et al.

Such persons would be in violation of appropriate Federal and State statutes.

PROVISION OF LICENSING AGREEMENTS – Recognized educational, commercial, industrial, and governmental institutions and organizations, and others legitimately engaged in educational pursuits, including training, testing, and measurement activities, may address request for a licensing agreement to the copyright owners, who will determine whether, and under what conditions, including fees and charges, the materials in this book may be used them. In other words, a licensing facility exists for the legitimate use of the material in this book on other than an individual basis. However, it is asseverated and affirmed here that the material in this book CANNOT be used without the receipt of the express permission of such a licensing agreement from the Publishers. Inquiries re licensing should be addressed to the company, attention rights and permissions department.

All rights reserved, including the right of reproduction in whole or in part, in any form or by any means, electronic or mechanical, including photocopying, recording, or by any information storage and retrieval system, without permission in writing from the Publisher.

Copyright © 2024 by
National Learning Corporation

212 Michael Drive, Syosset, NY 11791
(516) 921-8888 • www.passbooks.com
E-mail: info@passbooks.com

PUBLISHED IN THE UNITED STATES OF AMERICA

PASSBOOK® SERIES

THE *PASSBOOK® SERIES* has been created to prepare applicants and candidates for the ultimate academic battlefield – the examination room.

At some time in our lives, each and every one of us may be required to take an examination – for validation, matriculation, admission, qualification, registration, certification, or licensure.

Based on the assumption that every applicant or candidate has met the basic formal educational standards, has taken the required number of courses, and read the necessary texts, the *PASSBOOK® SERIES* furnishes the one special preparation which may assure passing with confidence, instead of failing with insecurity. Examination questions – together with answers – are furnished as the basic vehicle for study so that the mysteries of the examination and its compounding difficulties may be eliminated or diminished by a sure method.

This book is meant to help you pass your examination provided that you qualify and are serious in your objective.

The entire field is reviewed through the huge store of content information which is succinctly presented through a provocative and challenging approach – the question-and-answer method.

A climate of success is established by furnishing the correct answers at the end of each test.

You soon learn to recognize types of questions, forms of questions, and patterns of questioning. You may even begin to anticipate expected outcomes.

You perceive that many questions are repeated or adapted so that you can gain acute insights, which may enable you to score many sure points.

You learn how to confront new questions, or types of questions, and to attack them confidently and work out the correct answers.

You note objectives and emphases, and recognize pitfalls and dangers, so that you may make positive educational adjustments.

Moreover, you are kept fully informed in relation to new concepts, methods, practices, and directions in the field.

You discover that you are actually taking the examination all the time: you are preparing for the examination by "taking" an examination, not by reading extraneous and/or supererogatory textbooks.

In short, this PASSBOOK®, used directedly, should be an important factor in helping you to pass your test.

ASSISTANT HOUSING MANAGER

DUTIES AND RESPONSIBILITIES
Under direction, performs managerial work of moderate difficulty and responsibility in the administration of the public housing programs; performs related work.

EXAMPLES OF TYPICAL TASKS
Manages a small housing project or clearance site; assists the manager of a large project, or a group of projects, or a large or difficult clearance site in the management of the project or site, including the handling of tenant and community relations and recreational activities; secures public and private agency cooperation; supervises project personnel and controls the assignments of apartments and the collection of rents; keeps records and accounts; prepares reports; may supervise the operation of a small administrative unit.

TESTS
The written test will be of the multiple-choice type and may include questions on: project office management and managerial aspects of maintenance; employee training, evaluation, and supervision, and general administration; tenant, community and public relations; comprehension and communication of pertinent written material, including mathematical concepts; interrelationships with other housing authority departments, governmental agencies, and governmental housing programs; and other related areas including written comprehension, written expression, concern for others, teamwork, integrity and self-control.

HOW TO TAKE A TEST

I. YOU MUST PASS AN EXAMINATION

A. WHAT EVERY CANDIDATE SHOULD KNOW

Examination applicants often ask us for help in preparing for the written test. What can I study in advance? What kinds of questions will be asked? How will the test be given? How will the papers be graded?

As an applicant for a civil service examination, you may be wondering about some of these things. Our purpose here is to suggest effective methods of advance study and to describe civil service examinations.

Your chances for success on this examination can be increased if you know how to prepare. Those "pre-examination jitters" can be reduced if you know what to expect. You can even experience an adventure in good citizenship if you know why civil service exams are given.

B. WHY ARE CIVIL SERVICE EXAMINATIONS GIVEN?

Civil service examinations are important to you in two ways. As a citizen, you want public jobs filled by employees who know how to do their work. As a job seeker, you want a fair chance to compete for that job on an equal footing with other candidates. The best-known means of accomplishing this two-fold goal is the competitive examination.

Exams are widely publicized throughout the nation. They may be administered for jobs in federal, state, city, municipal, town or village governments or agencies.

Any citizen may apply, with some limitations, such as the age or residence of applicants. Your experience and education may be reviewed to see whether you meet the requirements for the particular examination. When these requirements exist, they are reasonable and applied consistently to all applicants. Thus, a competitive examination may cause you some uneasiness now, but it is your privilege and safeguard.

C. HOW ARE CIVIL SERVICE EXAMS DEVELOPED?

Examinations are carefully written by trained technicians who are specialists in the field known as "psychological measurement," in consultation with recognized authorities in the field of work that the test will cover. These experts recommend the subject matter areas or skills to be tested; only those knowledges or skills important to your success on the job are included. The most reliable books and source materials available are used as references. Together, the experts and technicians judge the difficulty level of the questions.

Test technicians know how to phrase questions so that the problem is clearly stated. Their ethics do not permit "trick" or "catch" questions. Questions may have been tried out on sample groups, or subjected to statistical analysis, to determine their usefulness.

Written tests are often used in combination with performance tests, ratings of training and experience, and oral interviews. All of these measures combine to form the best-known means of finding the right person for the right job.

II. HOW TO PASS THE WRITTEN TEST

A. NATURE OF THE EXAMINATION

To prepare intelligently for civil service examinations, you should know how they differ from school examinations you have taken. In school you were assigned certain definite pages to read or subjects to cover. The examination questions were quite detailed and usually emphasized memory. Civil service exams, on the other hand, try to discover your present ability to perform the duties of a position, plus your potentiality to learn these duties. In other words, a civil service exam attempts to predict how successful you will be. Questions cover such a broad area that they cannot be as minute and detailed as school exam questions.

In the public service similar kinds of work, or positions, are grouped together in one "class." This process is known as *position-classification*. All the positions in a class are paid according to the salary range for that class. One class title covers all of these positions, and they are all tested by the same examination.

B. FOUR BASIC STEPS

1) Study the announcement

How, then, can you know what subjects to study? Our best answer is: "Learn as much as possible about the class of positions for which you've applied." The exam will test the knowledge, skills and abilities needed to do the work.

Your most valuable source of information about the position you want is the official exam announcement. This announcement lists the training and experience qualifications. Check these standards and apply only if you come reasonably close to meeting them.

The brief description of the position in the examination announcement offers some clues to the subjects which will be tested. Think about the job itself. Review the duties in your mind. Can you perform them, or are there some in which you are rusty? Fill in the blank spots in your preparation.

Many jurisdictions preview the written test in the exam announcement by including a section called "Knowledge and Abilities Required," "Scope of the Examination," or some similar heading. Here you will find out specifically what fields will be tested.

2) Review your own background

Once you learn in general what the position is all about, and what you need to know to do the work, ask yourself which subjects you already know fairly well and which need improvement. You may wonder whether to concentrate on improving your strong areas or on building some background in your fields of weakness. When the announcement has specified "some knowledge" or "considerable knowledge," or has used adjectives like "beginning principles of..." or "advanced ... methods," you can get a clue as to the number and difficulty of questions to be asked in any given field. More questions, and hence broader coverage, would be included for those subjects which are more important in the work. Now weigh your strengths and weaknesses against the job requirements and prepare accordingly.

3) Determine the level of the position

Another way to tell how intensively you should prepare is to understand the level of the job for which you are applying. Is it the entering level? In other words, is this the position in which beginners in a field of work are hired? Or is it an intermediate or advanced level? Sometimes this is indicated by such words as "Junior" or "Senior" in the class title. Other jurisdictions use Roman numerals to designate the level – Clerk I, Clerk II, for example. The word "Supervisor" sometimes appears in the title. If the level is not indicated by the title, check the description of duties. Will you be working under very close supervision, or will you have responsibility for independent decisions in this work?

4) Choose appropriate study materials

Now that you know the subjects to be examined and the relative amount of each subject to be covered, you can choose suitable study materials. For beginning level jobs, or even advanced ones, if you have a pronounced weakness in some aspect of your training, read a modern, standard textbook in that field. Be sure it is up to date and has general coverage. Such books are normally available at your library, and the librarian will be glad to help you locate one. For entry-level positions, questions of appropriate difficulty are chosen – neither highly advanced questions, nor those too simple. Such questions require careful thought but not advanced training.

If the position for which you are applying is technical or advanced, you will read more advanced, specialized material. If you are already familiar with the basic principles of your field, elementary textbooks would waste your time. Concentrate on advanced textbooks and technical periodicals. Think through the concepts and review difficult problems in your field.

These are all general sources. You can get more ideas on your own initiative, following these leads. For example, training manuals and publications of the government agency which employs workers in your field can be useful, particularly for technical and professional positions. A letter or visit to the government department involved may result in more specific study suggestions, and certainly will provide you with a more definite idea of the exact nature of the position you are seeking.

III. KINDS OF TESTS

Tests are used for purposes other than measuring knowledge and ability to perform specified duties. For some positions, it is equally important to test ability to make adjustments to new situations or to profit from training. In others, basic mental abilities not dependent on information are essential. Questions which test these things may not appear as pertinent to the duties of the position as those which test for knowledge and information. Yet they are often highly important parts of a fair examination. For very general questions, it is almost impossible to help you direct your study efforts. What we can do is to point out some of the more common of these general abilities needed in public service positions and describe some typical questions.

1) General information

Broad, general information has been found useful for predicting job success in some kinds of work. This is tested in a variety of ways, from vocabulary lists to questions about current events. Basic background in some field of work, such as sociology or economics, may be sampled in a group of questions. Often these are principles which have become familiar to most persons through exposure rather than through formal training. It is difficult to advise you how to study for these questions; being alert to the world around you is our best suggestion.

2) Verbal ability

An example of an ability needed in many positions is verbal or language ability. Verbal ability is, in brief, the ability to use and understand words. Vocabulary and grammar tests are typical measures of this ability. Reading comprehension or paragraph interpretation questions are common in many kinds of civil service tests. You are given a paragraph of written material and asked to find its central meaning.

3) Numerical ability

Number skills can be tested by the familiar arithmetic problem, by checking paired lists of numbers to see which are alike and which are different, or by interpreting charts and graphs. In the latter test, a graph may be printed in the test booklet which you are asked to use as the basis for answering questions.

4) Observation

A popular test for law-enforcement positions is the observation test. A picture is shown to you for several minutes, then taken away. Questions about the picture test your ability to observe both details and larger elements.

5) Following directions

In many positions in the public service, the employee must be able to carry out written instructions dependably and accurately. You may be given a chart with several columns, each column listing a variety of information. The questions require you to carry out directions involving the information given in the chart.

6) Skills and aptitudes

Performance tests effectively measure some manual skills and aptitudes. When the skill is one in which you are trained, such as typing or shorthand, you can practice. These tests are often very much like those given in business school or high school courses. For many of the other skills and aptitudes, however, no short-time preparation can be made. Skills and abilities natural to you or that you have developed throughout your lifetime are being tested.

Many of the general questions just described provide all the data needed to answer the questions and ask you to use your reasoning ability to find the answers. Your best preparation for these tests, as well as for tests of facts and ideas, is to be at your physical and mental best. You, no doubt, have your own methods of getting into an exam-taking mood and keeping "in shape." The next section lists some ideas on this subject.

IV. KINDS OF QUESTIONS

Only rarely is the "essay" question, which you answer in narrative form, used in civil service tests. Civil service tests are usually of the short-answer type. Full instructions for answering these questions will be given to you at the examination. But in case this is your first experience with short-answer questions and separate answer sheets, here is what you need to know:

1) Multiple-choice Questions

Most popular of the short-answer questions is the "multiple choice" or "best answer" question. It can be used, for example, to test for factual knowledge, ability to solve problems or judgment in meeting situations found at work.

A multiple-choice question is normally one of three types—
- It can begin with an incomplete statement followed by several possible endings. You are to find the one ending which *best* completes the statement, although some of the others may not be entirely wrong.
- It can also be a complete statement in the form of a question which is answered by choosing one of the statements listed.

- It can be in the form of a problem – again you select the best answer.

Here is an example of a multiple-choice question with a discussion which should give you some clues as to the method for choosing the right answer:

When an employee has a complaint about his assignment, the action which will *best* help him overcome his difficulty is to
    A. discuss his difficulty with his coworkers
    B. take the problem to the head of the organization
    C. take the problem to the person who gave him the assignment
    D. say nothing to anyone about his complaint

In answering this question, you should study each of the choices to find which is best. Consider choice "A" – Certainly an employee may discuss his complaint with fellow employees, but no change or improvement can result, and the complaint remains unresolved. Choice "B" is a poor choice since the head of the organization probably does not know what assignment you have been given, and taking your problem to him is known as "going over the head" of the supervisor. The supervisor, or person who made the assignment, is the person who can clarify it or correct any injustice. Choice "C" is, therefore, correct. To say nothing, as in choice "D," is unwise. Supervisors have and interest in knowing the problems employees are facing, and the employee is seeking a solution to his problem.

2) True/False Questions

The "true/false" or "right/wrong" form of question is sometimes used. Here a complete statement is given. Your job is to decide whether the statement is right or wrong.

SAMPLE: A roaming cell-phone call to a nearby city costs less than a non-roaming call to a distant city.

This statement is wrong, or false, since roaming calls are more expensive.

This is not a complete list of all possible question forms, although most of the others are variations of these common types. You will always get complete directions for answering questions. Be sure you understand *how* to mark your answers – ask questions until you do.

V. RECORDING YOUR ANSWERS

Computer terminals are used more and more today for many different kinds of exams.
For an examination with very few applicants, you may be told to record your answers in the test booklet itself. Separate answer sheets are much more common. If this separate answer sheet is to be scored by machine – and this is often the case – it is highly important that you mark your answers correctly in order to get credit.
An electronic scoring machine is often used in civil service offices because of the speed with which papers can be scored. Machine-scored answer sheets must be marked with a pencil, which will be given to you. This pencil has a high graphite content which responds to the electronic scoring machine. As a matter of fact, stray dots may register as answers, so do not let your pencil rest on the answer sheet while you are pondering the correct answer. Also, if your pencil lead breaks or is otherwise defective, ask for another.

Since the answer sheet will be dropped in a slot in the scoring machine, be careful not to bend the corners or get the paper crumpled.

The answer sheet normally has five vertical columns of numbers, with 30 numbers to a column. These numbers correspond to the question numbers in your test booklet. After each number, going across the page are four or five pairs of dotted lines. These short dotted lines have small letters or numbers above them. The first two pairs may also have a "T" or "F" above the letters. This indicates that the first two pairs only are to be used if the questions are of the true-false type. If the questions are multiple choice, disregard the "T" and "F" and pay attention only to the small letters or numbers.

Answer your questions in the manner of the sample that follows:

32. The largest city in the United States is
    A. Washington, D.C.
    B. New York City
    C. Chicago
    D. Detroit
    E. San Francisco

1) Choose the answer you think is best. (New York City is the largest, so "B" is correct.)
2) Find the row of dotted lines numbered the same as the question you are answering. (Find row number 32)
3) Find the pair of dotted lines corresponding to the answer. (Find the pair of lines under the mark "B.")
4) Make a solid black mark between the dotted lines.

VI. BEFORE THE TEST

Common sense will help you find procedures to follow to get ready for an examination. Too many of us, however, overlook these sensible measures. Indeed, nervousness and fatigue have been found to be the most serious reasons why applicants fail to do their best on civil service tests. Here is a list of reminders:

- Begin your preparation early – Don't wait until the last minute to go scurrying around for books and materials or to find out what the position is all about.
- Prepare continuously – An hour a night for a week is better than an all-night cram session. This has been definitely established. What is more, a night a week for a month will return better dividends than crowding your study into a shorter period of time.
- Locate the place of the exam – You have been sent a notice telling you when and where to report for the examination. If the location is in a different town or otherwise unfamiliar to you, it would be well to inquire the best route and learn something about the building.
- Relax the night before the test – Allow your mind to rest. Do not study at all that night. Plan some mild recreation or diversion; then go to bed early and get a good night's sleep.
- Get up early enough to make a leisurely trip to the place for the test – This way unforeseen events, traffic snarls, unfamiliar buildings, etc. will not upset you.
- Dress comfortably – A written test is not a fashion show. You will be known by number and not by name, so wear something comfortable.

- Leave excess paraphernalia at home – Shopping bags and odd bundles will get in your way. You need bring only the items mentioned in the official notice you received; usually everything you need is provided. Do not bring reference books to the exam. They will only confuse those last minutes and be taken away from you when in the test room.
- Arrive somewhat ahead of time – If because of transportation schedules you must get there very early, bring a newspaper or magazine to take your mind off yourself while waiting.
- Locate the examination room – When you have found the proper room, you will be directed to the seat or part of the room where you will sit. Sometimes you are given a sheet of instructions to read while you are waiting. Do not fill out any forms until you are told to do so; just read them and be prepared.
- Relax and prepare to listen to the instructions
- If you have any physical problem that may keep you from doing your best, be sure to tell the test administrator. If you are sick or in poor health, you really cannot do your best on the exam. You can come back and take the test some other time.

VII. AT THE TEST

The day of the test is here and you have the test booklet in your hand. The temptation to get going is very strong. Caution! There is more to success than knowing the right answers. You must know how to identify your papers and understand variations in the type of short-answer question used in this particular examination. Follow these suggestions for maximum results from your efforts:

1) Cooperate with the monitor
The test administrator has a duty to create a situation in which you can be as much at ease as possible. He will give instructions, tell you when to begin, check to see that you are marking your answer sheet correctly, and so on. He is not there to guard you, although he will see that your competitors do not take unfair advantage. He wants to help you do your best.

2) Listen to all instructions
Don't jump the gun! Wait until you understand all directions. In most civil service tests you get more time than you need to answer the questions. So don't be in a hurry. Read each word of instructions until you clearly understand the meaning. Study the examples, listen to all announcements and follow directions. Ask questions if you do not understand what to do.

3) Identify your papers
Civil service exams are usually identified by number only. You will be assigned a number; you must not put your name on your test papers. Be sure to copy your number correctly. Since more than one exam may be given, copy your exact examination title.

4) Plan your time
Unless you are told that a test is a "speed" or "rate of work" test, speed itself is usually not important. Time enough to answer all the questions will be provided, but this does not mean that you have all day. An overall time limit has been set. Divide the total time (in minutes) by the number of questions to determine the approximate time you have for each question.

5) Do not linger over difficult questions

If you come across a difficult question, mark it with a paper clip (useful to have along) and come back to it when you have been through the booklet. One caution if you do this – be sure to skip a number on your answer sheet as well. Check often to be sure that you have not lost your place and that you are marking in the row numbered the same as the question you are answering.

6) Read the questions

Be sure you know what the question asks! Many capable people are unsuccessful because they failed to *read* the questions correctly.

7) Answer all questions

Unless you have been instructed that a penalty will be deducted for incorrect answers, it is better to guess than to omit a question.

8) Speed tests

It is often better NOT to guess on speed tests. It has been found that on timed tests people are tempted to spend the last few seconds before time is called in marking answers at random – without even reading them – in the hope of picking up a few extra points. To discourage this practice, the instructions may warn you that your score will be "corrected" for guessing. That is, a penalty will be applied. The incorrect answers will be deducted from the correct ones, or some other penalty formula will be used.

9) Review your answers

If you finish before time is called, go back to the questions you guessed or omitted to give them further thought. Review other answers if you have time.

10) Return your test materials

If you are ready to leave before others have finished or time is called, take ALL your materials to the monitor and leave quietly. Never take any test material with you. The monitor can discover whose papers are not complete, and taking a test booklet may be grounds for disqualification.

VIII. EXAMINATION TECHNIQUES

1) Read the general instructions carefully. These are usually printed on the first page of the exam booklet. As a rule, these instructions refer to the timing of the examination; the fact that you should not start work until the signal and must stop work at a signal, etc. If there are any *special* instructions, such as a choice of questions to be answered, make sure that you note this instruction carefully.

2) When you are ready to start work on the examination, that is as soon as the signal has been given, read the instructions to each question booklet, underline any key words or phrases, such as *least, best, outline, describe* and the like. In this way you will tend to answer as requested rather than discover on reviewing your paper that you *listed without describing*, that you selected the *worst* choice rather than the *best* choice, etc.

3) If the examination is of the objective or multiple-choice type – that is, each question will also give a series of possible answers: A, B, C or D, and you are called upon to select the best answer and write the letter next to that answer on your answer paper – it is advisable to start answering each question in turn. There may be anywhere from 50 to 100 such questions in the three or four hours allotted and you can see how much time would be taken if you read through all the questions before beginning to answer any. Furthermore, if you come across a question or group of questions which you know would be difficult to answer, it would undoubtedly affect your handling of all the other questions.

4) If the examination is of the essay type and contains but a few questions, it is a moot point as to whether you should read all the questions before starting to answer any one. Of course, if you are given a choice – say five out of seven and the like – then it is essential to read all the questions so you can eliminate the two that are most difficult. If, however, you are asked to answer all the questions, there may be danger in trying to answer the easiest one first because you may find that you will spend too much time on it. The best technique is to answer the first question, then proceed to the second, etc.

5) Time your answers. Before the exam begins, write down the time it started, then add the time allowed for the examination and write down the time it must be completed, then divide the time available somewhat as follows:
   - If 3-1/2 hours are allowed, that would be 210 minutes. If you have 80 objective-type questions, that would be an average of 2-1/2 minutes per question. Allow yourself no more than 2 minutes per question, or a total of 160 minutes, which will permit about 50 minutes to review.
   - If for the time allotment of 210 minutes there are 7 essay questions to answer, that would average about 30 minutes a question. Give yourself only 25 minutes per question so that you have about 35 minutes to review.

6) The most important instruction is to *read each question* and make sure you know what is wanted. The second most important instruction is to *time yourself properly* so that you answer every question. The third most important instruction is to *answer every question*. Guess if you have to but include something for each question. Remember that you will receive no credit for a blank and will probably receive some credit if you write something in answer to an essay question. If you guess a letter – say "B" for a multiple-choice question – you may have guessed right. If you leave a blank as an answer to a multiple-choice question, the examiners may respect your feelings but it will not add a point to your score. Some exams may penalize you for wrong answers, so in such cases *only*, you may not want to guess unless you have some basis for your answer.

7) Suggestions
   a. Objective-type questions
      1. Examine the question booklet for proper sequence of pages and questions
      2. Read all instructions carefully
      3. Skip any question which seems too difficult; return to it after all other questions have been answered
      4. Apportion your time properly; do not spend too much time on any single question or group of questions

5. Note and underline key words – *all, most, fewest, least, best, worst, same, opposite,* etc.
6. Pay particular attention to negatives
7. Note unusual option, e.g., unduly long, short, complex, different or similar in content to the body of the question
8. Observe the use of "hedging" words – *probably, may, most likely,* etc.
9. Make sure that your answer is put next to the same number as the question
10. Do not second-guess unless you have good reason to believe the second answer is definitely more correct
11. Cross out original answer if you decide another answer is more accurate; do not erase until you are ready to hand your paper in
12. Answer all questions; guess unless instructed otherwise
13. Leave time for review

   b. Essay questions
   1. Read each question carefully
   2. Determine exactly what is wanted. Underline key words or phrases.
   3. Decide on outline or paragraph answer
   4. Include many different points and elements unless asked to develop any one or two points or elements
   5. Show impartiality by giving pros and cons unless directed to select one side only
   6. Make and write down any assumptions you find necessary to answer the questions
   7. Watch your English, grammar, punctuation and choice of words
   8. Time your answers; don't crowd material

8) Answering the essay question

Most essay questions can be answered by framing the specific response around several key words or ideas. Here are a few such key words or ideas:

M's: manpower, materials, methods, money, management
P's: purpose, program, policy, plan, procedure, practice, problems, pitfalls, personnel, public relations

   a. Six basic steps in handling problems:
   1. Preliminary plan and background development
   2. Collect information, data and facts
   3. Analyze and interpret information, data and facts
   4. Analyze and develop solutions as well as make recommendations
   5. Prepare report and sell recommendations
   6. Install recommendations and follow up effectiveness

   b. Pitfalls to avoid
   1. *Taking things for granted* – A statement of the situation does not necessarily imply that each of the elements is necessarily true; for example, a complaint may be invalid and biased so that all that can be taken for granted is that a complaint has been registered

2. *Considering only one side of a situation* – Wherever possible, indicate several alternatives and then point out the reasons you selected the best one
3. *Failing to indicate follow up* – Whenever your answer indicates action on your part, make certain that you will take proper follow-up action to see how successful your recommendations, procedures or actions turn out to be
4. *Taking too long in answering any single question* – Remember to time your answers properly

IX. AFTER THE TEST

Scoring procedures differ in detail among civil service jurisdictions although the general principles are the same. Whether the papers are hand-scored or graded by machine we have described, they are nearly always graded by number. That is, the person who marks the paper knows only the number – never the name – of the applicant. Not until all the papers have been graded will they be matched with names. If other tests, such as training and experience or oral interview ratings have been given, scores will be combined. Different parts of the examination usually have different weights. For example, the written test might count 60 percent of the final grade, and a rating of training and experience 40 percent. In many jurisdictions, veterans will have a certain number of points added to their grades.

After the final grade has been determined, the names are placed in grade order and an eligible list is established. There are various methods for resolving ties between those who get the same final grade – probably the most common is to place first the name of the person whose application was received first. Job offers are made from the eligible list in the order the names appear on it. You will be notified of your grade and your rank as soon as all these computations have been made. This will be done as rapidly as possible.

People who are found to meet the requirements in the announcement are called "eligibles." Their names are put on a list of eligible candidates. An eligible's chances of getting a job depend on how high he stands on this list and how fast agencies are filling jobs from the list.

When a job is to be filled from a list of eligibles, the agency asks for the names of people on the list of eligibles for that job. When the civil service commission receives this request, it sends to the agency the names of the three people highest on this list. Or, if the job to be filled has specialized requirements, the office sends the agency the names of the top three persons who meet these requirements from the general list.

The appointing officer makes a choice from among the three people whose names were sent to him. If the selected person accepts the appointment, the names of the others are put back on the list to be considered for future openings.

That is the rule in hiring from all kinds of eligible lists, whether they are for typist, carpenter, chemist, or something else. For every vacancy, the appointing officer has his choice of any one of the top three eligibles on the list. This explains why the person whose name is on top of the list sometimes does not get an appointment when some of the persons lower on the list do. If the appointing officer chooses the second or third eligible, the No. 1 eligible does not get a job at once, but stays on the list until he is appointed or the list is terminated.

X. HOW TO PASS THE INTERVIEW TEST

The examination for which you applied requires an oral interview test. You have already taken the written test and you are now being called for the interview test – the final part of the formal examination.

You may think that it is not possible to prepare for an interview test and that there are no procedures to follow during an interview. Our purpose is to point out some things you can do in advance that will help you and some good rules to follow and pitfalls to avoid while you are being interviewed.

What is an interview supposed to test?

The written examination is designed to test the technical knowledge and competence of the candidate; the oral is designed to evaluate intangible qualities, not readily measured otherwise, and to establish a list showing the relative fitness of each candidate – as measured against his competitors – for the position sought. Scoring is not on the basis of "right" and "wrong," but on a sliding scale of values ranging from "not passable" to "outstanding." As a matter of fact, it is possible to achieve a relatively low score without a single "incorrect" answer because of evident weakness in the qualities being measured.

Occasionally, an examination may consist entirely of an oral test – either an individual or a group oral. In such cases, information is sought concerning the technical knowledges and abilities of the candidate, since there has been no written examination for this purpose. More commonly, however, an oral test is used to supplement a written examination.

Who conducts interviews?

The composition of oral boards varies among different jurisdictions. In nearly all, a representative of the personnel department serves as chairman. One of the members of the board may be a representative of the department in which the candidate would work. In some cases, "outside experts" are used, and, frequently, a businessman or some other representative of the general public is asked to serve. Labor and management or other special groups may be represented. The aim is to secure the services of experts in the appropriate field.

However the board is composed, it is a good idea (and not at all improper or unethical) to ascertain in advance of the interview who the members are and what groups they represent. When you are introduced to them, you will have some idea of their backgrounds and interests, and at least you will not stutter and stammer over their names.

What should be done before the interview?

While knowledge about the board members is useful and takes some of the surprise element out of the interview, there is other preparation which is more substantive. It *is* possible to prepare for an oral interview – in several ways:

1) Keep a copy of your application and review it carefully before the interview

This may be the only document before the oral board, and the starting point of the interview. Know what education and experience you have listed there, and the sequence and dates of all of it. Sometimes the board will ask you to review the highlights of your experience for them; you should not have to hem and haw doing it.

2) Study the class specification and the examination announcement

Usually, the oral board has one or both of these to guide them. The qualities, characteristics or knowledges required by the position sought are stated in these documents. They offer valuable clues as to the nature of the oral interview. For example, if the job involves supervisory responsibilities, the announcement will usually indicate that knowledge of modern supervisory methods and the qualifications of the candidate as a supervisor will be tested. If so, you can expect such questions, frequently in the form of a hypothetical situation which you are expected to solve. NEVER go into an oral without knowledge of the duties and responsibilities of the job you seek.

3) Think through each qualification required

Try to visualize the kind of questions you would ask if you were a board member. How well could you answer them? Try especially to appraise your own knowledge and background in each area, *measured against the job sought*, and identify any areas in which you are weak. Be critical and realistic – do not flatter yourself.

4) Do some general reading in areas in which you feel you may be weak

For example, if the job involves supervision and your past experience has NOT, some general reading in supervisory methods and practices, particularly in the field of human relations, might be useful. Do NOT study agency procedures or detailed manuals. The oral board will be testing your understanding and capacity, not your memory.

5) Get a good night's sleep and watch your general health and mental attitude

You will want a clear head at the interview. Take care of a cold or any other minor ailment, and of course, no hangovers.

What should be done on the day of the interview?

Now comes the day of the interview itself. Give yourself plenty of time to get there. Plan to arrive somewhat ahead of the scheduled time, particularly if your appointment is in the fore part of the day. If a previous candidate fails to appear, the board might be ready for you a bit early. By early afternoon an oral board is almost invariably behind schedule if there are many candidates, and you may have to wait. Take along a book or magazine to read, or your application to review, but leave any extraneous material in the waiting room when you go in for your interview. In any event, relax and compose yourself.

The matter of dress is important. The board is forming impressions about you – from your experience, your manners, your attitude, and your appearance. Give your personal appearance careful attention. Dress your best, but not your flashiest. Choose conservative, appropriate clothing, and be sure it is immaculate. This is a business interview, and your appearance should indicate that you regard it as such. Besides, being well groomed and properly dressed will help boost your confidence.

Sooner or later, someone will call your name and escort you into the interview room. *This is it.* From here on you are on your own. It is too late for any more preparation. But remember, you asked for this opportunity to prove your fitness, and you are here because your request was granted.

What happens when you go in?

The usual sequence of events will be as follows: The clerk (who is often the board stenographer) will introduce you to the chairman of the oral board, who will introduce you to the other members of the board. Acknowledge the introductions before you sit down. Do not be surprised if you find a microphone facing you or a stenotypist sitting by. Oral interviews are usually recorded in the event of an appeal or other review.

Usually the chairman of the board will open the interview by reviewing the highlights of your education and work experience from your application – primarily for the benefit of the other members of the board, as well as to get the material into the record. Do not interrupt or comment unless there is an error or significant misinterpretation; if that is the case, do not hesitate. But do not quibble about insignificant matters. Also, he will usually ask you some question about your education, experience or your present job – partly to get you to start talking and to establish the interviewing "rapport." He may start the actual questioning, or turn it over to one of the other members. Frequently, each member undertakes the questioning on a particular area, one in which he is perhaps most competent, so you can expect each member to participate in the examination. Because time is limited, you may also expect some rather abrupt switches in the direction the questioning takes, so do not be upset by it. Normally, a board member will not pursue a single line of questioning unless he discovers a particular strength or weakness.

After each member has participated, the chairman will usually ask whether any member has any further questions, then will ask you if you have anything you wish to add. Unless you are expecting this question, it may floor you. Worse, it may start you off on an extended, extemporaneous speech. The board is not usually seeking more information. The question is principally to offer you a last opportunity to present further qualifications or to indicate that you have nothing to add. So, if you feel that a significant qualification or characteristic has been overlooked, it is proper to point it out in a sentence or so. Do not compliment the board on the thoroughness of their examination – they have been sketchy, and you know it. If you wish, merely say, "No thank you, I have nothing further to add." This is a point where you can "talk yourself out" of a good impression or fail to present an important bit of information. Remember, *you close the interview yourself.*

The chairman will then say, "That is all, Mr. _____, thank you." Do not be startled; the interview is over, and quicker than you think. Thank him, gather your belongings and take your leave. Save your sigh of relief for the other side of the door.

How to put your best foot forward

Throughout this entire process, you may feel that the board individually and collectively is trying to pierce your defenses, seek out your hidden weaknesses and embarrass and confuse you. Actually, this is not true. They are obliged to make an appraisal of your qualifications for the job you are seeking, and they want to see you in your best light. Remember, they must interview all candidates and a non-cooperative candidate may become a failure in spite of their best efforts to bring out his qualifications. Here are 15 suggestions that will help you:

1) Be natural – Keep your attitude confident, not cocky

If you are not confident that you can do the job, do not expect the board to be. Do not apologize for your weaknesses, try to bring out your strong points. The board is interested in a positive, not negative, presentation. Cockiness will antagonize any board member and make him wonder if you are covering up a weakness by a false show of strength.

2) Get comfortable, but don't lounge or sprawl

Sit erectly but not stiffly. A careless posture may lead the board to conclude that you are careless in other things, or at least that you are not impressed by the importance of the occasion. Either conclusion is natural, even if incorrect. Do not fuss with your clothing, a pencil or an ashtray. Your hands may occasionally be useful to emphasize a point; do not let them become a point of distraction.

3) Do not wisecrack or make small talk

This is a serious situation, and your attitude should show that you consider it as such. Further, the time of the board is limited – they do not want to waste it, and neither should you.

4) Do not exaggerate your experience or abilities

In the first place, from information in the application or other interviews and sources, the board may know more about you than you think. Secondly, you probably will not get away with it. An experienced board is rather adept at spotting such a situation, so do not take the chance.

5) If you know a board member, do not make a point of it, yet do not hide it

Certainly you are not fooling him, and probably not the other members of the board. Do not try to take advantage of your acquaintanceship – it will probably do you little good.

6) Do not dominate the interview

Let the board do that. They will give you the clues – do not assume that you have to do all the talking. Realize that the board has a number of questions to ask you, and do not try to take up all the interview time by showing off your extensive knowledge of the answer to the first one.

7) Be attentive

You only have 20 minutes or so, and you should keep your attention at its sharpest throughout. When a member is addressing a problem or question to you, give him your undivided attention. Address your reply principally to him, but do not exclude the other board members.

8) Do not interrupt

A board member may be stating a problem for you to analyze. He will ask you a question when the time comes. Let him state the problem, and wait for the question.

9) Make sure you understand the question

Do not try to answer until you are sure what the question is. If it is not clear, restate it in your own words or ask the board member to clarify it for you. However, do not haggle about minor elements.

10) Reply promptly but not hastily

A common entry on oral board rating sheets is "candidate responded readily," or "candidate hesitated in replies." Respond as promptly and quickly as you can, but do not jump to a hasty, ill-considered answer.

11) Do not be peremptory in your answers

A brief answer is proper – but do not fire your answer back. That is a losing game from your point of view. The board member can probably ask questions much faster than you can answer them.

12) Do not try to create the answer you think the board member wants

He is interested in what kind of mind you have and how it works – not in playing games. Furthermore, he can usually spot this practice and will actually grade you down on it.

13) Do not switch sides in your reply merely to agree with a board member

Frequently, a member will take a contrary position merely to draw you out and to see if you are willing and able to defend your point of view. Do not start a debate, yet do not surrender a good position. If a position is worth taking, it is worth defending.

14) Do not be afraid to admit an error in judgment if you are shown to be wrong

The board knows that you are forced to reply without any opportunity for careful consideration. Your answer may be demonstrably wrong. If so, admit it and get on with the interview.

15) Do not dwell at length on your present job

The opening question may relate to your present assignment. Answer the question but do not go into an extended discussion. You are being examined for a *new* job, not your present one. As a matter of fact, try to phrase ALL your answers in terms of the job for which you are being examined.

Basis of Rating

Probably you will forget most of these "do's" and "don'ts" when you walk into the oral interview room. Even remembering them all will not ensure you a passing grade. Perhaps you did not have the qualifications in the first place. But remembering them will help you to put your best foot forward, without treading on the toes of the board members.

Rumor and popular opinion to the contrary notwithstanding, an oral board wants you to make the best appearance possible. They know you are under pressure – but they also want to see how you respond to it as a guide to what your reaction would be under the pressures of the job you seek. They will be influenced by the degree of poise you display, the personal traits you show and the manner in which you respond.

ABOUT THIS BOOK

This book contains tests divided into Examination Sections. Go through each test, answering every question in the margin. We have also attached a sample answer sheet at the back of the book that can be removed and used. At the end of each test look at the answer key and check your answers. On the ones you got wrong, look at the right answer choice and learn. Do not fill in the answers first. Do not memorize the questions and answers, but understand the answer and principles involved. On your test, the questions will likely be different from the samples. Questions are changed and new ones added. If you understand these past questions you should have success with any changes that arise. Tests may consist of several types of questions. We have additional books on each subject should more study be advisable or necessary for you. Finally, the more you study, the better prepared you will be. This book is intended to be the last thing you study before you walk into the examination room. Prior study of relevant texts is also recommended. NLC publishes some of these in our Fundamental Series. Knowledge and good sense are important factors in passing your exam. Good luck also helps. So now study this Passbook, absorb the material contained within and take that knowledge into the examination. Then do your best to pass that exam.

EXAMINATION SECTION

EXAMINATION SECTION
TEST 1

DIRECTIONS: Each question or incomplete statement is followed by several suggested answers or completions. Select the one that BEST answers the question or completes the statement. *PRINT THE LETTER OF THE CORRECT ANSWER IN THE SPACE AT THE RIGHT.*

1. Because of the severe housing shortage, the state legislature has decided that, notwithstanding statutory limits for continuing occupancy, a public housing authority may permit a family to remain in occupancy if it finds that the family is genuinely unable to find adequate and affordable local housing. The legislation provides that the rent of such a family remaining in occupancy shall be increased on the basis of the
    A. family's composition
    B. family's income
    C. age of the head of household
    D. number of wage earners

1._____

2. In federally aided projects having fixed rent, excess income families who are eligible for continued occupancy because they qualify for transfer to a larger apartment in the project are
    A. required to pay the same rent while awaiting transfer as charged for the apartment to which they are moving
    B. subject to a designated fractional rent increase while awaiting transfer
    C. not subject to a rent increase before or after transfer
    D. not subject to a rent increase while awaiting transfer

2._____

3. A residual single person who refuses to transfer to an apartment of appropriate size should generally have his tenancy terminated on the ground of
    A. breach of rules and regulations
    B. excess income
    C. non-desirability
    D. residual single-person occupancy

3._____

4. The Housing Authority sometimes uses Herculite K glass rather than ordinary glass PRIMARILY because it can
    A. be installed with special low-cost materials other than putty and clips
    B. withstand greater impact
    C. be cut to size at the project
    D. resist yellowing which is typical of ordinary glass

4._____

5. A tenant whose apartment is to be painted is responsible for
    A. moving all furniture to the center of the room
    B. taping electric switch and receptacle plates
    C. washing ceiling fixtures free of grease and grime
    D. washing all walls prior to the application of paint

5._____

6. When a project painting contract is completed, the Housing Manager may attach to the final request for payment a memorandum to the Chief of Maintenance recommending that a certain portion of payment be withheld in order to
    A. pay the required premiums to the covering bonding company
    B. meet unpaid wage claims filed against the painting contractor by his employees
    C. cover all outstanding tenant and Housing Authority claims for property damage against the painting contractor
    D. pay the mandatory fees incurred in meeting federal affirmative action requirements

7. Housing Authority project staff have, at times, been asked to reveal confidential information about tenants on the telephone to persons who have misrepresented themselves as members of the central office staff. To avoid divulging confidential information to unauthorized persons, project staff should
    A. ask the caller several technical questions concerning the Housing Authority to determine if he is an imposter
    B. ask the caller to put his inquiry in writing and submit it through prescribed office channels
    C. inform the caller that he should communicate directly with any tenant about whom he desires information
    D. inform the caller that his call will be returned, and then verify the number and name the caller has given

8. Project personnel are NOT to become involved in opening a tenant's door for a marshal or a sheriff in connection with a civil suit UNLESS
    A. the marshal or sheriff agrees in writing to reimburse the Housing Authority for damage to the door
    B. the marshal or sheriff specifically orders them to do so
    C. the Housing Authority itself is a party in an action to repossess the project apartment
    D. the tenant refuses admittance after being shown a court-issued writ or warrant

9. Whenever a dangerous weapon is found by a project staff member in a project apartment, public space or on the project grounds, the staff member should notify the project's Housing Patrolmen or security department, and should
    A. notify the local precinct of the Police Department
    B. question anyone who looks suspicious
    C. safeguard the weapon without disturbing it in any way
    D. take the weapon to the project office for safekeeping

10. Public assistance payment checks issued by the Department of Social Services are usually payable on the
    A. 1st and 16th of each month
    B. 5th and 20th of each month
    C. 8th and 23rd of each month
    D. 10th and 25th of each month

11. The better supervisor sees that the work for which he is responsible is done efficiently by
    A. delegating to his subordinates as much authority as possible
    B. handling as many details of the job as possible himself
    C. keeping for himself authority over all important parts of the job
    D. maintaining close supervision over all his subordinates

11._____

12. A person who inquires at a project or site about applying for public housing should be referred to the
    A. Applications Information Section
    B. Department of Community and Social Services
    C. local Community Corporation
    D. Tenant Selection Division

12._____

13. At the renting interview for an apartment available for immediate occupancy, the new tenant asks for an allowance of time, in order to make necessary moving arrangements, before her occupancy begins. Without special approval from the Chief Manager, the project manager may grant up to
    A. 3 days   B. 5 days   C. 10 days   D. 15 days

13._____

14. A termination-of-tenancy interview may properly be conducted by a Housing Assistant if the reason for termination is
    A. excess income
    B. misrepresentation
    C. non-desirability
    D. residual single-person occupancy

14._____

15. The primary purpose of an annual apartment visit to a tenant by a Housing Assistant is to
    A. determine tenant desirability
    B. discover faulty housekeeping
    C. improve tenant-management cooperation
    D. prepare necessary work orders

15._____

16. When a Housing Assistant conducts an annual apartment visit, if the tenant has no record of poor housekeeping and the apartment appears to be in reasonably good condition, it would usually be most suitable for the Housing Assistant, as the next step, to
    A. check for possible rodent or insect infestation
    B. inquire about unauthorized occupancy
    C. inspect the range and the refrigerator for cleanliness
    D. prepare requested work orders, if any

16._____

4 (#1)

17. Potential problem families should be referred to public or voluntary agencies for specialized assistance if the project staff is unable to remedy the problem within a reasonable time. The main purpose of making these referrals is to
    A. justify referral to the Tenant Review Board
    B. prevent or correct situations that could result in termination of tenancy
    C. develop sufficient data on the family to justify termination of tenancy
    D. reduce the amount of crime taking place on Housing Authority property

17._____

18. Home relief recipients who are Public Works Project Assignees may be assigned to lobby and stairwell duties in a project where a tenant patrol is functioning provided that their assignment is acceptable to the tenant patrol and
    A. their duties can be performed between the hours of 9:00 a.m. and 5:00 p.m.
    B. the Public Works Project Assignees are eligible for the customary surety bond
    C. such home relief recipients have had previous experience in performing similar duties
    D. their assignment will not tend to undermine tenant patrol interest and activity

18._____

19. All of the following statements concerning Public Works Project Assignees (home relief recipients) are correct EXCEPT:
    A. Assignees are not, in legal terms, employees of the Housing Authority or the city
    B. Assignees may perform any kind of work ordinarily and actually performed by regular employees
    C. Assignees may be accorded some benefits equal to those received by a regular employee with equal length of service
    D. Assignees may be assigned to duties other than those suggested by the title in which the Assignee is referred

19._____

20. Of the following notices, the one considered desirable for display on a project bulletin board is the one which
    A. gives tenants information abut the process of voter registration and elections
    B. informs tenants that the Housing Authority has endorsed a community candidate who is an Authority tenant
    C. presents the views on public housing of a candidate seeking reelection
    D. urges an affirmative vote for a bipartisan housing construction bond proposition

20._____

21. A project included in its communications a listing of some local physicians, dentists, optometrists and pharmacists. This practice should be considered
    A. advisable, mainly because it shows that the Authority is concerned with the well-being of tenants
    B. advisable, mainly because it provides essential information
    C. inadvisable, mainly because it raises ethical questions
    D. inadvisable, mainly because tenants tend to resent this paternalistic approach

21._____

22. The one of the following which is correct regarding the keeping of records of the race, color or ethnic background of tenants who have rented apartments and signed leases with the Housing Authority is that such records should be kept
    A. only for tenants who were not born in the state
    B. only for multi-problem families
    C. only for tenants receiving public assistance
    D. for all tenants

22._____

23. Housing Assistants who are on a promotion eligible list for Assistant Housing Manager and who are likely to be promoted within one year should be given the opportunity to learn the duties of this higher position before their appointment. All of the following are considered to be proper in accomplishing this EXCEPT:
    A. Give such Housing Assistants supervisory authority over other Housing Assistants at the work location
    B. Make arrangements to minimize interference with regular project activities performed by such Housing Assistants
    C. Permit such Housing Assistants to carry out some of the duties of an Assistant Housing Manager
    D. Schedule a weekly time period for such Housing Assistants to study with, and observe, an Assistant Housing Manager

23._____

24. The one of the following employees who may be employed at a project where he or she is a tenant is a(n)
    A. housing guard
    B. housing supplyman
    C. assistant accountant
    D. assistant housing manager

24._____

25. A Housing Assistant asks permission to use the project garage for his car. He points out that he regularly transports several of his coworkers to the project. His request should be
    A. granted; he may use the garage if he signs a statement relieving the Housing Authority from responsibility for damage caused by his car
    B. granted; he may use the garage as long as he does not violate internal parking regulations
    C. denied; the garage may be used only by resident employees
    D. denied; the garage may be used only for Housing Authority equipment

25._____

26. A major research finding regarding employee absenteeism is that
    A. absenteeism is likely to be higher on hot days
    B. male employees tend to be absent more than female employees
    C. the way an employee is treated has a definite bearing on absenteeism
    D. the distance employees have to travel is one of the most important factors in absenteeism

27. "The 'unguided interview' technique permits the interviewee to talk about anything that happens to be on his mind. When using this technique the interviewer avoids asking direct questions." Of the following, the main criticism of the unguided interview is that, generally,
    A. interviewees resist giving information to interviewers
    B. it is too time-consuming
    C. it reveals too many personal details about the interviewee
    D. interviewers, to be effective, must be trained psychologists

28. In interviewing, the tendency to judge the total personality of the interviewee on the basis of a single trait is known as the
    A. halo effect
    B. objective factor
    C. rapport ratio
    D. suggestibility quotient

29. Of the following, the supervisory behavior that is of greatest benefit to the organization is exhibited by supervisors who
    A. are strict with subordinates about following rules and regulations
    B. encourage subordinates to be interested in the work
    C. are willing to assist with subordinates' work on most occasions
    D. get the most done with available staff and resources

30. Before making a definite decision where group problems were involved, an Assistant Housing Manager frequently asked his subordinates for their opinions and recommendations. When the situation warranted he suggested to his subordinates that they make their own decisions. This approach to supervision is called "participative management." Of the following, probably the greatest benefit the Assistant Housing Manager gains from the use of "participative management" is that it
    A. permits him to pass the responsibility for faulty decisions on to his subordinates
    B. eliminates friction among his subordinates
    C. reduces the demands made on his time and attention
    D. enables him to achieve broader acceptance of agreed-upon goals and greater unity of purpose

KEY (CORRECT ANSWERS)

1. B	11. A	21. C
2. D	12. A	22. D
3. A	13. B	23. A
4. B	14. A	24. B
5. A	15. C	25. D
6. C	16. D	26. C
7. D	17. B	27. B
8. C	18. D	28. A
9. C	19. B	29. D
10. A	20. A	30. D

TEST 2

DIRECTIONS: Each question or incomplete statement is followed by several suggested answers or completions. Select the one that BEST answers the question or completes the statement. *PRINT THE LETTER OF THE CORRECT ANSWER IN THE SPACE AT THE RIGHT.*

1. Every public agency should adequately inform the public of its work, since public opinion affects public agencies. Of the following, which is usually the single greatest barrier to effective communications by public agencies?
   A. The inborn tendency to place too much faith in the printed word
   B. Giving too much attention to persons holding opposing views
   C. Professionally developed public information campaigns containing information which is repetitious in character are often relied upon by the agencies
   D. Lack of appropriate skill and insight on the part of the communicators

   1.____

2. In order to develop effective public relations, a public agency must identify the feelings and beliefs of the groups it seeks to reach. The MAIN reason for carefully studying such groups is to
   A. be able to counteract negative group attitudes regarding the future of public employment
   B. facilitate selecting the means, context and timing of informational efforts
   C. create a strong impression that public opinion is important to the agency
   D. demonstrate openly the abilities and skills of competent public relations people

   2.____

3. "Communications research strongly indicates that persuasive mass communication is, in general, more likely to reinforce the existing opinions of its audience than it is to change such opinions." For a public agency wishing to communicate effectively and to influence public opinion, the major implication of this statement is that
   A. most people tend to ignore a message if it is presented in an unusual manner
   B. the prestige of the source determines whether information will be accepted wholly or only in part
   C. public information campaigns should, if possible, begin by stressing widely accepted beliefs in order to strengthen the credibility of the agency's message
   D. an audience low in self-esteem is easily persuaded because it lacks self-confidence

   3.____

4. A public agency's public relations efforts should not only be honest but should also clearly appear to be honest primarily because
    A. an audience develops resistance when it perceives communications as being manipulative
    B. communications are usually interpreted in a greatly different manner by each recipient
    C. government agencies, more than private advertisers, have a low public image which they must overcome
    D. many persons have private economic interests in the outcome of a public relations campaign

4._____

5. A public relations program of a governmental agency should be designed primarily to
    A. build good human relations in order to improve the agency's ability to serve
    B. increase the agency's activities for the purpose of gaining recognition
    C. persuade various media to provide free or low-cost exposure
    D. reduce the public's resistance to new or increased taxes

5._____

6. The managements of some large organizations encourage lower-level supervisors to take necessary risks in decision-making, especially when immediate decisions must be made in the absence of complete information. The one of the following which is most likely to discourage such decision-making is
    A. management's expectation that necessary decisions be made with promptness
    B. lack of policy guidelines to provide insight into past experiences
    C. the unwillingness of employees to follow special or unusual instructions issued by lower-level supervisors
    D. the lower-level supervisor's fear of making mistakes

6._____

7. Of the following, the most effective way for an Assistant Housing Manager to gain the cooperation of Housing Assistants is for him to give them instructions
    A. exactly as given to him by higher officials
    B. which emphasize competitive standards
    C. in the form of suggestions or requests
    D. as much as possible in private

7._____

8. "Since each person sees things in his own way, even 'factual' things may be seen differently. Relevance to a person's needs is the most important determinant of his view of the world." Of the following, the most logical conclusion to be drawn from this quotation is that most subordinates
    A. alter their behavior for reasons which cannot be understood
    B. oppose organizational policies which are based on reasons beyond their understanding
    C. respond most favorably when communications with them are uniform and forceful
    D. tend to pay attention to things which they feel relate to them

8._____

9. A newly appointed employee, Mr. Jones, was added to the staff of a supervisor who, because of pressure of other work, turned him over to an experienced subordinate by saying, "Show Mr. Jones around and give him something to do." On the basis of this experience, Mr. Jones' first impression of his new position was most likely to have been
   A. negative, mainly because it appeared that his job was not worth his supervisor's attention
   B. negative, mainly because the more experienced subordinate would tend to emphasize the unpleasant aspects of the work
   C. positive, mainly because the supervisor wasted no time in assigning him to a subordinate
   D. positive, mainly because he saw himself working for a dynamic supervisor who expected immediate results

9._____

10. An employee who stays in one assignment for a number of years often develops a feeling of possessiveness concerning his knowledge of the job which may develop into a problem. Of the following, the best way for a supervisor to remedy this difficulty is to
    A. give the employee less important work to do
    B. point out minor errors as often as possible
    C. raise performance standards for all employees
    D. rotate the employee to a different assignment

10._____

11. A supervisor who tends to be supportive of his subordinates, in contrast to a supervisor who relies upon an authoritarian style of leadership, is more likely, in dealing with his staff, to have to listen to complaints, tolerate emotionally upset employees and even hear unreasonable and insulting remarks. Compared to the authoritarian supervisor, he is more likely to
    A. be unconsciously fearful of failure
    B. have an overriding interest in production
    C. have subordinates who are better educated
    D. receive accurate feedback information

11._____

12. Assume that you are an Assistant Housing Manager and have been assigned to assist the head of a large agency unit. He asks you to prepare a simple, functional organization chart of the unit. Such a chart would be useful for
    A. favorably impressing members of the public with the important nature of the agency's work
    B. graphically presenting staff relationships which may indicate previously unknown duplications, overlaps and gaps in job duties
    C. motivating all employees toward better performance because they will have a better understanding of job procedures
    D. subtly and inoffensively making known to the staff in the unit that you are now in a position of responsibility

12._____

13. In some large organizations, management's traditional means of learning about employee dissatisfaction has been the "open door policy." This policy usually means that
    A. management lets it be known that a management representative is generally available to discuss employees' questions, suggestions and complaints
    B. management sets up an informal employee organization to establish a democratic procedure for orderly representation of employees
    C. employees are encouraged to attempt to resolve dissatisfactions at the lowest possible level of authority
    D. employees are provided with an address or box so that they may safely and anonymously register complaints

13._____

14. Recent research shows that some lower-level professional employees feel that they accomplish little in their work that is worthwhile. Management experts usually say that the one of the following which best explains such feelings is
    A. dissatisfaction among employees provoked by the activities of labor unions
    B. frequent salary increases unmatched by any significant increase in productivity
    C. the failure to properly develop in these employees an understanding of the significance of their work
    D. the almost total indifference of employees to the vital issues of the times

14._____

15. One way to get maximum effort from employees is for management to give employees the maximum possible personal freedom in accomplishing agency objectives. This encourages a feeling of self-management which is most basic to
    A. high levels of motivation
    B. tightly coordinated team effort
    C. an impartial approach to work
    D. uniformity of action

15._____

16. "In an organization where each supervisor has only three or four subordinates, the result may be over-management and a tendency to stifle creativity." Such over-management is most likely to result from
    A. the desire on the part of competent supervisors to delegate responsibility too soon when subordinates show promise
    B. the over-training of supervisors in office routines and procedures
    C. the supervisors' having so few subordinates that supervisors are free to direct nearly all the actions of their subordinates
    D. the general tendency of organizations to regard strict supervisors as being efficient

16._____

17. It has been said, "In a democratic administrative climate, employees are often encouraged, within reasonable limits, to learn by their own errors. The unfailing benefit of this is the growth of both human abilities and organizational capabilities."
The development of employees as described in this passage takes place in most organizations mainly by means of appropriate
    A. committee assignments
    B. delegation of authority
    C. training publications
    D. close and careful supervision

18. An effective system of evaluating employees' suggestions should provide for evaluation without the evaluators knowing the identities of suggesters. The MAIN purpose of maintaining such anonymity is to
    A. concentrate attention on the needs of the organization, not on the rewarding of suggesters
    B. reduce the normal, but potentially harmful, urge for individual recognition
    C. encourage a spirit of competition among employees
    D. increase the probability that ideas are judged on their merits

19. Of the following forms of training, the one that is usually most similar to an actual work situation is the
    A. case-study method
    B. training conference technique
    C. lecture method
    D. role-playing method

20. Assume that you are an Assistant Housing Manager and that you have been attempting to improve the work performance of one of your subordinates by providing informal on-the-job training. He is making satisfactory, although slow, progress. In these circumstances, in order to further his progress, it would be best for you to
    A. avoid praise except when he implicitly asks for it
    B. imply approval by not criticizing his mistakes
    C. withhold praise until he has reached the final desired level of skill
    D. tell him he is doing well as his performance improves

21. One of the best ways of finding out whether training or retraining of employees is needed is to use
    A. confidential questionnaires directed to taxpayer groups
    B. employee questionnaires
    C. performance appraisals
    D. standardized intelligence tests

22. Within every organization, policies on most matters exist, either in written or oral form. A unique advantage of having policies expressed in writing is that it
    A. raises employee morale by creating the feeling that management has recognized employees' feelings
    B. increases employee confidence by reducing confusion, since management's positions are on record
    C. inhibits individual employees from asking for special treatment based on personal circumstances
    D. bridges the understanding gap between management and the less educated employees

23. An Assistant Housing Manager who believes that one of his subordinates has a mental health problem should consider taking, or recommending, appropriate referral action primarily when the problem
    A. affects the employee's job performance or adjustment to his work environment
    B. appears trivial on the surface but may have an underlying cause
    C. involves behavior which generally is different from prevailing social customs
    D. is of such nature that the supervisor is in danger of becoming personally involved

Answer questions 24 though 28 on the basis of the following paragraph:

"It is probable that supervisors who arouse anxiety in employees with early threats of low ratings and failure interfere with learning instead of *facilitating* it. It may well be that such threats serve to increase the employees' concern, but there is no guarantee that they will increase learning. In fact, experimental evidence gained from studies of college students suggests that, with very simple tasks, learning is enhanced by conditions of high motivation; but with complex tasks, the most efficient learning condition is one of low motivation. Moreover, when the motivation of the learner is raised artificially, as by a threat of failure, in the face of a complex task, there often occurs irrelevant learning not under the control of the supervisor, such as learning to worry. This emotional learning is likely to interfere with learning the task at hand."

24. According to the passage, studies have indicated that persons who attempt to learn difficult tasks
    A. are motivated most efficiently by an indirect approach despite the danger of unwanted side effects
    B. are more likely to learn if they are not especially concerned about learning
    C. usually begin in a state of tension provoked by supervisory intervention
    D. cannot learn efficiently unless motivated by a moderate fear of failure

25. Of the following, the most appropriate title for the passage is
    A. Blocks to Learning
    B. How to Prepare Employees for Advancement
    C. Experimentation in Training
    D. The Role of Psychology in Human Relations

    25._____

26. Of the following, the most reasonable conclusion to be drawn from the passage is that
    A. learning progress should be measured by a single standard
    B. college graduates are relatively easily motivated to perform difficult tasks
    C. inexperienced supervisors generally rely upon threats in order to facilitate learning
    D. employee training requires that employees be appropriately motivated

    26._____

27. The underlined word, facilitating, as used in the passage means, most nearly,
    A. establishing   B. assuring   C. assisting   D. evaluating

    27._____

28. According to the passage, a supervisor who causes an employee to be strongly motivated in connection with the learning of a task of low complexity is most likely to
    A. decrease anxiety   B. facilitate learning
    C. prevent worrying   D. reduce motivation

    28._____

29. The majority of public housing tenants in the nation are classified, socio-economically, as
    A. a downwardly mobile, highly stable, lower-class population
    B. a lower-income, stable-family, upper-working-class population
    C. a poverty-afflicted, non-mobile, lower-class population
    D. an upwardly mobile, intact-family, working-class population

    29._____

30. Although 17% of the area of a given city consists of parks and recreation space, most of the space is underutilized, inaccessible, peripheral or even underwater; the rest is unevenly distributed. The immediate remedy usually proposed for this maldistribution of space is to
    A. decrease facilities in the over-utilized parks
    B. create additional small parks
    C. divide large parks into community sections
    D. establish a unified system of user fees

    30._____

KEY (CORRECT ANSWERS)

1. D	11. D	21. C
2. B	12. B	22. B
3. C	13. A	23. A
4. A	14. C	24. B
5. A	15. A	25. A
6. D	16. C	26. D
7. C	17. B	27. C
8. D	18. D	28. B
9. A	19. D	29. C
10. D	20. D	30. B

TEST 3

DIRECTIONS: Each question or incomplete statement is followed by several suggested answers or completions. Select the one that BEST answers the question or completes the statement. *PRINT THE LETTER OF THE CORRECT ANSWER IN THE SPACE AT THE RIGHT.*

1. Modular housing refers most specifically to housing that
    A. is partly pre-fabricated
    B. is covered by an insured mortgage
    C. uses electricity exclusively as a power and heat source
    D. stresses uniform interior decoration

    1._____

2. In a rehabilitation program, rundown buildings are being turned into modernized units for low-income and moderate-income families. A common courtyard in the block's interior will feature trees, benches and a landscaped play area. A <u>major</u> reason for having such a courtyard, rather than a vacant area, is to reduce
    A. garbage throwing from windows facing the courtyard
    B. initial construction costs
    C. area-wide air pollution
    D. the rent levels of all the buildings

    2._____

3. In connection with housing construction, "economies of scale" would most likely result from
    A. allowing purchasers of condominiums to specify individual modifications prior to construction
    B. constructing small, low-cost frame houses of different layouts based on age and the family composition of prospective purchasers
    C. erecting several high-rise buildings at the same time on one plot of land
    D. permitting cooperators to vote on the architectural design of their building

    3._____

4. In many parts of the United States, the poor have been prevented from residing in the suburbs by
    A. low-density residential zoning
    B. large business organizations relocating to the suburbs
    C. lack of vacant suburban land
    D. low property taxes

    4._____

Questions 5 through 7 are to be answered solely on the basis of the following passage:

"In the early 1900's, the two major ingredients of slums (overcrowding and physical obsolescence and deterioration) were increasingly evident in the core of most of our major cities. Other ingredients of slums were: poor original construction, lack of facilities, inadequate city services, unplanned development and overcrowding.

"The widespread incidence of these abject living conditions became a matter of concern among students of our social structure, progressive legislators and many apprehensive public officials. For example, in England, a Labor Government was in control after World War I and a serious housing shortage resulted from the urbanization drives being manifested by the people. Parliament passed a law in 1919 providing for state-assistance in the creation of new housing, which was the forerunner to our own housing legislation.

"The complete and unfettered right of private ownership was a part of the American creed. People were loath to sponsor or promote public action which would violate these rights. The first tenement house law was enacted in 1867 in New York and further legislation was passed in the year 1901. However, the continuing consumer pressure for housing made old, obsolete and substandard buildings a scarce commodity and hence preserved their earning power and their value. As in all cities, these old buildings were too valuable an 'asset' to destroy. Only recently have U.S. cities tightened up their enforcement programs as well as their housing and building codes."

5. Of the following, the most suitable title for the passage would be
    A. Government Action to Deal With Slums
    B. Maximizing Profits From Slum Growth
    C. Parliamentary Interest in Slums
    D. The Focus on Tenant Responsibility for Slum Conditions

6. Of the following factors, which was probably the most important in eventually bringing about housing legislation in England in 1919?
    A. A desire on the part of the public to improve the physical appearance of slum areas
    B. A pledge by the Labor Government to repair and renovate deteriorated housing
    C. The movement of people from rural areas to urban areas
    D. The new enlightenment of land owners

7. According to the above passage, at one time most Americans generally believed that, with regard to real estate,
    A. a man had a right to put his land to use in whatever way he wished
    B. limiting owner's profits from slums would also prevent the creation of slums
    C. slums could be largely eliminated by concentrating on the enforcement of existing housing legislation
    D. the worst features of slums could be remedied by insisting that tenants maintain the property they had leased

Answer questions 8 and 9 solely on the basis of the following paragraph:

"Public housing planners are caught in a dilemma. They want to rid the cities of the most deteriorated housing, which are unsightly and sometimes dangerous. They want to reduce crowding, improve the physical environment, admit light and air, and bring trees and grass to the heart of the city. But their aspirations are usually frustrated by the scarcity and high cost of land that dictate intensive use and dense occupancy. Public housing, therefore, tends to increase the number of persons per acre even though the amount of space between buildings is greater than before the slums were cleared."

8. Based on the paragraph, it would be most reasonable to conclude that public housing, compared to the housing which it replaces, usually
    A. fails to increase the total supply of housing
    B. has a longer economic life
    C. increases gross rental profits
    D. provides more open areas

9. According to the paragraph, public housing planners are often unable to achieve their goals because they generally
    A. are forced to increase the concentration of tenants
    B. advocate public rather than private housing
    C. select sites located in unreceptive communities
    D. fail to take into account tenant wishes

Questions 10 through 14 consist of short paragraphs. Each paragraph contains one word which is INCORRECTLY used because it is not in keeping with the meaning of the paragraph. Find the word in each paragraph which is incorrectly used and then select as your answer the suggested word which should be substituted for the incorrect word.

SAMPLE: "One of your lowest responsibilities is to assign work so that it is fairly distributed and that everyone uses his best talents."
    A. complain   B. exclude   C. important   D. return

The word not in keeping with the meaning of the paragraph is <u>lowest</u>. The suggested word most in keeping with the meaning is <u>important</u> and should therefore be substituted. Thus, the correct answer is "C."

10. "Careful proofreading of all reports and correspondence is always necessary, since errors can have reductions ranging from simple embarrassment to serious misunderstanding. Common errors include omissions, transpositions, confused syntax and misspellings."
    A. emotions   B. requirements
    C. overly   D. consequences

11. "The assumption that the average person dislikes work and will seek to avoid it has been shown to be wrong. And the companion assumption that most employees must be coerced, controlled and threatened before they will avoid effort toward organizational goals is equally in error. Scientific research has demonstrated that the opposite concepts are true."
    A. establish   B. exert   C. identify   D. verify

12. "The administrative climate – the lines of authority, the confidence in staff, the minimizing of status or class, the style of executive direction – should be sufficiently motivating and supportive that it evaluates the release of human energies and ideas in the interest of the public service."
    A. ceases   B. discusses   C. modernizes   D. stimulates

13. "H.L. Menken once said: 'There is always an easy solution to every human problem – neat, plausible and wrong.' If this bit of cynicism means that we should be wary of simplistic formulas to solve human problems, it is worthwhile. If, on the other hand, it means to encourage our having any guideposts, it is seriously overdrawn."
    A. aversion   B. disparage   C. hesitate   D. speculate

14. "Public employees, like any other group of employees, deserve being regarded by their employer not only as workers performing essential services but as human beings worthy of care and cultivation. Of all those organizations in our civilization that examine the services of people, the government can least justify disregard for the welfare of its employees."
    A. accumulate   B. employ   C. predict   D. restrict

15. In order for a supervisor to employ the system of democratic leadership in his supervision, it would generally be best for him to
    A. allow his subordinates to assist in deciding on methods of work performance and job assignments but only in those areas where decisions have not been made on higher administrative levels
    B. allow his subordinates to decide how to do the required work, interposing his authority when work is not completed on schedule or is improperly completed
    C. attempt to make assignments of work to individuals only of the type which they enjoy doing
    D. maintain control over the job assignments and work production, but allow the subordinates to select methods of work and internal conditions of work at democratically conducted staff conferences

16. In an office in which supervision has been considered quite effective, it has become necessary to press for above-normal production for a limited period to achieve a required goal. The one of the following which is a LEAST likely result of this pressure is that
    A. there will be more griping by employees
    B. some workers will do both more and better work than has been normal for them
    C. there will be an enhanced feeling of group unity
    D. there will be increased absenteeism

17. The practice whereby the Assistant Housing Manager at a large site with many Housing Assistants delegates to one of them who is highly competent and experienced the task of initially training a newly employed Housing Assistant in the routines and procedures of the site office is one which should be followed
    A. frequently, since the experienced Housing Assistant will himself learn by the act of teacing and the time of the Assistant Manager will be free for other work
    B. very frequently, since it enhances the status of the experienced Housing Assistant and sets a pattern for continuing differentiation between the more experienced and less experienced Housing Assistants
    C. rarely, since the newly employed Housing Assistant is likely to feel resentful that the Assistant Manager does not think him important enough to do the training personally
    D. very rarely, since it delegates to a non-supervisory employee supervisory functions over someone on his own level and with whom he will later have to work on an equal basis

17._____

18. Assume that you are an Assistant Housing Manager in charge of a staff of three Housing Assistants: "A," who is a very competent individual; "B," who is very experienced but only of average ability; and "C," who has been recently assigned to you, although he has been employed at another location for about a year. Your operation is currently going through a slack period. You are given a job to be done of a type requiring work by only one individual. It is a rather difficult and complex job. "A" has not done this job before but has competently done similar work. "B" has done this job before but only with the moderate competence that he does all jobs. "C" has no experience with this job or a similar one. To accomplish this task while at the same time accomplishing other supervisory aims, it would generally be best that you assign it to
    A. "A," since he has experience with similar work and can be expected to do this task competently
    B. "B," since his work is acceptable even though not outstanding, and he has already had experience with this job
    C. "C," since the slack period will give you a good opportunity to train him in the job and to form your own evaluation of his competence
    D. yourself, since it is a slack period and the job is a difficult and complex one

18._____

19. An Assistant Housing Manager happens to be passing by when one of his experienced Housing Assistants is interviewing a tenant, asking questions concerning pertinent and important matters. The Assistant Manager becomes aware that the questions are being asked in a way that is annoying the tenant, a way that the Assistant Manager believes can be improved upon. It would generally be best for the Assistant Manager to

    A. introduce himself to the tenant, explain that there is no intention of annoying her, that the questions asked are necessary and important, and that the Housing Assistant is just doing his job
    B. introduce himself to the tenant and join in the conversation, asking the questions in an improved way, and, at an early opportunity, discuss interviewing techniques with the Housing Assistant
    C. pass by without comment but, at an early opportunity, discuss with the Housing Assistant some methods which may improve his interviewing techniques
    D. take no action in the matter at this time, with the intention of discussing methods of improving interviewing techniques in some later in-service training conferences

19._____

20. It is the practice of some supervisors, when they believe that it would be desirable for a subordinate to take a particular action in a case, to inform the subordinate of this in the form of a suggestion rather than in the form of a direct order. In general, this method of getting a subordinate to take the desired action is

    A. inadvisable; it may create in the mind of the subordinate the impression that the supervisor is uncertain about the efficacy of his plan and is trying to avoid whatever responsibility he may have in resolving the case
    B. advisable; it provides the subordinate with the maximum opportunity to use his own judgment in handling the case
    C. inadvisable; it provides the subordinate with no clear-cut direction and, therefore, is likely to leave him with a feeling of uncertainty and frustration
    D. advisable; it presents the supervisor's view in a manner which will be most likely to evoke the subordinate's cooperation

20._____

7 (#3)

21. At a group training conference of Housing Assistants conducted by an Assistant Housing Manager, one of the Housing Assistants asks a question which is only partially related to the subject under discussion. The Assistant Manager does not know the answer to the question and believes the question was asked to embarrass him since he recently reprimanded the Housing Assistant for inattention to his work. Under the circumstances, it would generally be best for the Assistant Manager to

    A. pointedly ignore the question and the questioner and go on to other matters
    B. request the questioner to remain after the group session, at which time the question and the questioner's attitude will be considered
    C. state that he does not know the answer and ask for a volunteer to give a brief answer, because the question is only partially relevant
    D. tell the questioner that the question is not pertinent, show wherein it is not pertinent and state that the time of the group should not be wasted on it

21._____

22. The one of the following circumstances when it would generally be most proper for a supervisor to do a job himself rather than train a subordinate to do the job is when it is

    A. a job which the supervisor enjoys doing and does well
    B. not a very time-consuming job but an important one
    C. difficult to train another to do the job yet is not difficult for the supervisor to do
    D. unlikely that this or any similar job will have to be done again at any future time

22._____

23. Effective training of subordinates requires that the supervisor understand certain facts about learning and forgetting processes. Among these is the fact that people generally

    A. both learn and forget at a relatively constant rate and this rate is dependent upon their general intellectual capacity
    B. forget what they learned at a much greater rate during the first day than during subsequent periods
    C. learn at a relatively constant rate except for periods of assimilation when the quantity of retained learning decreases while information is becoming firmly fixed in the mind
    D. learn very slowly at first when introduced to a new topic, after which there is a great increase in the rate of learning

23._____

24. It has been suggested that a subordinate who likes his supervisor tends to do better work than one who does not. According to the most widely held theories of supervision, this suggestion is a

    A. bad one, since personal relationships tend to interfere with proper professional relationships
    B. bad one, since the strongest motivating factors are fear and uncertainty
    C. good one, since liking one's supervisor is a motivating factor for good work performance
    D. good one, since liking one's supervisor is the most important factor in employee performance

24._____

8 (#3)

25. An Assistant Housing Manager is supervising a Housing Assistant who is very soon to complete his six-months' probationary period. The Assistant Housing Manager finds him to be slow, to make many errors, to do work poorly, to be antagonistic toward the Assistant Housing Manager and to be disliked by many of his co-workers. The Assistant Manager is aware that he is the sole support of his wife and two children. He has never been late or absent during his service with the Housing Authority. If he is terminated, there will be considerable delay before a replacement arrives. It would generally be best for the Assistant Housing Manager to recommend that this Housing Assistant be

   A. transferred to work with another supervisor and other staff members with whom he may get along better
   B. retained but be very closely supervised until his work shows marked improvement
   C. retained since his services are needed with the expectation that he be terminated at some later date when a replacement is readily available
   D. terminated

25._____

26. Assume that you are an Assistant Housing Manager recently assigned to a new unit. You notice that, for the past few days, one of the Housing Assistants in your unit whose work is about average has been stopping work at about 4:00 and has been spending the rest of the afternoon relaxing at his desk. The best of the following actions for you to take in this situation is to

   A. assign more work to this Housing Assistant since it is apparent that he does not have enough work to keep him busy
   B. observe the Housing Assistant's conduct more closely for about ten days before taking any more positive action
   C. discuss the matter with the Housing Assistant, pointing out to him how he can use the extra hour daily to raise the level of his job performance
   D. question the previous supervisor in charge of the unit in order to determine whether he had sanctioned such conduct when he supervised that unit

26._____

27. It has long been recognized that relationships exist between worker morale and working conditions. The one of the following which best clarifies these existing relationships is that morale is

   A. affected for better or worse in direct relationship to the magnitude of the changes in working conditions for better or worse
   B. better when working conditions are better
   C. little affected by working conditions so long as the working conditions do not approach the intolerable
   D. more affected by the degree of interest shown in providing good working conditions than in the actual conditions, and may, perversely, be highest when working conditions are worst

27._____

28. An Assistant Housing Manager, newly assigned in charge of a small project, discovers that the previous Assistant Housing Manger and one of the Housing Assistants supervised by him put all their business communications with each other in written form. The newly assigned Assistant Housing Manager finds that the Housing Assistant is continuing to put his communications in writing and has requested that the Manager do the same in order to prevent misunderstandings. It would generally be best for the Assistant Housing Manager to
    A. accede to the request since the likelihood of misunderstandings will be reduced and since, as a newly assigned supervisor, he should not make changes until he is well established and accepted
    B. allow the Housing Assistant to communicate with him in the way in which he chooses but refuse to communicate back to him in writing except in cases where he would generally consider written communications to be desirable, on the grounds that too much of the Assistant Housing Manager's time would be wasted thereby
    C. inform the Housing Assistant that neither one of them is to use written communications excessively in order to reduce the time consumed by communication but with the understanding that the Housing Assistant may resort to writing in cases where he has serious reason to fear a misunderstanding
    D. instruct the Housing Assistant to cease the use of written communications in excess of the use of them by the other Housing Assistants and refuse to accede to his request since the result would be excessive waste of time

28._____

29. A policy of direct crosswise communication at a project between a member of the management staff and a member of the maintenance staff of equal or superior status rather than following the chain of command upward through the manager and down through the top maintenance supervisors is a policy to be
    A. discouraged, primarily because it places responsibility where it does not belong and makes the quality of communication erratic and undependable
    B. discouraged, primarily because the manager and upper-level supervisors will fail to receive the full information they need to make policy and administrative decisions
    C. encouraged, primarily because it results in decision making at the lowest practical level
    D. encouraged, primarily because it shortens the communication time and improves the quality of communication

29._____

30. Assume that a tenant has made a claim against the Housing Authority which is being handled by an Authority insurance carrier. Further, assume that you are aware of certain information in the tenant's folder which would be helpful in determining the merits of the claim. With regard to releasing this information to the insurance carrier, it would generally be considered best

    A. to refer the matter to the central office because of its effect on tenant relations and its legal implications
    B. not to reveal the information because of the legal requirement that tenant folder information be considered confidential
    C. not to reveal the information because of the likelihood that tenants will conceal or falsify information which they believe might in future be used to their detriment
    D. to reveal the information so as to increase the amount of information upon which the decision on the claim will be based

30._____

KEY (CORRECT ANSWERS)

1. A	11. B	21. C
2. A	12. D	22. D
3. C	13. B	23. B
4. A	14. B	24. C
5. A	15. A	25. D
6. C	16. D	26. C
7. A	17. A	27. D
8. D	18. C	28. C
9. A	19. C	29. D
10. D	20. D	30. D

TEST 4

DIRECTIONS: Each question or incomplete statement is followed by several suggested answers or completions. Select the one that BEST answers the question or completes the statement. *PRINT THE LETTER OF THE CORRECT ANSWER IN THE SPACE AT THE RIGHT.*

1. The director of the community center in a housing project has asked the Housing Manager for any information he may have about the character and interests of a certain boy living in the project. The tenant folder contains information about several infractions of rules and incidents involving this boy. For the Housing Manager to give the director of the center a summary of this information about the boy would generally be
    A. improper, if the director is not an employee of the Housing Authority, since information in tenant folders is confidential
    B. improper, since the boy might be stigmatized at the center by the revealed information, which in turn might cause a worsening in his attitude and actions
    C. proper, because of the help it gives the director in justifying the elimination from the center of a disturbing or disruptive influence
    D. proper, because of the help it might give the director in understanding the boy and improving ways in which to handle him

1._____

2. The one of the following which most fully and accurately describes the attitude which would be best for project management to maintain toward door-to-door fund solicitations by well-known reputable charitable organizations is to
    A. allow the solicitation but without assisting the operation
    B. allow the solicitation, giving minor assistance by such methods as suggesting the names of reliable tenants who might be interested in soliciting for a worthy cause within the project
    C. allow the solicitation, assisting the operation where possible by encouraging the staff to make collections after working hours
    D. ignore the matter unless a complaint is received from a tenant after which the solicitors must be politely informed that it will be necessary to enforce the laws against trespass if they visit tenants without appointments

2._____

3. A project tenant requests permission from the Assistant Housing Manager to post on the management office bulletin board in the rent collection office a notice to other tenants that she is available for hire as a babysitter. It would generally be best for the Assistant Housing Manager to
    A. deny the request because it might be considered as implying Housing Authority approval of the caliber of the service advertised
    B. deny the request because the use of this bulletin board should be restricted to those official matters which the management wishes to bring to the attention of the tenants
    C. grant the request because it is a service not only to the tenant making the request but also to other tenants with children
    D. grant the request in order to encourage the development of community living and the building of meaningful inter-relationships among the tenants

3._____

4. Housing Assistants should be instructed that in timing initial apartment inspection and orientation visits to new tenants, it is generally best to make the first visit
   A. within 24 hours after the tenant moves in
   B. about two days after the tenant moves in
   C. about two weeks after the tenant moves in
   D. about two months after the tenant moves in

4._____

5. On the 30th day of the month, a Housing Assistant visits a chronic rent delinquent in his apartment to discuss the rent for that month which has not yet been paid. The tenant, cash in hand, offers to pay the rent money to the Housing Assistant, in the apartment, explaining that she cannot leave the apartment until she gets someone to baby-sit for her ill two-month-old son. The Housing Assistant is aware that on previous occasions, when he refused to accept rent offered in the apartment, the money was not brought to the office for many days. In such an instance, the Housing Assistant should
   A. accept the money, giving a handwritten receipt, with instructions to the tenant to return this receipt when she next comes to the office to be replaced by the regulation machine entry in her rent book
   B. call in a neighbor to be a witness, accept the money and the rent book and return the latter after a regulation machine entry has been made in the rent book
   C. refuse to accept the money but offer to baby-sit while the mother brings the rent to the rent office, impressing upon her the importance of paying the money immediately
   D. refuse to accept the money, insisting that the mother make payment in the normal way, and warning her of the serious consequences of continued rent delinquencies

5._____

6. The Housing Authority has certain policies concerning the use of community space for dances sponsored by private, non-profit agencies. Dances may be of the invitation type, wherein admission is by invitation or ticket procured in advance, or of the open-type, wherein there is no limit on admission of non-members of the community center. According to these policies,
   A. both open dances and invitation dances are permitted so long as no admission fees are charged and proper arrangements for control of behavior are made and enforced
   B. both open and invitation dances are permitted and admission fees may be charged
   C. open dances are not permitted but invitation dances are permitted and admission fees may be charged
   D. open dances are not permitted but invitation dances are permitted as long as no admission fees are charged

6._____

7. The one of the following conditions under which it is necessary to make an interim change in income and rent for a tenant in federal or state subsidized housing is a condition wherein
    A. a non-welfare family contains a member who had been receiving welfare assistance which has now been terminated
    B. a member of the tenant household has graduated from high school and secured a permanent full-time job
    C. a regularly employed tenant has left his full-time job in one industry and received a full-time job in another industry at a substantial increase in salary
    D. a tenant with non-fixed employment in an industry characterized by long-term unemployment during slack seasons has now been without work for over three months during such a slack period

8. The one of the following which is the most complete and accurate description of the information contained in the Tenants' Charges and Credits Book (TCC Book) is that this book contains
    A. daily entries and monthly summaries of retroactive surcharges and credits broken down into categories by months to which attributed
    B. daily entries of total charges or debits, all the credits to the tenants' accounts, and all cash receipts broken down into categories of charges or credits but not by tenant or apartment account numbers
    C. monthly entries of total miscellaneous charges or debits, credits and receipts broken down into categories of such charges and credits and by tenant account number
    D. monthly summaries of all charges or debits and credits to tenants other than minimum or basic rent, broken down into categories of such charges and credits and by tenant account number

9. Assume that interest is paid on security deposits at the rate of 2% per annum, compounded annually, and paid to the nearest quarter of a year. A tenant who paid a security deposit of $100 on January 2, 1997 moved out with a charge-through date of February 10, 2001. He should have refunded to him, most nearly (assuming that there are no charges to be deducted from the security deposit),
    A. $107   B. $108   C. $109   D. $110
    E. $111

10. The peculiarities of the payment system of a particular employer have resulted in payments during a particular year of 53 weekly paychecks although only 52 paychecks were earned during the year. Assuming that there has been no change in salary during the year and that a tenant working for this employer has a statement of income for that year of $5,550 (covering 53 payments), his year's income for 52 weeks is most nearly
    A. $5,442   B. $5,445   C. $5,456   D. $5,495
    E. $5,549

Questions 11 through 15 are to be answered on the basis of the following graphs:

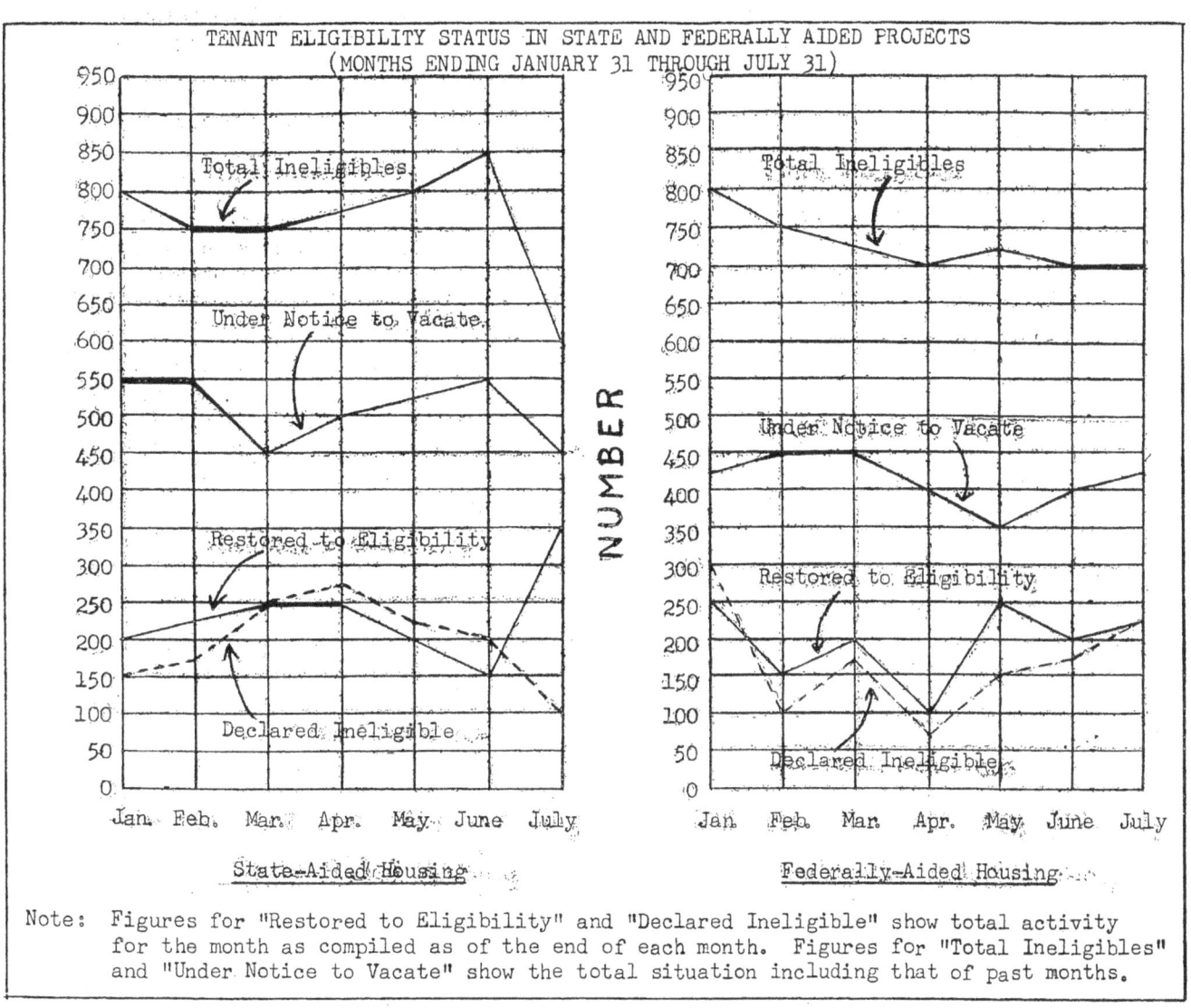

11. In Federally-aided housing, the average number of tenants restored to eligibility during the first six months of the year is, most nearly
    A. 100   B. 188   C. 192   D. 196
    E. 200

12. For the months covered by the graphs, in State-aided housing, the ratio of the average number of total ineligibles to the average number under notice to vacate is, most nearly
    A. 1:2   B. 2:3   C. 3:2   D. 2:1
    E. 3:1

13. For State-aided housing, assume that it has been decided to predict figures for the end of August and the end of September on the basis that the number of tenants expected to be declared ineligible in each future month will be 30% less than the average for the previous three months. The number of tenants expected to be declared ineligible during the month of September is expected to be, most nearly
    A. 100　　B. 122　　C. 141　　D. 158
    E. 175

14. Of the four categories of tenant status in the graph, the number of categories in which, at the end of May as compared with the end of April, there was a greater <u>numerical</u> increase in State-aided housing as compared with the same category in Federally-aided housing, is
    A. 0　　B. 1　　C. 2　　D. 3
    E. 4

15. Assume that, at the end of March, in State-aided housing, the total number of ineligibles was 10% greater than shown on the graph, and that this 10% increase was due entirely to a greater number of tenants being declared ineligible in that month than is shown on the graph. Under this assumption, the percentage increase in the number *declared ineligible*, as compared with the figure in the graph would be, most nearly
    A. 3%　　B. 10%　　C. 17%　　D. 23%
    E. 30%

16. In a housing project, the term <u>hatch door</u> is generally used to describe a door
    A. between the outdoors and the basement
    B. giving access from the boiler room to the fire tubes of a boiler
    C. giving access to the roof from the top of the stairway
    D. giving entrance from the hallway to the elevator shaft

17. A <u>parapet</u> is
    A. a device through which a fine spray of oil enters the firebox of an oil burner
    B. a hot water drain used in mornings to bleed off cold water which has accumulated overnight
    C. a protective low wall at the edge of a roof
    D. the primary support of an arch

18. <u>2-4-D</u> is used to designate
    A. an oil mixture used to start an oil burner in operation
    B. a size of threaded pipe of the type used to carry waste water
    C. a type of weed killer for use on lawns
    D. a type of pre-mixed cement for patching walks

19. A <u>condenser</u> is part of a
    A. boiler where the oil is preheated
    B. fertilizer spreader where concentrated fertilizer is mixed with water
    C. radiator where the return water forms from steam
    D. refrigerator where the refrigerant takes liquid form

20. In a housing project, a <u>low water cut-off</u> is usually a device to   20._____
    A. close the waste line opening when the waste has flushed out of the toilet bowl
    B. shut down the automatic lawn-watering system when the moisture level in the lawn reaches a pre-determined level of saturation
    C. stop a sum pump when the water level is below floor level in the sump wall
    D. stop an oil burner motor when the water level in the system falls below a pre-determined level

21. The purpose of a <u>check valve</u> is to   21._____
    A. interrupt the flow of electricity in an overloaded circuit
    B. limit the amount of electrical current which can flow from a main line into a branch circuit
    C. prevent water from flowing in a pipe system in a direction opposite to that desired
    D. stop the flow of water when the water in a system reaches a pre-determined level

22. In deteriorating slum neighborhoods which have high rates of crime and juvenile delinquency, the attitude of the majority of the residents toward the neighborhood is that it is   22._____
    A. a neighborhood which they understand and which understands them, so that it is to be preferred over any neighborhood except one with much better physical amenities
    B. a neighborhood with faults, but as good a neighborhood as most
    C. a bad place to live, one they would like to be able to leave
    D. a fine place to live and one which meets their needs

23. The one of the following which is NOT considered an *essential* criterion in the determination that an apartment is standard is that   23._____
    A. heat be provided centrally
    B. there be a fully enclosed bath in the apartment
    C. it have a kitchen or kitchenette
    D. there be a window in every room

24. The one of the following circumstances under which it would be proper for the Assistant Housing Manager at a project to unlock the door to a tenant's apartment for a law enforcement official without first contacting the Legal Department for an opinion is when
    A. an agent of the FBI, without a warrant, wishes to further an investigation by searching an apartment where, he states, he has reason to believe a crime is being committed
    B. a city patrolman wants to enter an apartment at night to make an arrest pursuant to a warrant in which the crime specified is a misdemeanor and the warrant makes no specification as to the time when it may be served
    C. a city patrolman, without a warrant, wishes to enter an apartment where he is in hot pursuit of someone whom, he states, he saw commit a felony
    D. a United States Army military policeman has a warrant for the arrest of a deserter whom, he states, he has just seen entering the apartment

25. The Assistant Manager of a large project becomes aware that two of the Housing Assistants do not get along with each other and have not gotten along for some time. In view of this fact, it would be best for the Assistant Manager to
    A. arrange assignments in such a way that these two assistants have as little contact with each other as possible
    B. call a staff meeting and emphasize the need for teamwork
    C. suggest that both assistants apply for transfers
    D. try to determine which of the two is at fault and insist that the one at fault correct his attitude

26. On the basis of a complaint by a site tenant that a certain Housing Assistant had refused to listen to her complaint about a lack of services, an Assistant Housing Manager has reprimanded the Housing Assistant. The Assistant Manager later becomes aware that the assistant reprimanded is not the one who was at fault. It would be best for the Assistant Manager to
    A. apologize privately to the assistant as soon as possible
    B. give the assistant certain desirable assignments in partial redress of the past error
    C. make a public apology at the next staff meeting
    D. say nothing about this incident but investigate such complaints much more carefully in the future

27. The manager called one of the Housing Assistants into his office and told him that his work was very unsatisfactory and pointed out exactly wherein it was so poor. He also stated that an improvement was expected. This method of approaching the situation is generally
    A. desirable; the discussion and criticism was carried on in private
    B. desirable; the Housing Assistant knows exactly where he stands
    C. poor; some praise or favorable comment should also be made if possible
    D. poor; a better approach would be to ask the Housing Assistant to explain why his work is unsatisfactory

28. Assume that you are the manager of a project. You have found it necessary to successively warn, reprimand and then severely reprimand a Housing Assistant for failure to carry out your orders. If the Housing Assistant again does not carry out your orders, it would be best for you to
    A. confer with the assistant privately, again explain the reason for the orders, and in most serious terms indicate the necessity for carrying them out
    B. bring the assistant up on charges of failure to perform his duties properly
    C. recommend that the assistant be transferred elsewhere
    D. severely reprimand the assistant again and warn him that more drastic action will be taken if it happens again

29. A junior accountant requests a transfer from the project where he is presently working to another project where he would be doing the same type of work. This transfer would be of no apparent advantage either to the Housing Authority or to the junior accountant. It would be best for the manager of the project to
    A. base his approval or rejection of the request on whether the junior accountant will be acceptable in the other project
    B. recommend the transfer if there is no apparent disadvantage to the Housing Authority
    C. refer the matter to the supervising manager without recommendation
    D. refuse the request and explain to the junior accountant that it is not in his best interest

30. A typist at a Housing Authority site comes to the Assistant Manager with a request that she be transferred to a project because she does not like site work, which she defines as making families move from their homes. It would be best for the Assistant Manager to
    A. explain to the typist the need for making families move in order to accomplish the slum clearance job of the Housing Authority and ask her to reconsider the request
    B. explain to the typist the need for making families move in order to accomplish the slum clearance job of the Housing Authority and refuse the request since it was based on a misunderstanding of the situation
    C. grant the request
    D. point out to the typist that the responsibility for making families move is not hers and ask her to reconsider the request

KEY (CORRECT ANSWERS)

1. D	11. C	21. C
2. A	12. C	22. C
3. A	13. A	23. D
4. C	14. B	24. C
5. D	15. E	25. A
6. C	16. D	26. A
7. B	17. C	27. C
8. B	18. C	28. B
9. B	19. D	29. A
10. B	20. D	30. A

EXAMINATION SECTION
TEST 1

DIRECTIONS: Each question or incomplete statement is followed by several suggested answers or completions. Select the one that BEST answers the question or completes the statement. *PRINT THE LETTER OF THE CORRECT ANSWER IN THE SPACE AT THE RIGHT.*

1. An Assistant Housing Manager has called a subordinate into his office in order to discuss the subordinate's failure to perform some task adequately. The subordinate, when criticized, accused the Assistant Manager of being prejudiced against him. If this is the first time that such an incident has occurred, it would be best for the manager to

    A. assure the subordinate that the facts upon which the criticism was based will be reviewed, since the subordinate feels so strongly about the matter
    B. insist that the subordinate listen to the criticism and that he make no comment on it unless he can do so in an objective manner
    C. listen to whatever the subordinate has to say and indicate the basis for the criticism
    D. terminate the interview immediately and suggest that the discussion be continued at some other time

2. Faced with a subordinate who is excessively dependent upon his superior in arriving at decisions, the superior should

    A. arrange to have the subordinate transferred to work which will not involve decision making
    B. continue to assist him in making decisions while instilling a feeling of confidence in the subordinate
    C. direct the subordinate to make his own decisions in areas assigned to him
    D. reprimand the subordinate for failing to perform the job properly

3. A supervisor has called one of his subordinates into his office to inform him of his service rating. During the interview, the supervisor has praised the subordinate for his good points and also criticized his shortcomings. The subordinate has agreed without discussion to every criticism leveled against him by the supervisor. It would now be best for the supervisor to

    A. get the employee to review his shortcomings and to suggest a plan for minimizing them, before terminating the interview
    B. suggest that the employee reserve any opinion on the criticisms until the service rating appeal period
    C. terminate the interview after having outlined all of the employee's shortcomings and points of merit
    D. terminate the interview after praising the employee's general receptiveness to criticism and emphasizing that past mistakes will not count against him in the coming year

4. A report to be sent to another subdivision of the Housing Authority has been prepared by a competent subordinate, in the name of the supervisor. It would be best for the supervisor to

   A. check the report in detail since it bears his name
   B. have the report checked in detail by another competent subordinate
   C. review the report briefly to pick up any obvious errors or omissions
   D. send the report forward without reading it

5. In establishing a work schedule for the performance of a particular job, the one of the following which is of LEAST importance is the

   A. number of employees available for assignment
   B. time by which the job must be finished
   C. time required for each separate part of the total job
   D. time required under very difficult or adverse conditions

6. One of the chief responsibilities of the supervisor is to make sure that the work is completed on time. In order to achieve this aim, it would be desirable for the supervisor to

   A. assign one employee to each specific task
   B. delegate responsibility in accordance with the abilities and capacities of his subordinates
   C. help out by doing as much of the work himself as he can
   D. schedule the work and keep informed of its progress

7. Effective supervisors apply proper principles of human relations. Application of such principles has what kind of effect on the need for detailed rules and regulations covering every aspect of the job?

   A. has no effect upon it
   B. increases the need for it
   C. reduces the need for it
   D. supersedes rules and regulations

8. Of the following, the most important generally approved method of maintaining high morale in one's staff is to

   A. advise the staff that personal problems must be left at home
   B. employ a jocular manner in issuing such reprimands as are necessary
   C. keep the staff informed of new developments and policies of the Housing Authority
   D. praise employees whenever such praise is warranted and refrain from direct criticism of their faults

9. When you become aware that a Housing Assistant under your supervision has failed to follow the proper procedure in making apartment inspections and has concealed this failure, it would be best for you to

   A. discuss with him both the failure to follow the proper procedure and the reason for this concealment, with the aim of improving the relationship between superior and subordinate
   B. make no mention of the matter to the assistant, but watch him more closely in the future

C. inform the assistant that the proper apartment inspection procedure must be followed since a uniform procedure is necessary for effective project management
D. review the proper apartment inspection procedure with the assistant and reprimand him for having concealed his failure to follow it

10. "The project manager does not formulate Housing Authority policy, but is responsible for executing policy formulated by top management. He is the administrative person closest to the employee group carrying out actual operations."
On this basis, a chLief function of the manager is to

10.____

A. dissuade employees from giving suggestions on translating policy into action
B. interpret policy in a way which will respect the personal interests and needs of the employees
C. recommend promotion of personnel to top management
D. report work schedules, work delays and staff assignments to top management so all the facts are available for decision making

11. The one of the following which is NOT a principle of effective operation in an organization is the need to

11.____

A. coordinate the work of different divisions
B. delegate to subordinates as much authority as they can assume within the scope of their jobs
C. provide sufficient overlapping of authority to insure coverage of all aspects of operation
D. trace and isolate problems, obstructions and other difficulties

12. A supervisor is most likely to achieve increased production by setting

12.____

A. high but attainable goals, and according high praise to those subordinates who reach the goals
B. low goals, and according high praise to those subordinates who exceed the goals
C. moderately high goals, raising them as the more efficient subordinates approach them
D. very high goals, and pressing the subordinates to reach them

13. Of the following, the most practical method of acquainting new employees with the details of routine rules and regulations of the Housing Authority is to

13.____

A. assign each new employee to an older employee for instruction and clarification of procedures
B. discuss with each new employee the nature of such rules and regulations shortly after he begins work
C. hold a conference with all new employees to inform them of the rules and regulations
D. provide a manual of rules and regulations for each employee

14. The practice of supervisors making themselves available to subordinates in order to listen to and help solve the subordinates' personal (off the job) problems is regarded as

    A. a form of paternalism rejected by both management and labor
    B. inadvisable since supervisors are seldom equipped to do such counseling
    C. proper in the maintenance of good personal relations
    D. undesirable since it represents the intrusion into the subordinates' personal affairs

14.____

15. An important educational principle that should be recognized by supervisors who are training subordinates is that

    A. any effective method of instruction will work equally well with all subordinates in a given title
    B. individual instruction is the only reliable method of training the average individual
    C. interested and capable persons will learn at different rates of speed when taking the same course of training
    D. people over 60 years of age have little capacity for learning

15.____

16. Assume that a Housing Manager disagrees with a new policy which has just been adopted by the central office. When he explains to his staff the policy and its application, there are criticisms and objections, many of which reflect his own point of view. It would be best for the manager to

    A. agree that the policy is defective but direct that it must be carried out
    B. explain the basis for the policy and order the staff to follow it
    C. modify the policy to meet the most valid objections to insure willing compliance with the policy
    D. refute the criticisms and objections regardless of his own opinion in the matter

16.____

17. A staff conference has been called by a supervisor for the purpose of considering means which may be used to solve a particular problem. In this situation, it is most important for the supervisor to

    A. encourage discussion, but discourage argument
    B. express his own views and opinions first
    C. permit the discussion to continue until everyone attending the conference is satisfied he has had his full say
    D. remain impartial, indicating neither approval or disapproval of any suggestions which may be presented

17.____

18. At staff meetings a manager is faced with a subordinate who takes every opportunity to make comments and gripe about one particular procedure. It would be best for the manager to

    A. assert his authority and warn the griper that publicly aired complaints will not be tolerated
    B. briefly explain management's reason for the procedure griped about
    C. ignore the gripes
    D. tell the griper that the problem at hand is how best to operate under the established procedure

18.____

19. One member of the staff, at staff meetings, likes to argue frequently and at length. It would be best for the supervisor to

    A. exclude him from staff meetings
    B. hear his arguments and answer them briefly
    C. talk to him privately and enlist his help in reducing arguments at staff meetings
    D. talk to other members of the staff, requesting that they not become involved in arguments with the offending member

20. At a staff conference conducted by you, there are frequent interruptions of the general discussion which indicate lack of understanding of the objectives of the conference. Of the following, the most reasonable conclusion to draw from this situation is that

    A. adequate control over the trend of the discussion was lacking
    B. conferees were probably antagonistic to the objectives of the conference
    C. content of the discussion bore little relation to the actual work assignments of the conferees
    D. objectives of the conference may not have been clearly expressed at the start of the conference

21. One of the staff members at a project frequently has good ideas but expresses them poorly when presenting them at staff meetings. It would be best for the manager to

    A. accept the ideas as they are presented, without commenting on the method of expression
    B. allow the staff member to state his ideas and for the manager to paraphrase them so they are easily understood
    C. defer consideration of the ideas until the next staff meeting so that the staff member can have time to put them in clearer form
    D. suggest to the staff member that he inform the manager of his ideas before the meeting so that the manager can rephrase them and present them so that they are more easily understood

22. In the course of several interviews with a certain tenant, you notice several incidents of peculiar behavior on the part of her child whom she has brought along with her to the office. The behavior appears to indicate an emotional disturbance requiring psychiatric help. The most advisable course of action for you to follow is to

    A. bring the situation to the attention of a child guidance clinic so that they may take appropriate action
    B. discuss the situation with the mother in an attempt to make her aware of the problem and the possible need for treatment
    C. tactfully point out to the mother that the child is emotionally disturbed and should be treated by a psychiatrist
    D. take no action on the situation but make a note of it in the tenant folder

23. An accepted concept of management of public housing is that it should "studiously avoid attitudes of paternalism." To avoid the paternalistic approach in dealing with tenants, management should

    A. deal with tenants as individuals rather than in organized groups
    B. emphasize its interest in good tenant relations, but avoid making specific recommendations on problems brought to it by tenants

C. emphasize objective uniform procedures in dealing with tenant problems
D. not interest itself in an unemployment problem brought to its attention by a tenant

24. Housing management should realize that the most essential factor contributing to the success of a community activities program is   24.____

   A. adequacy of facilities
   B. availability of funds
   C. existence of a sponsoring agency
   D. quality of leadership in activities

25. The one of the following which LEAST characterizes the dealings of the Housing Authority with agencies sponsoring community activities programs in projects is that the Authority   25.____

   A. gives certain forms of financial assistance
   B. permits retention of agency identity
   C. provides government direction
   D. requires reports on activities and progress

KEY (CORRECT ANSWERS)

1. C	11. C
2. B	12. A
3. A	13. D
4. C	14. C
5. D	15. C
6. D	16. B
7. C	17. A
8. C	18. D
9. A	19. C
10. B	20. D

21. B
22. B
23. C
24. D
25. C

TEST 2

DIRECTIONS: Each question or incomplete statement is followed by several suggested answers or completions. Select the one that BEST answers the question or completes the statement. *PRINT THE LETTER OF THE CORRECT ANSWER IN THE SPACE AT THE RIGHT.*

1. The one of the following which best indicates the extent to which teenage boys and girls may be permitted to plan their own leisure-time activities program is:

    A. Give the teenagers full responsibility for planning
    B. Leave the planning in the hands of the community activities coordinator or other professional leadership
    C. Permit certain selected teenagers to offer suggestions on planning, but leave all decisions up to the community activities coordinator
    D. Provide for joint responsibility of teenagers and professional leadership in planning

    1.____

2. A frequent criticism of the construction of public housing developments in slum areas has been the

    A. failure to consider the transportation needs of tenants
    B. failure to modify in any way the established gridiron pattern of slum thoroughfares
    C. failure to reduce population densities to desirable density standards
    D. lack of provision for slum site families in public housing developments

    2.____

3. As part of a report to the central office, a graph is to be prepared to show the rental income of a housing project, the amount which has been spent on heating, and the amount which has been spent on maintenance, each year for a five-year period. The best type of graph to use is a

    A. bar graph
    B. circle graph
    C. pictorial graph
    D. proportional graph

    3.____

4. Of the following arguments which may be used in an effort to urge residential site tenants to move, the LEAST suitable is to

    A. assure displaced families that they will be given first preference in choice of apartments in the new project
    B. explain that new projects will provide wholesome housing quarters for many families
    C. indicate why a slum area is not a desirable place in which to live and raise a family
    D. point out that stores, movies and other similar services will soon go out of business to make room for the new project

    4.____

5. The Housing Authority does not usually attempt to replace or make major improvements in the heating and plumbing systems of site buildings, even when such systems are somewhat defective or present operating difficulties. The chief reason for this policy is that

    A. buildings on sites are of such a heterogeneous nature and generally so out-of-date that repair and replacement parts are unobtainable
    B. it is economically unsound to make major improvements in buildings which will soon be demolished

    5.____

41

C. poor heating and plumbing services are very effective in encouraging tenants to move as quickly as possible
D. there is no need for the Authority to make repairs which the previous owner was unwilling to make

6. A site building has a coal-fired steam boiler as the heating plant. While using the boiler, proper examination of the water gauge fails to reveal the presence of any water. Of the following, it would be best that

    A. a small amount of water be let into the boiler immediately, increasing the amount of water gradually until the proper level is reached
    B. the fire be put out immediately by covering with sand
    C. the fire be put out immediately by spraying with warm water
    D. the required amount of water be put into the boiler immediately

7. The principal reason why a record is kept of "removable items" (so designated by the city's appraisers) which are left behind by commercial site tenants when they move out is that the

    A. award for moving expenses may be appropriately reduced
    B. commercial tenant may receive an award for the removable items
    C. items may be enumerated and taken into account in demolition contracts
    D. presence of the items will be known in the event they are reclassified as fixtures

8. When a commercial tenant, occupying space in a building purchased by the Housing Authority for demolition, moves prior to the date of condemnation, leaving behind certain fixtures, he is ordinarily entitled to

    A. a fixture award plus moving expenses
    B. a fixture award to be paid by the former owner as determined by the court at the time of condemnation
    C. no fixture award
    D. the same fixture award he would receive if he had waited until after the date of condemnation

9. To expedite the clearance of one site it may be necessary to transfer a residential tenant to a second site. In this event, the tenant is entitled, in so far as priority for admission to a project is concerned, to

    A. former site occupant status at the first site but no preference at the second site
    B. no former site occupant status but preference for admission to a project so long as he remains a site tenant
    C. site occupant status at the second site but no preference at the first site
    D. site tenant status at the second site and former site occupant status at the first site

10. Security deposits are required of all project tenants EXCEPT the following:

    A. recipients of assistance from the Department of Welfare
    B. resident employees
    C. resident employees and recipients of full assistance from the Department of Welfare
    D. resident employees and recipients of full Old Age Assistance

11. The most accurate statement concerning the eligibility for public housing of persons engaged in professional occupations, such as doctors, dentists or lawyers, is that they are

    A. eligible on the same basis as non-professionals
    B. eligible when engaged in their profession only part time, and if they meet the standards of eligibility, including income
    C. eligible when not self-employed, and if they meet the standards of eligibility, including income
    D. ineligible under all circumstances

12. A family group consisting of a husband, wife, son and an unrelated individual who has resided with them for 20 years applies for a project apartment. Considering family composition only, this family group is

    A. eligible for admission only to federally aided and city-aided projects
    B. eligible for admission only to state-aided and city-aided projects
    C. eligible for admission to all projects
    D. not eligible for public housing

13. A natural family group contains, in addition, one or more foster children for the support of whom the family receives remuneration from an accredited social agency. If the family meets other eligibility requirements, it is eligible for admission to

    A. all projects, the remuneration not to be considered income
    B. all projects, the remuneration not to be considered in determining eligibility, but to be considered in determining rent
    C. all projects, but, in the case of federally aided projects, the remuneration is to be considered income in determining rent and eligibility
    D. federally and city-aided projects only

14. The one of the following which is the most complete list of requirements for eligibility for an apartment in a public housing project for a single-person family is:

    A. 55 years of age or older; has been maintaining his own separate living quarters, or is a roomer in a hotel, rooming house or lodging house
    B. physically able to care for himself; able to maintain his apartment; 55 years of age or older; has been maintaining his own separate living quarters
    C. physically able to care for himself; 50 years of age or older; has been maintaining his own separate living quarters, or is a roomer in a hotel, rooming house or lodging house
    D. physically able to care for himself; 50 years of age or older

15. If a tenant who has been served with a notice of ineligibility, but not with a notice to vacate, moves from his apartment without notifying the Housing Authority prior to the date of move-out, he shall be charged rent

    A. for a period not to exceed seven days after the date of move-out, depending on the vacancy loss
    B. for a period not to exceed 15 days after the date of move-out, depending on the vacancy loss
    C. only through the date of move-out
    D. for the full calendar month, regardless of vacancy loss

16. As the population of cities increases, there is a decrease in the proportion of the developed urban land area which is used for

    A. commercial purposes
    B. industrial purposes
    C. parks and open areas
    D. residential purposes
    E. streets and thoroughfares

17. If valid criteria have been used in tenant selection for public housing projects, the result most likely to be attained is

    A. homogeneity of tenant characteristics will be assured
    B. larger Federal subsidies will be required
    C. neediest families will receive the greatest proportion of aid
    D. the underlying conditions of slums will be ameliorated
    E. management problems will be satisfied

18. On August 26 a tenant notifies the project of an increase in income which became effective on August 12. This increased income will require a rent increase for the tenant. His new increased rent becomes effective on the first of

    A. August   B. September   C. October   D. November

19. In calculating the anticipated income of a project tenant, the one of the following which shall NOT be included is

    A. unemployment insurance benefits
    B. veteran's mustering-out payments
    C. Workmen's Compensation payments
    D. Workmen's Compensation payments, when the employee also has income from other employment

20. An investigation has been made of a broken window pane in an apartment on the third floor which the tenant claims was broken by children playing outside. The investigation disclosed that there were several small holes in the window pane. Each hole is approximately cone-shaped and is about 3/16 inch in diameter on the inside of the glass (room side) and about 1/2 inch in diameter on the outside. Cracks connected some of these holes. On the basis of this information, the tenant should

    A. be charged for the window pane since the damage is not normal wear-and-tear and it is not possible to substantiate the tenant's claim
    B. be charged for the window pane since the nature of the damage indicates that it was caused from inside
    C. not be charged for the window pane since it is not possible to determine the cause of the damage and the low floor involved does not tend to support the tenant's explanation
    D. not be charged for the window pane since the nature of the damage indicates that it was caused from outside

21. Suppose you are studying the need for improving the effectiveness of operation of a particular activity. In making this study, you should pay LEAST attention to the

    A. amount of time which is consumed in this activity
    B. degree of prestige which will accrue to you
    C. number of persons engaged in this activity
    D. possible revision of employee work schedules
    E. value of the end product resulting from the activity

22. In training employees under your supervision, a basic fact to recognize is that

    A. instruction should be the same for all, since learning rates are uniform for all employees in a given title
    B. it is difficult to train persons above the age of 40 years
    C. persons differ in the amount they learn in a given period of time
    D. the training process should begin on a highly technical level if the subject matter to be learned is highly technical
    E. training can seldom achieve its purpose unless individual instruction is the method used

23. A group of newly appointed Housing Assistants has been assigned to your project. Of the following, the most important thing for you to do when they report for work on their first day is to

    A. acquaint them with the general features of the duties they are to perform
    B. allow them to ask questions freely about the conditions of work and the possibilities of advancement
    C. ascertain their sympathy with the social philosophy behind low-rent public housing
    D. distribute a schedule of visits to tenants to acquaint the Housing Assistants with the typical situations they will encounter
    E. inform them about time, sickness, absence and vacation regulations

24. Of the following, the best incentive to better work to employ in the supervision of a recently appointed Housing Assistant is, in general, to compare his present progress with

    A. previous progress made by him at the project
    B. progress of Housing Assistants of average ability at the project
    C. progress of the least competent Housing Assistant at the project
    D. progress of the most efficient Housing Assistant at the project
    E. progress of Housing Assistants in general at all projects

25. Of the following, the most important basis upon which to evaluate the efficiency of a subordinate is his

    A. accuracy and promptness in execution of assignments
    B. awareness of the social aspects of the assignments given to him
    C. confidence in the handling of difficult assignments
    D. observance of the rules and regulations of the Authority
    E. relationship with fellow employees

KEY (CORRECT ANSWERS)

1. D
2. C
3. A
4. A
5. B

6. B
7. D
8. C
9. D
10. D

11. C
12. C
13. A
14. C
15. C

16. D
17. C
18. C
19. B
20. B or C

21. B
22. C
23. A
24. A
25. A

TEST 3

DIRECTIONS: Each question or incomplete statement is followed by several suggested answers or completions. Select the one that BEST answers the question or completes the statement. *PRINT THE LETTER OF THE CORRECT ANSWER IN THE SPACE AT THE RIGHT.*

1. A Housing Assistant under your supervision attempts to conceal the fact that he has made an error. Of the following, the most reasonable interpretation of this action is that the

    A. action of the Housing Assistant indicates an independent attitude
    B. desire for concealment of the error demonstrates an antisocial attitude
    C. error was probably a minor one which the Housing Assistant felt did not have to be reported to superior authority
    D. evasion indicates the possibility of an inadequate relationship between you and the Housing Assistant
    E. Housing Assistant does not know the proper procedure to follow

1.____

2. A Housing Assistant under your supervision complains that he deserves a higher service rating than the one he received recently. Your review of his work indicates that his work performance was average and that the standard rating he received was a just rating. Of the following, the most appropriate reply to his complaint is to

    A. advise him that he may appeal to the Civil Service Commission for a higher rating
    B. point out the below-average aspects of his work which were not included in his service rating report
    C. tell him not to be too concerned about his rating since he was considered a satisfactory employee
    D. tell him that the Departmental Personnel Board, and not you, is responsible for the allocation of service ratings
    E. tell him why his work was considered average and did not deserve more than a standard rating

2.____

3. A subject which is LEAST desirable as a topic in group discussion of interviewing problems is

    A. effect of the setting of an interview on the success of the interview
    B. evaluation of the interviews handled by the least efficient staff member
    C. handling language difficulties at interviews
    D. maximum utilization of application forms on which interviews are based
    E. subjective attitudes of applicants for low-rent public housing

3.____

4. A Housing Assistant criticizes a form which has been used in connection with applications for low-rent housing as poor because it limits the interviewer to specified areas of discussion with applicants. Of the following, the most appropriate course of action for you, as his supervisor, to take is to

    A. ascertain the need for further guidance of this Housing Assistant by reviewing his past use of this form
    B. ask the Housing Assistant to explain the limitations of the form in relation to required job performance

4.____

47

C. make a study of records of interviews by other Housing Assistants to determine the validity of the criticism
D. tell the Housing Assistant that such limitation is necessary to avoid interviews of undue length
E. tell the Housing Assistant that the ability of an employee to adhere to the form in his interviews is related to his understanding of standard procedures

5. One of your Housing Assistants has shown himself to be inaccurate in checking tenant income records. The action most likely to result in improvement in the work habits of this employee is to

   A. assign him to work that will not require close attention to details
   B. have him study a group of tenant income records which have been accurately checked
   C. review with him some of the records he has checked
   D. tell him that it is just as easy to do his job the right way
   E. warn that he will receive an unsatisfactory rating if he persists in being careless

6. Assume that a new procedure of interviewing has been adopted by the management division which you think may meet with some staff resistance. To reduce such possible resistance to a minimum, the best of the following steps to take is to

   A. advise the staff that they will have to accept the new procedure regardless of their personal feelings about it
   B. appoint a staff committee to study the procedure and report on its objectionable and desirable features
   C. ask staff members who in the past have been resistant to new procedures to comment on the new procedure before it is effective
   D. hold a staff meeting to discuss the meaning and application of the procedure prior to the date it is effective
   E. issue detailed instructions on the use of the new procedure to facilitate its application

7. To determine if assignments made to employees under your supervision are being carried out, the most practical supervisory method is to

   A. develop work-flow charts for use in checking work performance
   B. establish production quotas and work schedules
   C. evaluate periodic reports of work performed by subordinates
   D. give detailed instructions for all work assignments and delegate authority for work performance
   E. keep subordinates under constant surveillance to see that details of assignments are executed properly

8. "Samples of income re-examination records of Housing Assistants, in which no change in income or eligibility is involved, should be reviewed periodically." Of the following, the LEAST important reason for such periodic review is to

   A. correct errors in the application of re-examination procedures
   B. indicate a basis for efficiency ratings of these employees
   C. insure uniformity in application of re-examination procedures

D. obtain data as to the need for further training of Housing Assistants in eligibility review procedures
E. provide a means of determining the comparative production of each Housing Assistant

9. Suppose that a study is to be made of the adequacy of work schedules for maintenance personnel at your project. Of the following, the best first step to take is to

   A. arrange for detailed surveys of actual performance to obtain needed data
   B. discuss current work schedules with the building superintendent and his assistant superintendents
   C. have each employee submit a statement of his daily tasks and the time required for each task
   D. review typical work schedules of other projects to provide the basis for desired standards of work output
   E. utilize records of complaints as to service and breakdown of equipment as the starting point of the study

10. Of the following, the most important reason for planning work schedules for subordinates is that

    A. coverage of essential operations is more likely to be maintained
    B. emergency situations can be handled more expeditiously
    C. subordinates are more likely to be satisfied with their assignments if routinized
    D. supervisory relationships will be clarified and strengthened
    E. the basis for most tenant complaints will be eliminated

11. An employee under your supervision has shown difficulty in organizing his work. Consequently, the quality and quantity of his work output has been below acceptable standards. Of the following, the most effective way of improving the performance of this employee is to

    A. advise the employee to set up a tickler system so that he will not forget essential tasks
    B. encourage the employee to organize his work more efficiently
    C. explain the relationship of proper organization of work to work output
    D. help the employee discover the factors that may be hindering effective organization of work
    E. lay out the work of the employee until he is able to organize his work properly by himself

12. Suppose you have been assigned as site manager of a newly acquired slum clearance site. Of the following, the first major task you should undertake is to

    A. approach community agencies to solicit aid in tenant relocation
    B. establish criteria for determination of usability of residential buildings for which demolition may be deferred
    C. establish procedures for the acceptance from site tenants of applications for permanent low-rent housing
    D. establish reasonable time limits for removal of tenants from the site
    E. plan and administer a complete tenant and physical inventory

13. While walking down the steps of one of the project buildings, you notice a porter doing his work very poorly. Of the following, the proper action for you to take is to

   A. advise the building superintendent that the porter did not seem to know how to do his work
   B. analyze the porter's record to determine if it is satisfactory
   C. inform the building superintendent that a training program for porters appears advisable
   D. question the porter to ascertain whether he knows the proper way to do the job
   E. tell the porter that he is delinquent in his duties

14. After an accident has occurred and the injured employee has been given needed care, it is accepted practice to make a thorough determination of the cause of the accident. From the viewpoint of management, the most important purpose of such accident investigations is to

   A. establish the extent of liability of management in each case
   B. indicate to maintenance employees their responsibility in accident prevention
   C. maintain the morale of the staff and tenants
   D. obtain the necessary data for the liability insurer
   E. prevent the recurrence of such accidents

15. When a congested urban slum area is given over to a private or public housing project, the setting aside, at the same time, of additional space for school building is

   A. undesirable because it tends to decrease the amount of tax-producing property and thereby increase the tax burden on other property owners
   B. undesirable because the location of a school building depends on other additional factors which can be better determined at a later date
   C. desirable because property owners in the area raise fewer objections when land is condemned for both project and school at the same time
   D. desirable because suitable land may otherwise not be readily available for this purpose
   E. desirable because a school is an essential part of the community

16. The most important reason why Housing Assistants should be acquainted with the significant social foci of the housing project neighborhood is that

   A. a more constructive approach for the improvement of intra-family relations may be obtained
   B. better relations between project families and neighborhood families may be fostered
   C. fewer referrals to social agencies will need to be made
   D. neighborhood needs may be assessed more adequately
   E. tenants may be better advised how to budget their incomes

17. The most important positive result of tenant organization from the viewpoint of management is that it

   A. acts as a control on the possible slipshod work of subordinate members of the staff
   B. enables management to avoid complaints of an individual nature
   C. inevitably serves as a filter through which only important tenant problems affecting general welfare pass on to management

D. provides a means for bringing problems to the surface which otherwise might not be known or understood by management
E. usually engages the interests of tenants who will assume positions of leadership in the community

18. Where imminence of eviction of an applicant makes it impracticable to schedule a housing investigation, it is essential that prior to acceptance as an emergency applicant in a permanent project, he submit

    A. conclusive proof of residence at the address from which he is being evicted
    B. detailed proof of income eligibility
    C. evidence that he is unable to find suitable quarters pending completion of the housing investigation
    D. primary proof of citizenship
    E. proof that he is financially responsible or is a recipient of public assistance

19. When the building superintendent tells you that the transformer of one of the oil burners is defective, he is referring to the device which

    A. atomizes the liquid oil prior to ignition
    B. changes low-pressure steam to high-pressure steam
    C. increases the voltage for oil ignition
    D. regulates oil temperature prior to atomization
    E. supplies the proper voltage for operation of the motor

20. When a building superintendent reports corroded flashings resulting in leakage, the part of the building he is referring to is the

    A. basement piping
    B. boiler room
    C. pavement adjoining building
    D. roof
    E. stair halls

21. If an automatic elevator is not leveling properly at floor stops, the proper action to take is to

    A. allow the car to remain in service only if the distance between the car floor and floor landing is 3 inches or less
    B. post signs in the elevator to warn passengers
    C. station a maintenance man near the ground floor stop to warn passengers
    D. take the car out of service during slow periods to make necessary adjustments
    E. take the car out of service immediately to make necessary adjustments

22. Although rock salt is commonly used on the walks of the project when they are iced or heavily packed with snow, the chief disadvantage of its use is that it

    A. creates a very slushy condition
    B. generally causes deterioration of concrete walks
    C. increases cleaning costs if used intensively
    D. is harmful to adjacent trees and shrubs
    E. tends to increase the accident hazard

23. When instructing tenants how to clean enamel-painted woodwork, the tenant should be advised to wash the surfaces with   23.____

    A. ammonia water
    B. mild soap and water solution
    C. plain warm water
    D. strong soda solution
    E. vinegar and water solution

24. Of the following items included in the work schedule of porters, the one that should be assigned as a daily duty is   24.____

    A. cleaning incinerators
    B. cleaning stairhall windows and woodwork
    C. mopping all assigned stairhalls
    D. sweeping all stair landings
    E. washing down all sidewalks adjacent to assigned buildings

25. Some housing projects have, in the past, reduced their personnel cost for community activities by using tenant volunteers. The major disadvantage of this practice is that   25.____

    A. volunteers have no financial ties to oblige them to carry on the work regularly and efficiently
    B. tenant volunteers may not be aware of the most desirable methods of group work
    C. tenant volunteers are usually unable to obtain the respect and cooperation of fellow tenants
    D. demands of tenants for further participation in management operation will be fostered
    E. antagonism between tenant volunteers and tenants using community facilities is a general occurrence

26. "Studies in the cities of Hartford, Chicago, Philadelphia, Newark and New York showed that the rate of juvenile delinquency was highest in areas where housing was least adequate."   26.____
    On the basis of this quotation, it is most correct to say that

    A. no relationship can be established at all since bad housing is but one factor among many that may cause delinquent behavior
    B. areas of substandard housing are generally areas of high juvenile delinquency
    C. provision of adequate housing is probably the most effective tool in combating juvenile delinquency
    D. slum areas are less effectively policed than other areas in the cities mentioned
    E. the physical aspects of housing have direct causal relationship with the rate of juvenile delinquency

In questions 27 through 30, each paragraph contains five words in **bold** type, one of which is not in keeping with the meaning of the selection. In the space provided, write the letter of the one of the five words given that does not belong as written in the statement.

27. "The **minimum** amount that can be paid by the **Federal** government in any year as annual **contributions** to a low-rent housing project under a given contract of financial aid is a **fixed** percentage of the total **development** cost of the project."   27._____

    A. minimum   B. Federal   C. contributions   D. fixed
    E. development

28. "The existence and **dimensions** of the slums had long been **recognized** by State legislatures and municipalities, but these local public bodies and officers had **wasted** their efforts primarily on **unintegrated** remedial measures **restricted** in character to building and health codes."   28._____

    A. dimensions   B. recognized   C. wasted   D. unintegrated
    E. restricted

29. "One of the **major** purposes of a program of land **assembly** for urban redevelopment is to direct the location of new **home** building to **zoned** city land by erasing the margin that seems to favor unused **fringe** land."   29._____

    A. major   B. assembly   C. home   D. zoned
    E. fringe

30. Migration of **non-farm** families is estimated to **increase** the needs for housing construction only to the extent that **out-migration** from individual localities is so great as to leave an actual **deficit** of standard housing in those localities **after** demolition of all sub-standard units."   30._____

    A. non-farm   B. increase   C. out-migration   D. deficit
    E. after

KEY (CORRECT ANSWERS)

1.	D	16.	B
2.	E	17.	D
3.	B	18.	A
4.	B	19.	C
5.	C	20.	D
6.	D	21.	E
7.	C	22.	D
8.	E	23.	B
9.	B	24.	D
10.	A	25.	A
11.	D	26.	B
12.	E	27.	A
13.	A	28.	C
14.	E	29.	D
15.	D	30.	D

EXAMINATION SECTION
TEST 1

DIRECTIONS: Each question or incomplete statement is followed by several suggested answers or completions. Select the one that BEST answers the question or completes the statement. *PRINT THE LETTER OF THE CORRECT ANSWER IN THE SPACE AT THE RIGHT.*

1. While interviewing tenants, an assistant should use the technique of interruption, beginning to speak when a tenant has temporarily paused at the end of a phrase or sentence, in order to

    A. limit the tenant's ability to voice his objection or complaints
    B. shorten, terminate, or redirect a tenant's response
    C. assert authority when he feels that the tenant is too conceited
    D. demonstrate to the tenant that pauses in speech should be avoided

    1.____

2. An assistant might gain background information about a tenant by being aware of the person's speech during an interview.
Which one of the following patterns of speech would offer the LEAST accurate information about a tenant?
The

    A. number of slang expressions and the level of vocabulary
    B. presence and degree of an accent
    C. rate of speech and the audibility level
    D. presence of a physical speech defect

    2.____

3. Suppose that you are interviewing a distressed tenant who claims that he was just laid off from his job and has no money to pay his rent.
Your FIRST action should be to

    A. ask if he has sought other employment or has other sources of income
    B. express your sympathy but explain that he must pay the rent on time
    C. inquire about the reasons he was laid off from work
    D. try to transfer him to a smaller apartment which he can afford

    3.____

4. Suppose you have some background information on an applicant whom you are interviewing. During the interview, it appears that the applicant is giving you false information.
The BEST thing for you to do at that point is to

    A. pretend that you are not aware of the written facts and let him continue
    B. tell him what you already know and discuss the discrepancies with him
    C. terminate the interview and make a note that the applicant is untrustworthy
    D. tell him that because he is making false statements, he will not be eligible for an appointment

    4.____

5. Since at present there are not many Spanish-speaking assistants, a Spanish-speaking applicant may want to bring his bilingual child with him to an interview to act as an interpreter.
Which of the following would be LEAST likely to affect the value of an interview in which an applicant's child has acted as interpreter?

    5.____

A. It may make it undesirable for the assistant to ask certain questions.
B. A child may do an inadequate job of interpretation.
C. A child's answers may indicate his feelings toward his parents.
D. The applicant may not want to reveal all information in front of his child.

6. While you are showing families around a new project which will be ready for occupancy in a month, you are asked many questions concerning the present state of disorder in the halls and grounds of the buildings. These families are concerned that this condition will exist when they move in.
Of the following, the BEST way to handle this situation would be for you to

   A. assure the tenants that the buildings will all be clean and tidy when they are due to move in
   B. explain that almost everything will be completed when the tenants move in, but that temporary inconveniences tend to exist when one moves into a new project
   C. avoid answering the questions since the condition will exist, but emphasize the advantage of moving into a new project
   D. explain that because this is a low-income project, efficiency is reduced and it will, therefore, take more time to get the building ready

7. Assume that you are responsible for making apartment inspections.
To make a practice of setting up appointments with tenants before visiting is

   A. *good,* mainly because it allows the tenant time to become acquainted with household safety procedures
   B. *good,* mainly because it is demeaning and disrespectful of tenant's privacy to appear at the apartment unannounced
   C. *poor,* mainly because it will give the tenant an opportunity to clean the house, thus not giving a picture of normal conditions
   D. *poor,* mainly because tenants should be available at all times for inspections

8. Assume that you are approached by a tenant who seeks your help in dealing with her 12-year-old son, Joe. He apparently leaves for school each morning, but another child has just informed her that Joe has not been in school for a month. She is very upset and does not know what action to take.
The one of the following actions which you should recommend that she take as a FIRST step is to

   A. report the truancy to the school immediately so they can take action
   B. discuss the situation with Joe, inquiring as to the truth of the matter
   C. reprimand Joe or deprive him of something he wants to get him to go to school
   D. tell Joe to report to you to discuss an important matter

9. Suppose you have been informed by your supervisor that he has checked the applications that you have submitted and he found that you have categorized a disproportionate number of minority applicants as ineligible. You feel that you have impartially evaluated all of the applications.
Of the following, the MOST appropriate action for you to take is to

   A. request that he review the application forms with you to discuss the eligibility of specific applications
   B. tell him that you will look over the applications and change them to eligible

C. tell him that you will try to be more careful in the future when interviewing and qualifying applicants
D. provide as much evidence as possible showing your good treatment of members of minority groups in other situations

10. Suppose you have placed in an apartment a family that has recently arrived from a distant country. Other tenants have mentioned to you that they are puzzled by the new tenants' strange culture and wonder when they will adapt to our society.
Of the following, which aspect of their culture is MOST conducive to change?

    A. Religious beliefs
    B. Parent-child relationships
    C. Use of household appliances
    D. Customs observed at meal-time

11. Suppose a tenant, Mr. X, complains to you that the occupants of the apartment directly below his apartment play their boom box . very loudly, although he has repeatedly asked them to lower it.
Of the following, the BEST action for you to take is to

    A. suggest that Mr. X also play loud music in his apartment to show how annoying it can be
    B. inform Mr. X that there is nothing that you can do–Mr. X must deal with the tenants directly
    C. post a sign in the building lobby stating the Noise Abatement Laws
    D. speak with the other tenant and discuss the situation with him

12. Suppose one of your duties includes inspecting the apartments of all new tenants and suggesting proper care of equipment. A family you are visiting appears to be quite hostile to you, although you have explained the purpose of your visit. You notice that the stove is covered with grease and the sink drain is clogged with coffee grounds. Of the following, what is the BEST thing for you to do in this situation?

    A. Refrain from making comments on the situation at this time, but remember to report the conditions to your supervisor
    B. Describe the dangers or possible results of the clogged drain and greasy stove, and suggest easy ways to correct these conditions
    C. Offer to help clean the stove and sink drain and enumerate, on paper, the ways to take care of the equipment properly
    D. Make an appointment for the tenants to speak with you about the situation in your office

13. Assume you are assigned to interview applicants for low-rent apartments.
Of the following, which is the BEST attitude for you to take in dealing with applicants for apartments?

    A. Assume they will enjoy being interviewed because they believe that you, as a representative of the landlord, will get them an apartment
    B. Expect that they have had a history of anti-social behavior in the family, and probe deeply into the social development of family members
    C. Expect that they will try to control the interview, thus you should keep them on the defensive

D. Assume that they will be polite and cooperative and attempt to secure the information you need in a business-like manner

14. Assume that the following problem of a tenant family has come to your attention. The tenant, who is the main support of his family, has developed a health problem which prevents him from driving a car or traveling to work by subway. He can, however, walk up to a mile or travel by surface transportation. Because of the problem of traveling to work, he may lose his job.
Which of the following courses of action should you take FIRST?

    A. Put the tenant in touch with the department of social services. They may be able to arrange public assistance payments for him.
    B. Find out whether any housing projects meeting the new transportation restrictions of the tenant have any apartments available.
    C. Arrange a visit by a social worker. If the man stays home and his wife goes to work, they may be able to maintain their income.
    D. Send the man for employment counseling. He may have skills that are in demand, close to his present apartment.

15. Assume that an elderly single tenant who has habitually paid her rent on time is now two weeks late with her current month's rent. You have sent her an official notice of delinquency.
Assuming that you have taken no other action to collect the rent, the NEXT thing you should do is to

    A. send her a strong personal note demanding payment of her rent
    B. send a polite note to her daughter, who is listed on your records as next of kin, asking her to speak to her mother about her delinquency
    C. send her a note asking her to telephone you immediately
    D. telephone or visit her apartment because illness may be the cause of the late rent payment

16. Assume that you are working at a project and a tenant tells you that some equipment left on the grounds poses a hazard to the tenants and their children. She suggests that this equipment be surrounded by barricades and signs.
Of the following, the BEST response for you to make is to tell the tenant

    A. to route her complaint and suggestion through the tenants' association
    B. that you will pass her complaint and suggestion on to the manager of the project for consideration
    C. to be careful in making complaints; she may be labeled as a troublemaker
    D. suggest that she put her complaint and suggestion into writing so that it will be easier to understand

17. Assume that, in a public housing project, a tenant complains that the interior of the elevator has recently been defaced by graffiti. She claims that for the past two days, at about 3 P.M., she has seen a few teenage boys running from the building and suspects they are the culprits.
The FIRST thing that you should do is to

    A. station a housing patrolman by the elevator for the next few days to observe any unusual incidents
    B. explain to her that the incidents appear to be totally unrelated

C. have a housing patrolman patrol the outside of the building at 3 P.M. to watch for the boys
D. ask her why she feels the boys are responsible for the graffiti

Questions 18-20.

DIRECTIONS: Questions 18 through 20 each list various duties that you are to perform on a particular day. Assuming that you have arrived at the office at 9:00 A.M., indicate for each question which of the four duties listed should be taken care of FIRST.

18. A. You are informed that an elderly tenant has just been taken to the hospital and you must call his son, whose telephone number you have on file.
    B. Two tenants whose children have been involved in a series of complaints concerning damage to housing authority property are waiting to see you.
    C. You have a message from the central office of the housing authority requesting clarification of a single point in a report you prepared.
    D. A tenant who was already served with an eviction notice for non-payment of rent is waiting with a large back-rent check.

19. A. A tenant who is about to be evicted because of non-payment of rent is waiting to see you.
    B. A housing patrolman who must leave for court wants to speak to you about a tenant's child he has just arrested.
    C. It will take only ten minutes to finish your monthly activities report which is overdue.
    D. An insurance investigator is waiting to see you concerning an injury suffered by a tenant in his building's elevator.

20. A. The receptionist tells you that a woman is waiting to see you with a complaint about a repair to a toilet. The woman says she must leave for work by 9:30 A.M.
    B. You have an unfinished report in your desk which requires about 15 minutes to complete,
    C. A tenant is early for a 9:15 appointment for an interview that should take approximately 15 minutes.
    D. There is a note to you from the project manager which says, *Please see me as soon as you can spare 15 minutes.*

KEY (CORRECT ANSWERS)

1. B	6. B	11. D	16. B
2. C	7. B	12. B	17. D
3. A	8. B	13. D	18. A
4. B	9. A	14. B	19. B
5. C	10. C	15. D	20. A

TEST 2

DIRECTIONS: Each question or incomplete statement is followed by several suggested answers or completions. Select the one that BEST answers the question or completes the statement. *PRINT THE LETTER OF THE CORRECT ANSWER IN THE SPACE AT THE RIGHT.*

Questions 1-5.

DIRECTIONS: Questions 1 through 5 are to be answered SOLELY on the basis of the following passage.

At one time people thought that in the interview designed primarily to obtain information, the interviewer had to resort to clever and subtle lines of questioning in order to accomplish his ends. Some people still believe that this is necessary, but it is not so. An example of the "tricky" approach may be seen in the work of a recent study. The study deals with materials likely to be buried beneath deep defenses. Interviewers utilized methods of questioning which, in effect, trapped the interviewee and destroyed his defenses. Doubtless these methods succeeded in bringing out items of information which straightforward questions would have missed. Whether they missed more information than they obtained and whether they obtained the most important facts must remain unanswered questions. In defense of the "clever" approach, it is often said that, in many situations, the interviewee is motivated to conceal information or to distort what he chooses to report.

Technically, it is likely that a highly skilled interviewer can, given the time and the inclination, penetrate the interviewee's defenses and get information which the latter intended to keep hidden. It is unlikely that the interviewer can successfully elicit all of the information that might be relevant. If, for example, he found that an applicant for financial assistance was heavily in debt to gamblers, he might not care about getting any other information. There are situations in which one item, if answered in the "wrong" way, is enough. Ordinarily, this is not true. The usual situation is that there are many considerations and that the plus and minus features must be weighed before a decision may be made. It is, therefore, important to obtain complete information.

1. According to the above passage, it was generally believed that an interviewer would have difficulty in obtaining the information he sought from a person if he

    A. were tricky in his methods
    B. were open and frank in his approach
    C. were clever in his questioning
    D. utilized carefully prepared questions

1._____

2. The passage does NOT reveal whether the type of questions used

    A. trapped those being interviewed
    B. elicited facts which an open method of questioning might miss
    C. elicited the most important facts that were sought
    D. covered matters which those interviewed were reluctant to talk about openly

2._____

3. An argument in favor of the *tricky* or *clever* interviewing technique is that, unless this approach is used, the person interviewed will NOT

    A. offer to furnish all pertinent information
    B. answer questions concerning routine data

3._____

C. clearly understand what is being sought
D. want to continue the interview

4. According to the above passage, in favorable circumstances, a talented interviewer would be able to obtain from the person interviewed information 4.____

   A. which the person regards as irrelevant
   B. which the person intends to conceal
   C. about the person's family background
   D. which the person would normally have forgotten

5. According to the above passage, a highly skilled interviewer should concentrate, in most cases, on getting 5.____

   A. one outstanding fact about the interviewee which would do away with the need for prolonged questioning
   B. facts which the interviewee wanted to conceal because these would be the most relevant in making a decision
   C. all the facts so that he can consider their relative values before reaching any conclusion
   D. information about any bad habits of the interviewee, such as gambling, which would make further questioning

Questions 6-8.

DIRECTIONS: Questions 6 through 8 are to be answered SOLELY on the basis of the following passage.

City governments have long had building codes which set minimum standards for building and for human occupancy. The code (or series of codes) makes provisions for standards of lighting and ventilation sanitation, fire prevention and protection. As a result of demands from manufacturers, builders, real estate people, tenement owners, and building-trades unions, these codes often have established minimum standards well below those that the contemporary society would accept as a rock-bottom minimum. Codes often become outdated, so that meager standards in one era become seriously inadequate a few decades later as society's concept of a minimum standard of living changes. Out-of-date codes, when still in use, have sometimes prevented the introduction of new devices and modern building techniques. Thus, it is extremely important that building codes keep pace with changes in the accepted concept of a minimum standard of living.

6. According to the above passage, all of the following considerations in building planning would probably be covered in a building code EXCEPT 6.____

   A. closet space as a percentage of total floor area
   B. size and number of windows required for rooms of differing sizes
   C. placement of fire escapes in each line of apartments
   D. type of garbage disposal units to be installed

7. According to the above passage, if an ideal building code were to be created, how would the established minimum standards in it compare to the ones that are presently set by city governments? 7.____
They would

A. be lower than they are at present
B. be higher than they are at present
C. be comparable to the present minimum standards
D. vary according to the economic group that sets them

8. On the basis of the above passage, what is the reason for difficulties in introducing new building techniques?

   A. Builders prefer techniques which represent the rock-bottom minimum desired by society.
   B. Certain manufacturers have obtained patents on various building methods to the exclusion of new techniques.
   C. The government does not want to invest money in techniques that will soon be outdated,
   D. New techniques are not provided for in building codes which are not up to date.

Questions 9-11.

DIRECTIONS: Questions 9 through 11 are to be answered SOLELY on the basis of the following passage.

The agreement under which a tenant rents property from a landlord is known as a lease. Generally speaking, leases are classified as either short-term or long-term in duration. They are further subdivided according to the method used to determine the amount of periodic rent payments. Of the following types of leases in use, the more commonly used ones are the following;

1. *The straight or fixed lease is one in which rent may be paid in equal amounts throughout the duration of the lease. These are usually restricted to short-term leasing, or somewhat longer-term if clauses in the lease provide for periodic escalation of payments as the economy shifts.*
2. *Percentage leasing, used for short-term commercial leasing, provides the landlord with a stipulated percentage of a tenant's gross sales from goods and services sold on the premises, in addition to a fixed amount of rent.*
3. *The net lease, generally long-term (ten years or more), requires the tenant to pay all operating costs, including real estate taxes and insurance. In a net-net lease, the tenant further agrees to meet mortgage interest and principal payments.*
4. *An escalated lease, which is a long-term lease, requires rent to be of a stipulated base amount which periodically is subject to escalation in accordance with cost-of-living index scales, or in direct proportion to taxes, insurance, and operating costs.*

9. Based on the information given in the passage, which type of lease is MOST likely to be advantageous to a landlord if there is a high rate of inflation? _____ lease.

   A. Fixed   B. Percentage
   C. Net   D. Escalated

10. On the basis of the above passage, which types of lease would generally be MOST suitable for a well-established textile company which requires permanent facilities for its large operations?
    _____ lease and_____ lease.

    A. Percentage; escalated   B. Escalated; net
    C. Straight; net   D. Straight; percentage

11. According to the above passage, the ONLY type of lease which assures the same amount of rent throughout a specified interval is the _____ lease.   11.____

    A. straight   B. percentage   C. net-net   D. escalated

Questions 12-14.

DIRECTIONS: Questions 12 through 14 are to be answered SOLELY on the basis of the following passage.

Physical design plays a very significant role in crime rate. Crime rate has been found to increase almost proportionately with building height. The average number of crimes is much greater in higher buildings than in lower ones (equal or less than six stories). What is most interesting is that in buildings of six stories or less, the project size or total number of units does not make a difference. It seems that although larger projects encourage crime by fostering feelings of anonymity, isolation, irresponsibility, and lack of identity with surroundings, evidence indicates that larger projects encompassed in low buildings seem to offset what we may assume to be factors conducive to high crime rates. High-rise projects not only experience a higher rate of crime within the buildings, but a greater proportion of the crime occurs in the interior public spaces of these buildings as compared with those of the lower buildings. Lower buildings have more limited public space than higher ones. A criminal probably perceives that the interior public areas of buildings are where his victims are most vulnerable and where the possibility of his being seen or apprehended is minimal. Placement of elevators, entrance lobbies, fire stairs, and secondary exits all are factors related to the likelihood of crimes taking place in buildings. The study of all of these elements should bear some weight in the planning of new projects.

12. According to the above passage, which of the following BEST describes the relationship between building size and crime?   12.____

    A. Larger projects lead to a greater crime rate.
    B. Higher buildings tend to increase the crime rate.
    C. The smaller the number of project apartments in low buildings, the higher the crime rate.
    D. Anonymity and isolation serve to lower the crime rate in small buildings.

13. According to the passage, the likelihood of a criminal attempting a mugging in the interior public portions of a high-rise building is GOOD because   13.____

    A. tenants will be constantly flowing in and out of the area
    B. there is easy access to fire stairs and secondary exits
    C. there is a good chance that no one will see him
    D. tenants may not recognize the victims of crime as their neighbors

14. Which of the following is IMPLIED by the passage as an explanation for the fact that the crime rate is lower in large low-rise housing projects than in large high-rise projects?   14.____

    A. Tenants know each other better and take a greater interest in what happens in the project.
    B. There is more public space where tenants are likely to gather together.
    C. The total number of units in a low-rise project is fewer than the total number of units in a high-rise project.

D. Elevators in low-rise buildings travel quickly, thus limiting the amount of time in which a criminal can act.

Questions 15-19.

DIRECTIONS: Questions 15 through 19 are to be answered SOLELY on the basis of the following *total annual income adjustment* rules for household income.

The basic annual income is to be calculated by multiplying the total of the current weekly salaries of all adults (age 21 or over) by 52.
Upward and downward adjustments must be made to the basic annual salary to arrive at the *total adjusted annual income* for the household.

UPWARD ADJUSTMENTS

1. Add one-half of total overtime payments in the previous two years.
2. Add that part of the earnings of any minor in the household that exceeded $2,000 in the previous 12 months.

DOWNWARD ADJUSTMENTS

1. Deduct one-third of all educational tuition payments for household members in the previous 12 months.
2. Deduct the expense of going to and from work in excess of $20 per week per household member. This adjustment is made on the basis of the previous 12 months and should be computed for each household member individually for each week in which excess travel expenses were incurred.
3. Deduct that part of child care expenses which exceeded $1000 in the previous 12 months.

15. In household A, the husband has a weekly salary of $390 and the wife has just had her salary increased from $260 to $280 per week. In the previous 12 months, each had a paid continuous vacation of four weeks; the husband had to travel to a secondary work location every fourth week. His travel costs during those weeks were $28 per week. In the previous 12 months, they had child care costs of $980.
What is the total annual adjusted income for the household?

   A. $34,744   B. $34,736   C. $34,552   D. $34,156

16. In household B, the husband has a weekly salary of $360. In the past year, he received overtime payments of $170. In the year before that he received overtime payments of $814. His wife has just begun a job with a weekly salary of $220. As a result of this, annual child care expenses will be $1420.
What is the total annual adjusted income for the household?

   A. $30,160   B. $30,232   C. $30,652   D. $31,216

17. In household C, the husband has a weekly salary of $370, The wife has a weekly salary of $260. They each had expenses of $22 per week when traveling to and from work in the previous 12 months. The husband had an annual paid vacation of five weeks, and the wife had an annual paid vacation of three weeks in the previous year. There is a daughter in college for whom annual tuition payments of $1140 were made in the previous 12 months.
    What is the total annual adjusted income for the household?

    A. $32,172   B. $32,188   C. $32,760   D. $33,348

18. In household D, the husband has a weekly salary of $310, the wife has a weekly salary of $220, and an adult daughter has a weekly salary of $190. The husband received overtime payments of $1260 in the past year. In the year before that, he received no overtime payments. In the past year, there were weekly child care expenses of $140 per week for 47 weeks.
    What is the total annual adjusted income for the household?

    A. $38,070   B. $32,490   C. $31,490   D. $31,230

19. In household E, the husband has a weekly salary of $410. The wife has a weekly salary of $130. During the past year, there were tuition payments of $170 per month for 10 months per year for children in grade school and annual tuition payments of $1540 for a boy in high school.
    What is the total annual adjusted income for the household?

    A. $26,380   B. $26,400   C. $27,000   D. $28,080

20. In the writing of reports or letters, the ideas presented in a paragraph are usually of unequal importance and require varying degrees of emphasis.
    All of the following are methods of placing extra stress on an idea EXCEPT

    A. repeating it in a number of forms
    B. placing it in the middle of the paragraph
    C. placing it either at the beginning or at the end of the paragraph
    D. underlining it

KEY (CORRECT ANSWERS)

1. B	6. A	11. A	16. C
2. C	7. B	12. B	17. B
3. A	8. D	13. C	18. B
4. B	9. D	14. A	19. C
5. C	10. B	15. A	20. B

TEST 3

DIRECTIONS: Each question or incomplete statement is followed by several suggested answers or completions. Select the one that BEST answers the question or completes the statement. *PRINT THE LETTER OF THE CORRECT ANSWER IN THE SPACE AT THE RIGHT.*

Questions 1-2.

DIRECTIONS: Questions 1 and 2 are to be answered SOLELY on the basis of the following paragraph.

A housing development has 450 apartments. The average monthly rent is $269 per apartment. The average amount of subsidy money added to the average monthly rent (to meet the total operating costs) is $136. Since the time when the amount of the subsidy was determined, operating costs for the development have increased by $7920.00 per month.

1. If the subsidy is increased by 6%, what increase in the average monthly rental will be necessary to meet monthly operating costs?   1.____

   A. $6.80
   C. $17.60
   B. $9.44
   D. No increase

2. What is the NEW total monthly operating cost per apartment?   2.____

   A. $153.60   B. $286.60   C. $422.60   D. $484.20

3. In a certain housing project, the average income of tenant families is $18,400 per annum and the average rent per apartment is $360 per month.   3.____
   If the average income increases 12% in a year while the average rent of an apartment increases 15%, how much more money will the average family have in a year after paying rent?

   A. $677.60   B. $1560.00   C. $2241.60   D. $4968.00

4. A certain housing project has 1860 tenant families. It has two playgrounds, both rectangular in shape. One measures 104 feet by 45 feet; the other is 74 feet by 53 feet.   4.____
   The number of square feet of playground space per family in this project is MOST NEARLY

   A. 3   B. 5   C. 7   D. 9

5. A particular housing project has 1460 occupied apartments. If there are 12 new tenants in January, 14 in February, and 16 in March, the turnover rate for the first quarter of the year is MOST NEARLY   5.____

   A. 2.9%   B. 3.2%   C. 3.5%   D. 3.8%

Questions 6-7.

DIRECTIONS: Questions 6 and 7 are to be answered SOLELY on the basis of the following paragraph.

A tenant in a housing development receives a semi-monthly public assistance check of $234 and pays a monthly rental of $142 from the proceeds. The tenant is about to begin paying $18 additional per month toward total rent arrears of $272. At the same time that the arrears payments begin, his semi-monthly check increases to $242.

6. What will be the TOTAL change in monthly net income after all rent payments. 6._____

   A. $6   B. $4   C. $2   D. No change

7. If, instead of paying only $18 per month toward the arrears, the total increase in public assistance payments is used to increase arrears payments, how many months will it take the tenant to pay off the arrears? 7._____
   _____ months.

   A. 8   B. 10   C. 12   D. 14

8. A tenant is offered two options in renewing a lease: (1) a one-year lease at a 10% increase in rent, or (2) a three-year lease at an 18% increase in rent. The tenant's current rent is $440 monthly. 8._____
   If the tenant takes the first option and continues to live in the apartment for three years with a 10% increase in rent each year, what would be the difference between the total rent he would pay and the rent he would have paid had he chosen the three-year lease?

   A. $533.28   B. $553.28   C. $2,851.20   D. $3,384.48

9. A certain task that an assistant performs takes approximately 45 minutes per unit of work. Seventy-five percent of his work day is spent on this task. 9._____
   Assuming that he works seven hours per day, how many work-days will it take him to finish 1,470 units of work?

   A. 153   B. 210   C. 240   D. 270

10. It takes 5 1/2 gallons of paint to paint an average apartment, and it requires 18 man-hours. 10._____
    If the price of paint increases 24 cents per gallon and the pay of the painters increases 26.5 cents per hour, what is the INCREASE in the cost of painting an apartment?

    A. $4.99   B. $5.09   C. $5.99   D. $6.09

11. A government employee can process a certain type of report in 23 minutes. 11._____
    How many such reports could he finish processing in a work day from 9:00 A.M. to 5:00 P.M., with a 45-minute lunch break and two 10-minute coffee breaks?

    A. 16   B. 17   C. 18   D. 19

12. The income of a tenant family is as follows: The husband has a gross income of $280 per week; the wife has a gross income of $220 per week. Deductions from gross family income total $116 per week, plus an allowable child care expense of $56 per week. What is the net annual income of the family after deductions and allowable child care expenses? 12._____

    A. $16,656   B. $17,056   C. $18,656   D. $19,056

Questions 13-15

DIRECTIONS: Questions 13 through 15 are to be answered on the basis of the following information and schedule.

Assume that, after having been appointed as an assistant at the Rumsey Housing Project, you are now ready to assume the same duties being performed by the other two assistants, X and Y, Their daily work schedules have already been prepared, and you are asked to work out a schedule which will be compatible with theirs and which will conform to the following stipulations:

a. At least one assistant is to be in the project office at all times between 9 A.M. and 5 P.M. Monday through Friday.
b. No more than two assistants are to conduct office interviews at one time.
c. All assistants must be in the project office between the hours of 4 P.M. and 5 P.M.
d. Each assistant is to take one hour for lunch between 11:30 A.M. and 2 P.M.
Following is the Monday schedule for assistants X and Y.

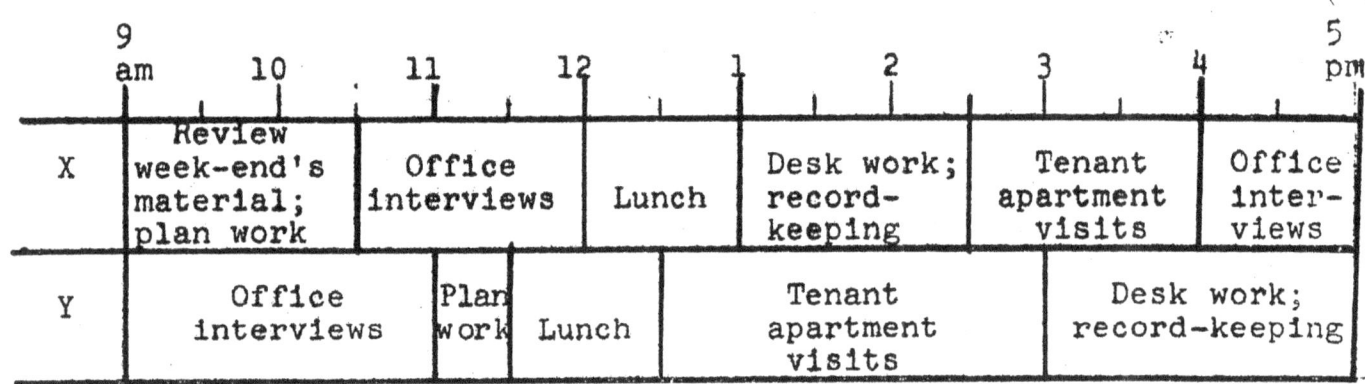

13. Which one of the following blocks of time would be BEST for you to plan 2 1/2 hours of office interviewing?

    A. 9:00-11:30   B. 11:00-1:30
    C. 1:30-4:00   D. 2:00-4:30

14. During what hours would it be BEST for you to schedule tenant apartment visits covering a two-hour block of time?

    A. 9:00-11:00   B. 10:30-12:30
    C. 1:00-3:00   D. 3:00-5:00

15. Of the following suggestions for scheduling your day's assignments, which one would NOT be acceptable?

    A. Desk work including weekly plans from 9:00-11:00 and 2:00-3:00
    B. Interviews from 11:00-1:00
    C. Lunch from 1:00-2:00
    D. Tenant apartment visits from 3:00-5:00

Questions 16-20.

DIRECTIONS: Questions 16 through 20 are to be answered SOLELY on the basis of the information contained in the following table of apartment availabilities and explanation of *Priority Codes for Admission* column.

PRIORITY CODES AND MAXIMUM ANNUAL INCOME FOR ADMISSION TO PROJECTS

Division	Projects	Priority Codes for Admission	Maximum Annual Income for Admission			
			One Bedroom	Two Bedrooms	Three Bedrooms	Four Bedrooms
Northern	Allan	1-3Cs 4B	$18,200	$20,000	$21,400	$23,000
	Boston	1-2C; 3-4A	13,600	15,800	18,000	19,800
	Danton	1-2C; 3Bs 4 A	14,800	16,400	18,200	20,200
	Miller	1-3B; 4 A	13,600	15,800	18,000	19,800
	Preston	1-2C, 3B; 4A	16,600	18,800	20,400	22,000
Central	Andrews	1-2D; SB; 4 A	13,600	15,800	18,000	19,800
	Clayton	1-2D, SB, 4 A	13,600	15,800	18,000	19,800
	Ivy Hill	1-3C; 4B	14,800	16,400	18,200	20,200
	Montrose	1-2B, 3-4A	18,200	20,000	21,400	23,000
Eastern	Bryan	1B; 2-4 A	16,600	18,800	20,400	22,000
	Farrar	1C; 2-4A	18,200	20,000	21,400	28,000
	Golden	1-2B; 3-4A	13,600	15,800	18,000	19,800
	Wagner	1B; 2-4A	18,200	20,000	21,400	23,000
Western	Colfax	1-3C; 4B	18,200	20,000	21,400	23,000
	Drexel	1-3B, 4 A	14,800	16,400	18,200	20,200
	Foxton	1-3C; 4A	13,600	15,800	18,000	19,800

EXPLANATION OF PRIORITY CODES FOR ADMISSION COLUMN

The letters A, B, C, and D represent four levels of priority for admission to a project. Level A priority is the most restrictive of the four priority levels and represents the highest level of need; level D priority is the least restrictive of the four priority levels and represents the lowest level of need. An applicant can be admitted only to an apartment with the same level of priority or to an apartment with a lower level of priority. For example, an applicant with a C priority can be admitted to an apartment with a C or D priority but not to an apartment with an A or B priority.

The numbers 1, 2, 3, and 4 represent the number of bedrooms in the apartments. For example, the notation after the Allan project, 1-3C; 4B, means that apartments with from one to three bedrooms have priority level C and apartments with four bedrooms have priority level In the Allan project, only applicants with a priority level of C or higher (levels A and B) can be admitted to apartments with one, two, or three bedrooms and only applicants with a priority level of B or higher (level A) can be admitted to a four-bedroom apartment.

16. An applicant with an annual income of $16,400 needs an apartment with two bedrooms. The applicant has a level B priority. Those projects in the Eastern and Central Divisions which have two-bedroom apartments for which the applicant is eligible are

    A. Allan and Ivy Hill
    B. Montrose, Bryan, and Golden
    C. Ivy Hill and Montrose
    D. Ivy Hill, Montrose, and Farrar

16.____

17. What is the LOWEST level of priority an applicant may have in order to be eligible for a three-bedroom apartment in the Western Division if he has an income of $18,200 a year?
Level

    A. A   B. B   C. C   D. D

18. Which division is MOST restrictive as to the level of priority required for three-bedroom apartments?

    A. Northern   B. Central   C. Eastern   D. Western

19. Which division contains the GREATEST number of projects with two-bedroom apartments in the LEAST restrictive level of priority?

    A. Northern   B. Central   C. Eastern   D. Western

20. How many projects have four-bedroom apartments available to an applicant with an A priority and an income of $22,000?

    A. 3   B. 5   C. 7   D. 12

KEY (CORRECT ANSWERS)

1. B	6. C	11. C	16. C
2. C	7. A	12. B	17. C
3. B	8. A	13. D	18. C
4. B	9. B	14. A	19. B
5. A	10. D	15. D	20. C

TEST 4

DIRECTIONS: Each question or incomplete statement is followed by several suggested answers or completions. Select the one that BEST answers the question or completes the statement. *PRINT THE LETTER OF THE CORRECT ANSWER IN THE SPACE AT THE RIGHT.*

Questions 1-4.

DIRECTIONS: Questions 1 through 4 are to be answered SOLELY on the basis of the following information and hypothetical schedule for the granting of priority points. These points determine the applicant's place on a waiting list for an apartment. The applicants may be awarded points for condition of present housing, for children, for veteran status, and for space falling below the minimum space standard. Categories not listed get no points. Points in all categories are added together to determine total number of priority points.

	Priority Points
Condition of Present Housing (choose one)	
Extremely substandard housing	5
Moderately substandard housing	3
Minimally substandard housing	1
Children (choose as many as apply)	
Two children over age eight, of different sexes, sleeping in same room	2
Two children of different sexes, one over age eight, the other under age eight, sleeping in same room	1
Family with child over age 18 months sleeping in same bedroom with parents	2
Veteran Status	
Veteran of Vietnam War in household	1
Minimum Space Standard	
For each 75 square feet or part thereof below minimum space standard, computed by totaling the following: 110 square feet for each person over age 18, 90 square feet for each person age 18 or under	1

1. A husband, wife, six-year-old son, and nine-year-old daughter live in a moderately substandard apartment of 280 square feet. The son and daughter sleep in the same bedroom. There are no war veterans in the household. How many priority points should be given?

    A. 6   B. 5   C. 4   D. 3

2. A husband, wife, wife's father, 16-year-old daughter, 14-year-old son, and 12-year-old son live in an extremely substandard apartment of 450 square feet. The daughter sleeps in her own room. The sons have their own room. The wife's father is a World War II veteran.
   How many priority points should be given?

    A. 9   B. 8   C. 7   D. 6

3. A widow, age 50, who is not a war veteran, lives with her son, age 15, in a minimally substandard two-bedroom apartment with 290 square feet of living space.
How many priority points should be given?

   A. 3   B. 2   C. 1   D. 0

3.____

4. A family has had to leave their former apartment because of fire damage. They are presently living in an extremely substandard storefront which is one room of 320 square feet, without partitions. The family consists of a father who is a Vietnam war veteran, a mother, and their two children: a girl, age 5; and a boy, age 7.
How many priority points should be given?

   A. 10   B. 9   C. 8   D. 7

4.____

Questions 5-8.

DIRECTIONS: In Questions 5 through 8, choose the sentence which contains NO errors in grammar, punctuation, or spelling.

5.   A. Certain changes in family income must be reported as they occur.
     B. When certain changes in family income occur, it must be reported.
     C. Certain family income changes must be reported as they occur.
     D. Certain changes in family income must be reported as they have been occuring.

5.____

6.   A. Each tenant has to complete the application themselves.
     B. Each of the tenants have to complete the application by himself.
     C. Each of the tenants has to complete the application himself.
     D. Each of the tenants has to complete the application by themselves.

6.____

7.   A. Yours is the only building that the construction will effect.
     B. Your's is the only building affected by the construction.
     C. The construction will only effect your building.
     D. Yours is the only building that will be affected by the construction.

7.____

8.   A. A copy of the lease, in addition to the Rules and Regulations, are to be given to each tenant.
     B. The Rules and Regulations and a copy of the lease is being given to each tenant.
     C. A copy of the lease, in addition to the Rules and Regulations, is to be given to each tenant.
     D. A copy of the lease, in addition to the Rules and Regulations, are being given to each tenant.

8.____

Questions 9-10.

DIRECTIONS: Each of Questions 9 and 10 consists of four numbered sentences which constitute a paragraph in a report. They are not in the right order. Choose the numbered arrangement appearing after letter A, B, C, or D which is MOST logical and which BEST expresses the thought of the paragraph.

9.
I. Congress made the commitment explicit in the Housing Act of 1949, establishing as a national goal the realization of *a decent home and suitable environment for every American family.*
II. The result has been that the goal of decent home and suitable environment is still as far distant as ever for the disadvantaged urban family.
III. In spite of this action by Congress, federal housing programs have continued to be fragmented and grossly underfunded.
IV. The passage of the National Housing Act signalled a new federal commitment to provide housing for the nation's citizens,

A. I, IV, III, II
B. IV, I, III, II
C. IV, I, II, III
D. II, IV, I, III

10.
I. The greater expense does not necessarily involve *exploitation,* but it is often perceived as exploitative and unfair by those who are aware of the price differences involved, but unaware of operating costs.
II. Ghetto residents believe they are *exploited* by local merchants and evidence substantiates some of these beliefs.
III. However, stores in low-income areas were more likely to be small independents, which could not achieve the economies available to supermarket chains and were, therefore, more likely to charge higher prices, and the customers were more likely to buy smaller-sized packages which are more expensive per unit of measure.
IV. A study conducted in one city showed that distinctly higher prices were charged for goods sold in ghetto stores than in other areas.

A. IV, II, I, III
B. IV, I, III, II
C. II, IV, III, I
D. II, III, IV, I

11. If an assistant is writing to an applicant who is a minority group member in reference to his eligibility for an apartment, it would be BEST for him to use language that is

A. informal, using ethnic expressions known to the applicant
B. technical, using the expressions commonly used in the housing authority
C. simple, using words and phrases which laymen understand
D. formal, to remind the applicant that he is dealing with a government agency

12. Assume that you have just informed an applicant for an apartment that he has a low priority and that it is unlikely that he will be assigned an apartment within the next two years. When informed of this, he becomes angry and abusive.
Of the following, the MOST effective action you can take is to

A. tell the applicant that you will do your best to get him a higher priority
B. let him know he cannot intimidate you
C. tell him to submit a new application that has greater emotional appeal
D. keep your self-control and try to calm the applicant

13. When interviewing an applicant to determine his eligibility for public housing, it is MOST important to

    A. have a prior mental picture of the typical eligible applicant
    B. conduct the interview strictly according to a previously prepared script
    C. keep in mind the goal of the interview, which is to determine eligibility
    D. get an accurate and detailed account of the applicant's life history

14. The practice of trying to imagine yourself in the applicant's place during an interview is

    A. *good,* mainly because you will be able to evaluate his responses better
    B. *good,* mainly because it will enable you to treat him as a friend rather than an applicant
    C. *poor,* mainly because it is important for the applicant to see you as an impartial person
    D. *poor,* mainly because it is too time-consuming to do this with each applicant

15. When dealing with tenants from different ethnic backgrounds, an assistant should be aware of certain tendencies toward prejudice.
    Which of the following statements is LEAST likely to be valid?

    A. Whites prejudiced against Blacks are more likely to be prejudiced against Puerto Ricans than whites not prejudiced against Blacks.
    B. The less a white is in competition with Blacks, the less likely he is to be prejudiced against them.
    C. Persons who have moved from one social group to another are likely to retain the attitudes and prejudices of their original social group.
    D. When there are few Blacks or Puerto Ricans in a project, whites are less likely to be prejudiced against them than when there are many.

16. Mr. Smith asks the assistant why his rent is higher than his neighbor's, although he claims that both apartments are the same size, and that his neighbor's income is the same as his. The assistant is aware of this but is also aware that the neighbor is allowed several deductions in computing income that are not available to Mr. Smith.
    The assistant should explain to Mr. Smith that

    A. the amount of his neighbor's rent is really no concern of his, but that the neighbor's rent will be raised if Mr. Smith can prove that the neighbor is not reporting income
    B. his neighbor receives more deductions in computing income
    C. he cannot discuss complaints presented by Mr. Smith concerning the rent of other tenants
    D. the amount of rent is based on the rules for computing rent and that there may be individual circumstances of which Mr. Smith is not aware

17. Of the following, the assistant who is MOST likely to be a good interviewer of people seeking low-rent housing from a public agency is one who

    A. tries to get applicants to seek private housing instead
    B. believes that it is necessary to get as much pertinent information as possible in order to determine the applicant's real needs
    C. believes that people who seek public housing are likely to have persons with a history of irresponsible behavior in their households
    D. is convinced that there is no need for public housing

18. An assistant must be familiar with the policies of both federal and state agencies which regulate public housing as well as with the many rules, regulations, and procedures of the housing authority.
The MOST important reason for an assistant to have a thorough knowledge and understanding of these policies and procedures is that he

   A. will know when to tell an applicant that his request for a particular project cannot be granted
   B. will be able to back up his actions by referring to the relevant rule or policy when making a report
   C. can give the best possible service to tenants and applicants
   D. will be able to show that he has the knowledge needed for his job

18.____

Questions 19-20.

DIRECTIONS: Questions 19 and 20 must be answered SOLELY on the basis of the following passage.

The new suburbia that is currently being built does not look much different from the old; there has, however, been an increase in the class and race polarization that has been developing between the suburbs and the cities for several generations now. The suburbs have become the home for an ever larger proportion of working-class, middle-class, and upper-class whitest the oities, for an even larger proportion of poor and non-white people. A great number of cities are 30 to 50 percent non-white in population, with more and larger ghettos than cities have ever had. Now, there is greater urban poverty on the one hand, and stronger suburban opposition to open housing and related policies to solve the cities' problems on the other hand. The urban crisis will worsen, and although there is no shortage of rational solutions, nothing much will be done about the crisis unless white America permits a radical change of public policy and undergoes a miraculous change of attitude towards it cities and their populations.

19. Which of the following statements is IMPLIED by the above passage?

    A. The percentage of non-whites in the suburbs is increasing.
    B. The policies of suburbanites have contributed to the seriousness of the urban crisis.
    C. The problems of the cities defy rational solutions.
    D. There has been a radical change in the appearance of both suburbia and the cities in the past few years.

19.____

20. Of the following, the title which BEST describes the passage's main them is:

    A. The New Suburbia
    B. Urban Poverty
    C. Urban-Suburban Polarization
    D. Why Americans Want to Live in the Suburbs

20.____

KEY (CORRECT ANSWERS)

1. A	6. C	11. C	16. D
2. C	7. D	12. D	17. B
3. C	8. C	13. C	18. C
4. A	9. B	14. A	19. B
5. A	10. C	15. C	20. C

EXAMINATION SECTION
TEST 1

DIRECTIONS: Each question or incomplete statement is followed by several suggested answers or completions. Select the one that BEST answers the question or completes the statement. *PRINT THE LETTER OF THE CORRECT ANSWER IN THE SPACE AT THE RIGHT.*

1. While in your office, your attention is attracted by the sound of loud crying. Looking out of the window, you see two small boys, each about ten years old, punching a little girl of about the same age. The incident is taking place off the project grounds but you recognize the children and know they live in the project.
   What is the BEST course of action to take?

   A. Do not interfere since it is off project grounds.
   B. Go out and stop the fighting.
   C. Notify the parents involved.
   D. Separate the children, scold the boys, and take the little girl back with you so the fighting will not recur.
   E. Shout, *"Stop that fighting. Boys, you should be ashamed of yourselves."*

2. One of the tenants tells you she is sure that the income of a certain family exceeds the permissible maximum.

   A. Ask the tenant how she learned of this information so you may verify it.
   B. Ask the tenant to write out the details and send it to the office.
   C. Notify your superior so he may take appropriate action.
   D. Tell the tenant that stirring up trouble for another family is detrimental to the smooth functioning of the project.
   E. Thank the tenant for the information and tell her you will look into it.

3. A tenant informs you that he is a member of a group which would like to use the project community room to hold card games on a certain evening each week.

   A. Advise the tenant that it will be permitted if he will assume the responsibility in case there is any gambling.
   B. Advise the tenant to make a written request to the manager.
   C. Ask the tenant for all details before making any decision
   D. Tactfully bring the conversation around to more desirable social activities and indicate that a request for a different activity will then be approved.
   E. Tell the tenant that the community room is already taken on that evening in order to avoid antagonizing him by criticizing the proposed activity.

4. Several tenants complain to you that they are frequently disturbed late at night by loud radio playing from an adjoining apartment. One or more of these tenants have, on several occasions, asked the neighbor to lower the radio but to no avail.

   A. Advise the tenants that they should complain to the department of health.
   B. Advise the tenants that they should complain to the police department.
   C. Ascertain whether the complaint is justified.
   D. Request the tenant to lower the radio and explain the reason for the request.
   E. Tell the tenants to present the matter at the next meeting of the tenants' association.

5. A tenant asks you whether it is permissible for him to bring several friends who live outside the project, but near it, to a special educational program which has been scheduled for the project meeting room.

   A. Advise the tenant to ask the manager for permission.
   B. Ask the tenant who his friends are before giving him any answer.
   C. Inform the tenant that he may do so.
   D. Refer the tenant to the president of the tenants' association.
   E. Tactfully explain to the tenant why outsiders are not permitted.

6. A tenant who has never made any previous complaints complains to you that the penetrating cooking odors of a certain tenant are frequently very objectionable.

   A. Arrange to move the tenant at fault to another section of the project.
   B. Ascertain whether the complaint is justified.
   C. Discuss the situation with the complaining tenant.
   D. Discuss the situation with the tenant at fault.
   E. Explain to the complaining tenant that you cannot interfere in such personal matters.

7. While walking through the corridor of the project, you see a tenant trip and fall down about half a flight of stairs. The tenant immediately picks himself up, states that he is perfectly all right, and begins to go on about his business.

   A. Advise the tenant to prepare a written statement at his own convenience and send it to the manager.
   B. Ask the tenant to accompany you to the office so he may sign a statement that he suffered no injury.
   C. Insist that the tenant accompany you to a doctor for examination for possible injury.
   D. Submit a report on the occurrence to your supervisor.
   E. Think no more of the situation since obviously no injury was incurred.

8. While walking on the court of the project, you notice a tenant's nine-year-old child destroying some of the shrubbery.

   A. Notify the parent that he will be held financially responsible for damages incurred.
   B. Provide socially desirable outlets for children's activities.
   C. Report the child's behavior to his parents.
   D. Report the incident to your superior so he may take appropriate action.
   E. Reprimand the child.

9. A tenant complains to you that it is very cold in her apartment.

   A. Advise her to make the complaint to the building superintendent.
   B. Ascertain if the complaint is justified.
   C. Pay no attention to the matter unless additional complaints are made by other tenants.
   D. Report the matter to the building superintendent.
   E. Tactfully tell her that it is her problem since heat is being supplied in accordance with the law.

10. A tenant who wants to buy a pressure cooker asks you what brand she should buy.

    A. Inform her that you must be impartial and, therefore, cannot make any recommendation.
    B. Refer her to a consumer cooperative where you know she can get a substantial discount.
    C. Refer her to a department store where a salesman can help her make a selection from the various types which you know they sell.
    D. Refer her to organizations which make comparative tests of consumers' goods.
    E. Tactfully explain that a pressure cooker is a luxury and that a serviceable cooking utensil can be bought for a small fraction of the cost.

11. To say that a housing assistant should apply the pragmatic test to his beliefs means MOST NEARLY that he should be

    A. certain of authoritative sources
    B. familiar with current philosophic thought
    C. guided by practical results
    D. skeptical of generally accepted conclusions
    E. trained in laboratory methods

12. A housing assistant who is *sanguine* is

    A. belligerent   B. cruel   C. lazy
    D. optimistic   E. sound in mind

13. An *abstemious* tenant is a desirable tenant.
    The word *abstemious* means, MOST NEARLY,

    A. adhering punctiliously to established rules and accepted practices
    B. exact in the observance of the usages of polite society
    C. indulging temperately in alcoholic beverages
    D. possessing abundant health and vitality
    E. totally abstaining from intoxicants

14. Public housing is not *indigenous* to the United States. The word *indigenous* means, MOST NEARLY,

    A. competing with housing constructed under private enterprise
    B. looked upon unfavorably
    C. originating in a specific country
    D. restricted to persons receiving public financial assistance
    E. taxable source of revenue

15. The report contained statements which were *equivocal*. The word *equivocal* means, MOST NEARLY,

    A. diametrically opposed
    B. not recognized as valid or authentic
    C. of the same degree in magnitude or value
    D. pertaining to principles of right and justice
    E. susceptible of different interpretations

16. The housing assistant pointed out the *hiatus* in the manual procedures.
    The word *hiatus* means, MOST NEARLY,

    A. error in fact
    B. explanation of policy
    C. incorrect word usage
    D. some part missing
    E. typographical inaccuracy

17. To say that the dose administered to the tenant was *innocuous* means, MOST NEARLY, that the dose was

    A. curative
    B. deadly
    C. harmless
    D. painful
    E. protective

18. A tenant who has been subjected to *ostracism* has been, MOST NEARLY,

    A. a victim of cruel and unusual punishment
    B. excluded from participating in social affairs
    C. exposed to personal indignities
    D. inoculated against contagious diseases
    E. the recipient of the contempt of his neighbors

19. When actions of a tenant are *condoned* by a housing assistant, the actions are, MOST NEARLY,

    A. approved
    B. condemned
    C. justified
    D. overlooked
    E. scrutinized

20. To say that a housing assistant sometimes encounters *extenuating* circumstances means, MOST NEARLY, that the housing assistant must consider

    A. facts pertinent only to the solution of the problem in hand
    B. facts which lessen the seriousness of an offense
    C. facts which require the immediate attention of his supervisor
    D. situations that call for very tactful handling
    E. situations where legal action is obligatory

21. Suppose you are assigned to make a home investigation of an applicant for an apartment in a public housing project at a time when there are vacancies. The applicant lives in grossly substandard housing and appears to be eligible in all respects. He begs you to tell him if he is eligible.
    The one of the following actions you should take is:

    A. Advise him that he keeps his apartment in such poor condition that he will probably be refused
    B. Assure him he will get an apartment since he meets the eligibility requirements
    C. Inform him that he will be notified of the status of his application as soon as it is acted upon
    D. Tell him that you are not permitted to inform him of the results of your investigation
    E. Tell him you will check with your office and let him know the next day

22. Suppose you are assigned to investigate an applicant for an apartment in a low-rent public housing project. He is 67 years old and works for a small firm whose only other employee is an office worker. You uncover certain facts which lead you to believe that the applicant's income exceeds the permissible maximum.
The one of the following which is PROBABLY least likely to be available as an indication of the applicant's real income is:

    A. state unemployment insurance records
    B. Social Security Board records
    C. sworn statement from employer
    D. sworn affidavit from the applicant
    E. withholding tax statement

23. In a certain city, 18,250 new dwelling units were built in 1986, thereby increasing the total number of dwelling units in the city by 1.6%.
The number of new dwelling units which had to be built in 1987 to maintain the same rate of increase is, MOST NEARLY,

    A. 18,250   B. 18,400   C. 18,500   D. 18,600
    E. an amount which cannot be determined from the given data

24. A housing project is to be erected on a site of S square feet. Unpaid taxes which must be paid on the X buildings now on the site total Y dollars; the cost of demolishing the buildings is estimated at Z dollars.
The cost, per square foot, of the site, when clear of buildings and free of tax delinquency, is

    A. $\dfrac{XY + Z}{S}$ B. $\dfrac{Y + Z}{S}$ C. $S(Z+Y)$ D. $S(XY+Z)$
    E. an expression which cannot be determined from the given data

25. The one of the following acts under the provisions of which financial assistance to housing was FIRST provided by the Federal government is:

    A. United States Housing Act
    B. Emergency Relief and Construction Act
    C. National Industrial Recovery Act
    D. National Housing Act
    E. Home Owners Loan Corporation Act

26. The Mutual Ownership Housing Plan, as originally conceived, is a plan

    A. for the cooperative ownership of a multiple dwelling
    B. sponsored by the Mutual Life Insurance Company to aid home owners
    C. whereby mutual savings banks promote home ownership
    D. whereby tenants of a project may purchase it from the Federal government
    E. whereby the tenants of a building form a housing company to own and operate the building

27. The one of the following statements concerning public low-rent housing projects which is NOT a provision of the United States Housing Act is:

    A. Federal subsidies are conditioned upon local contribution in certain forms equal to at least 20% of the subsidy
    B. Loans must not exceed 90% of the cost of the project
    C. Loans must be repaid within 60 years
    D. Not more than 25% of Federal funds may be expended within any state
    E. slum dwelling units must be eliminated in numbers equivalent to the number of newly constructed dwelling units

27.___

28. The permanent consolidation under one agency of all Federal activities relating to housing was accomplished by

    A. the Lanham Act
    B. Presidential executive order in 1942
    C. Reorganization Act of 1946
    D. the United States Housing Act
    E. none of the above

28.___

Questions 29-35.

DIRECTIONS: Column I lists seven items, each of which is to be matched with one of the choices given in Column II. For each item of Column I, write in the space at the right the letter in front of the BEST choice in Column II. (The choices in Column II may be used any number of times.)

COLUMN I	COLUMN II	
29. Managed war housing projects of the Federal government	A. FHA	29.___
30. Insures loans made by private sources for purchase of homes	B. FHLBA	30.___
31. Insures loans made by private sources for alteration or repair of homes	C. FPHA	31.___
32. Made loans for refinancing delinquent mortgages on private homes	D. HOLC	32.___
33. Provides credit reserve for home-mortgaging and home-financing institutions	E. NAHO	33.___
34. Administers low-rent public housing subsidies		34.___
35. The only one of the agencies in Column II which is a part of one of the other agencies listed		35.___

36. An applicant for an apartment in a federally-aided low-rent housing project MUST be   36.____

    A. a resident of the state in which the project is located
    B. a citizen of the United States
    C. gainfully employed
    D. living under unsafe or insanitary housing conditions
    E. all of the above

37. It is the present policy of federally-aided public housing projects to grant first preference to eligible applicants who are families   37.____

    A. displaced from the site of a slum clearance project
    B. displaced from a site on which the project was built
    C. of men still in military service
    D. of servicemen and of veterans
    E. who lack housing entirely

38. In determining the net family income of a family applying for admission to a low-rent public housing project, the one of the following which is NOT an allowable deduction is: 38.____

    A. Deductions from wages for pension funds if this is required as a condition of employment
    B. Payroll deductions for income tax
    C. Payroll deductions for social security
    D. Payroll deductions for unemployment insurance
    E. Special expenses incident to employment which are not reimbursed by the employer

39. The *20% gap* policy governing admission rents in Federally-aided public housing refers to the fact that in a given community,   39.____

    A. rents in public housing must be at least 20% below the rents at which private enterprise is supplying decent and safe dwellings
    B. rents in public housing must not be more than 20% below the rents at which private enterprise is supplying decent and safe dwellings
    C. maximum rent for a given dwelling unit must not be more than 20% greater than the minimum rent
    D. minimum rent for a given dwelling unit must not be more than 20% below the rental for the same accommodations in privately-owned buildings
    E. minimum rent for a given dwelling unit must be at least 20% below the rental for the same accommodations in privately-owned buildings

40. It was NOT a primary purpose of the United States Housing Act to   40.____

    A. alleviate unemployment
    B. make funds available to states for low-rent housing
    C. make credit available to cities for low-rent housing
    D. promote the general welfare of the nation
    E. stimulate construction of dwellings by private enterprise

KEY (CORRECT ANSWERS)

1.	B	11.	C	21.	C	31.	A
2.	E	12.	D	22.	A	32.	D
3.	B	13.	C	23.	C	33.	B
4.	D	14.	C	24.	E	34.	C
5.	C	15.	E	25.	B	35.	D
6.	B	16.	D	26.	D	36.	B
7.	D	17.	C	27.	D	37.	D
8.	E	18.	B	28.	E	38.	B
9.	D	19.	D	29.	C	39.	A
10.	D	20.	B	30.	A	40.	E

TEST 2

DIRECTIONS: Each question or incomplete statement is followed by several suggested answers or completions. Select the one that BEST answers the question or completes the statement. *PRINT THE LETTER OF THE CORRECT ANSWER IN THE SPACE AT THE RIGHT.*

Questions 1-6.

DIRECTIONS: Column I lists the titles and authors of six publications, each of which is to be matched with one of the subjects given in Column II. For each item of Column I, write in the space at the right the letter in front of the subject in Column II which BEST expresses the central theme or major area presented in each publication.

COLUMN I

1. AMERICAN HOUSING by 20th Century Fund
2. HOUSING FOR THE MACHINE AGE by Clarence A. Perry
3. HOUSING COMES OF AGE by Straus and Wegg
4. MODERN HOUSING by Catherine Bauer
5. THE FUTURE OF HOUSING by Charles Abrams
6. THEY SEEK A CITY by Bontemps and Conroy

COLUMN II

A. An account of the battle against slums and the progress in public housing
B. Compendium of articles on public housing in the United States
C. Defines adequate shelter and proposes a ten-year budget for better housing in America
D. European housing and American problems from the background of European experience
E. Housing policy of cities, with particular reference to the neighborhood unit idea
F. Official publication of an outstanding organization of persons interested in housing
G. PWA low-rent slum clearance program
H. Study of family and neighborhood life in four slum areas of the city
I. Survey of how the field of house-building is organized and operates
J. Study of Black life in a northern city of the United States
K. Very recent study of our housing problems and a program of housing reform
L. Growth of residential segregation and slums and other relevant housing factors in six cities of the United States

1.____

2.____

3.____

4.____

5.____

6.____

Questions 7-16.

DIRECTIONS: Each of Questions 7 through 16 contains five words in capital letters, one of which is NOT in keeping with the meaning which the selection is evidently intended to carry. The five words in capital letters in each selection are reprinted after the selection. Indicate the letter in front of the one of the one of the five words which does MOST to spoil the true meaning of the selection.

7. The MINIMUM amount that can be paid by the FEDERAL government in any year as annual CONTRIBUTIONS to a low-rent housing project under a given contract for financial aid is a FIXED percentage of the total DEVELOPMENT cost of the project. 7.___

   A. Minimum   B. Federal   C. Contributions
   D. Fixed   E. Development

8. The existence and DIMENSIONS of the slums had long been RECOGNIZED by state legislatures and municipalities, but these local public bodies and officers had WASTED their efforts primarily on UNINTEGRATED remedial measures RESTRICTED in character to building and health codes. 8.___

   A. Dimensions   B. Recognized   C. Wasted
   D. Unintegrated E. Restricted

9. One of the MAJOR purposes of a program of land ASSEMBLY for urban redevelopment is to direct the location of new HOME building to ZONED city land by erasing the margin that seems to favor unused FRINGE land. 9.___

   A. Major   B. Assembly   C. Home
   D. Zoned   E. Fringe

10. Postwar migration of NONFARM families is estimated (by the National Housing Agency) to INCREASE the need for housing construction only to the extent that OUT-MIGRATION from individual localities is so great as to leave an actual DEFICIT of standard housing in those localities AFTER demolition of all sub-standard units. 10.___

    A. Nonfarm   B. Increase   C. Out-migration
    D. Deficit   E. After

11. The choice of a site has GREAT influence on the degree of INTEGRATION the housing project will maintain in the development of long-range COMMUNITY plans. Careful deliberation about the PRESENT and expected future relation of different PROGRAMS to the whole community is necessary if the project is to succeed in being a natural and happy part of its surroundings. 11.___

    A. Great   B. Integration   C. Community
    D. Present E. Programs

12. FUTURE planning in the field of public housing must have for its goal not only the elimination of slum-blighted areas AND the providing of decent housing to families of low income, but also the opening of new areas for STREET IMPROVEMENT and development CONTINGENT upon the housing program. 12.___

    A. Future   B. And   C. Street
    D. Improvement E. Contingent

13. In general, farmers of low income are UNABLE to make payments over a period of years which will approximate the CAPITAL cost of an adequate house. Federal contributions would be available to meet INTEREST and other costs with respect to the house. The LOCAL contribution should be adjusted to recognize the LIMITED possibilities for such contributions.

    A. Unable
    B. Capital
    C. Interest
    D. Local
    E. Limited

14. LOCAL housing authorities have recognized that the COMMUNITY'S worst housing problems often are those connected with MINORITY groups and have already PRODUCED a SMALL proportion of low-rent housing for such families.

    A. Local
    B. Community's
    C. Minority
    D. Produced
    E. Small

15. The United States Housing Act LIMITS the Federal function to providing financial aid, seeing that the purposes and REQUIREMENTS of the Act are carried out, and COORDINATING COMMUNITIES in the BUILDING and operation of their projects at the lowest cost consistent with the purpose of the housing.

    A. Limits
    B. Requirements
    C. Coordinating
    D. Communities
    E. Building

16. A SEASONAL plan of maintenance has important ADVANTAGES for the homeowner and represents a LUCRATIVE field for the organization of special service companies which will undertake ALL types of home maintenance work and will maintain a PERMANENT staff of employees for this purpose.

    A. Seasonal
    B. Advantages
    C. Lucrative
    D. All
    E. Permanent

17. As the population of cities increases, there is a decrease in the proportion of the developed urban land area which is used for

    A. commercial purposes
    B. industrial purposes
    C. parks and open areas
    D. residential purposes
    E. streets and thoroughfares

18. The statement that building new homes for the upper income groups will thereby create a supply of older buildings for the lower income groups is NOT tenable unless

    A. the concurrent elimination of slum dwellings takes place
    B. the erection of potential new slums is prevented
    C. the housing shortage is replaced by an excess of housing
    D. the low-income groups are unable to afford the buildings thus vacated
    E. private enterprise has the facilities to build for all families in the upper income groups

19. Of the following, the MOST effective way to reduce the monthly cost of home ownership is to secure reductions in

    A. interest rates
    B. maintenance expenses
    C. property taxes
    D. the capital cost of the house
    E. the capital cost of the land

20. If valid criteria have been used in tenant selection for public housing projects, the result MOST likely to be attained is

    A. homogeneity of tenant characteristics will be assured
    B. larger Federal subsidies will be required
    C. neediest families will receive the greatest proportion of aid
    D. the underlying conditions of slums will be ameliorated
    E. management problems will be simplified

21. Impairment of desirability and usefulness resulting from changes in the arts or in design or from external influences which make a property less desirable for continued use is MOST NEARLY a definition of

    A. blight   B. depreciation   C. deterioration
    D. obsolescence   E. slum area

22. A collection of legal requirements, the purpose of which is to protect the safety, health, morals, and general welfare of those in and about buildings is, MOST NEARLY, a definition of the _____ Code.

    A. Administrative B. Building   C. Legal
    D. Sanitary   E. Welfare

23. The right to expropriate private property for public use is, MOST NEARLY, a definition of

    A. condemnation   B. eminent domain
    C. excess condemnation   D. police power
    E. prior lien

24. A study of the social effects of rehousing families from substandard dwellings showed that the GREATEST improvement occurred in the rate of

    A. fatal home accidents
    B. fire costs
    C. infant deaths
    D. juvenile delinquency
    E. new cases of tuberculosis

25. The one of the following which is NOT a major difference between the State and the United States housing laws for permanent low-rent housing projects is the provision concerning the

    A. base upon which maximum amount of subsidy for a given project is computed
    B. creation of housing companies
    C. maximum contributions required from the local political subdivision
    D. maximum duration of subsidy for a given project
    E. maximum percentage of project cost which may be advanced as a loan

26. The Multiple Dwelling Law does NOT contain basic requirements for multiple dwellings with reference to

    A. areas of yards and courts
    B. height and bulk of buildings
    C. sanitation and water closets
    D. strength of fire retarding construction
    E. ventilation and lighting of rooms

Questions 27-32.

DIRECTIONS: Carefully study the table on the following page. It is followed by Questions 27 through 32, which refer to it alone. You are to judge whether on the basis of the data given in the table each item is:
  A. entirely true
  B. entirely false
  C. partly true and partly false
  D. may or may not be true, but cannot be answered on the basis of these data alone

RESIDENTIAL STRUCTURES AND DWELLING UNITS

Area		Residential Structures		Residential Dwelling Units		Occupied Dwelling Units	
		Number	%	Number	%	Number	%
U.S. TOTAL		29,313,708	100.0	37,325,470	100.0	34,854,532	100.0
I. Inside metropolitan districts		11,482,330	39.2	18,185,020	48.8	17,217,317	49.4
	A. Nonfarm	11,413,959	38.9	17,902,692	48.0	16,948,731	48.6
	1. Urban	9,777,222	33.3	16,116,875	43.2	15,308,089	43.9
	2. Rural	1,636,737	5.6	1,785,817	4.8	1,640,642	4.7
	B. Farm	68,371	.3	282,328	.8	268,586	.8
II. Outside metropolitan districts		17,831,378	60.8	19,140,450	51.2	17,637,215	50.6
	A. Nonfarm	10,367,591	35.4	11,780,497	31.5	10,799,242	31.0
	1. Urban	4,490,156	15.3	5,499,477	14.7	5,288,411	15.2
	2. Rural	5,877,435	20.1	6,281,020	16.8	5,510,831	15.8
	B. Farm	7,463,787	25.4	7,359,953	19.7	6,837,973	19.6

27. In all categories, the figures for urban nonfarm areas represent a greater proportion of the United States total than rural nonfarm areas.

28. The ratio of total residential dwelling units to residential structures is less for nonfarm areas inside metropolitan districts than for such areas outside metropolitan districts.

29. In only one group does the number of unoccupied residential dwelling units exceed 10% of the total number of residential dwelling units.

30. The percentage of occupancy of residential structures with more than one dwelling unit is greater inside metropolitan districts than outside metropolitan districts. 30.___

31. In all categories, the figures for urban nonfarm areas, both inside and outside metropolitan districts, represent a greater proportion of the district totals than do rural nonfarm areas. 31.___

32. The average number of occupied dwelling units per structure is less in rural nonfarm areas than in the other areas for which data are given. 32.___

33. The solution of problems by a display of authority by the housing assistant is 33.___

    A. *desirable* because it is a necessary device in making the tenants conform to established policies
    B. *desirable* because it is inherent in his work
    C. *undesirable* because it indicates unwarranted assumption of power
    D. *undesirable* because it is natural only to the aggressive housing assistant
    E. *undesirable* because it violates the principle of delegation of authority

34. When conducting a first interview with an applicant for an apartment who speaks English poorly, the skill of the housing assistant is indicated by 34.___

    A. asking the applicant to return the following day when a staff member familiar with the applicant's language will be available
    B. creating a spirit of rapport in spite of the language difficulty
    C. explaining to the applicant how his language handicap affects his eligibility
    D. explaining to the applicant that he would probably find it difficult to get along with the other tenants because of their prejudice against foreigners
    E. impartially discussing the situation with the applicant without any particular consideration of his language background

35. In order to secure information on several specific points from all the tenants of a project, it has been suggested that a questionnaire be distributed to be completed and returned by the tenants. 35.___
    The use of such a procedure is GENERALLY

    A. *desirable* because it is a valuable means of building the cooperative relationship which should exist between tenants and management
    B. *desirable* because it provides a written record of each tenant's reply
    C. *undesirable* because distribution and collection of questionnaires is time-consuming
    D. *undesirable* because few tenants will probably fill out the questionnaires incorrectly
    E. *undesirable* because it makes no provision for the expression of related information or viewpoints

KEY (CORRECT ANSWERS)

1.	I	11.	E	21.	D	31.	B
2.	E	12.	C	22.	B	32.	C
3.	G	13.	A	23.	B	33.	C
4.	D	14.	E	24.	A	34.	B
5.	K	15.	C	25.	A	35.	B
6.	L	16.	A	26.	A		
7.	A	17.	D	27.	B		
8.	C	18.	C	28.	B		
9.	D	19.	D	29.	A		
10.	D	20.	C	30.	D		

EXAMINATION SECTION
TEST 1

DIRECTIONS: Each question or incomplete statement is followed by several suggested answers or completions. Select the one that BEST answers the question or completes the statement. *PRINT THE LETTER OF THE CORRECT ANSWER IN THE SPACE AT THE RIGHT.*

1. The following three statements relate to master keys:
   I. The use of the apartment master key by project maintenance employees is authorized for emergencies which require widespread entrance to apartments
   II. Housing patrolmen receive apartment master keys but not maintenance master keys
   III. Defective or broken master keys must be sent to the Bay View Lock Shop only by registered mail.

   Which of the following choices lists all the foregoing statements that are generally CORRECT?

   A. I only is generally correct.
   B. II only is generally correct.
   C. III only is generally correct.
   D. I and III only are generally correct.

   1.____

2. State legislation requires an owner, including the Authority, to install a bell, buzzer, and voice intercommunication system and to install self-closing and self-locking building entrance doors under certain conditions.
   The following three statements relate to such installations:
   I. The Authority is obligated to install such a system only when tenants occupying a majority of the apartments in a building make written request and agree to pay for the cost
   II. Tenants who do not request the installation need not pay for it
   III. Housing managers must meet with the executive committee of the tenant organization to discuss possible installation of the system.

   Which of the following choices list all the foregoing statements that are generally correct?

   A. I and II only are generally correct.
   B. II and III only are generally correct.
   C. I and III only are generally correct.
   D. I, II, and III are generally correct.

   2.____

3. The following three statements relate to underoccupied apartments:
   I. A tenant may not be transferred to a smaller apartment unless he is eligible on the basis of income for the smaller apartment
   II. The Authority will pay moving expenses according to its schedule for a non-welfare tenant transferring to a smaller apartment
   III. When underoccupancy arises from death, no attempt to have the tenant move to a smaller apartment should be made for six months.

   Which of the following choices lists all the foregoing statements that are generally CORRECT?

   3.____

A. I only is generally correct.
B. II only is generally correct.
C. I and II only are generally correct.
D. II and III only are generally correct.

4. The following three statements relate to the project operating budget:
   I. The second- and third-year figures of the three-year budget may be more of an estimate than those for the first year
   II. Housing managers may consult with technicians in the technical service division about budget matters
   III. Each housing manager and superintendent shall maintain a file to be known as *operating budget preparation folder.*
   Which of the following choices lists all the foregoing statements that are generally CORRECT?

   A. I and II only are generally correct.
   B. II and III only are generally correct.
   C. I and III only are generally correct.
   D. I, II, and III are generally correct.

5. The following three statements relate to apartment visits by housing assistants in subsidized projects:
   I. If there are indications of a problem situation or negligent use of the apartment, the housing assistant must visit all the rooms
   II. The tenant has the option of refusing both the orientation visit made after move-in and the annual visit
   III. If there is no record of poor housekeeping, and at first glance the apartment appears to be in reasonably good order, the housing assistant should limit his inspection to the range and the refrigerator.
   Which of the following choices lists all the foregoing statements that are generally CORRECT?

   A. I only is generally correct.
   B. I and II only are generally correct.
   C. II only is generally correct.
   D. II and III only are generally correct.

6. The following three statements relate to the use of project space for community purposes:
   I. All groups requesting space must first apply to the housing manager
   II. The housing manager must notify the legal department immediately upon the vacating of community space by the lessee or upon a major change in the use of space.
   III. The housing manager must maintain a ledger card for each community space under lease and collect rent for such space.
   Which of the following choices lists all the foregoing statements that are generally CORRECT?

   A. I, II, and III are generally correct.
   B. I and II only are generally correct.
   C. II and III only are generally correct.
   D. I and III only are generally correct.

7. A newspaper reporter calls to interview you about a fire that occurred the previous   7.____
   evening in a tenant's apartment. All their furnishings and clothing were destroyed either
   through fire or water damage. The family was forced to spend the night with several
   neighbors. You have been authorized to grant the interview.
   Which of the following statements would be PROPER for you to make?
   The family

   A. has been a problem to management because of poor apartment maintenance
   B. is being moved to a smaller apartment in the project because they are destitute
   C. is being relocated to another apartment because of complaints from neighbors
   D. is being moved into a vacant apartment, since it will take some days to rehabilitate
      their apartment

8. A press photographer requests permission to take pictures from the roof of a high-rise   8.____
   building. The housing manager at the project should

   A. reject the request in order to comply with the regulations
   B. reject the request because the Authority has no third-party insurance
   C. check his credentials and request permission from the public relations office
   D. verify his credentials and allow him to photograph from the roof

9. Assume that the tenant patrol has been very effective in a high-rise building in reducing   9.____
   crime and vandalism. However, an incident involving an argument between two youths
   brings a crowd to the lobby. A patrol volunteer in the lobby has supported the Puerto
   Rican boy involved, whereas the tenants congregated support the Chinese boy involved.
   The police are called to disperse the crowd. Later you receive complaints that the patrol
   in the lobby mistreats the Chinese boys. The incident seems to have stirred up unrest
   throughout the building.
   Of the following, the BEST way to handle this problem would be to

   A. investigate the charges and, if verified, disband the patrol
   B. request assistance from the office of community affairs at central office
   C. call in the parents and the boys involved in the incident and discuss continued
      occupancy reevalua-tions
   D. advise the complaining tenants that the patrol is dedicated to their security

10. Assume that tenant patrol volunteers in one of your 16 buildings request permission to   10.____
    store their lobby table and chairs in the electric meter room. Unless they can store their
    equipment, they will give up the work, since none of them is willing to continue cluttering
    his apartment with this equipment.
    You should reject this request and attempt to find another remedy because

    A. buildings serviced by other patrols do not have similar storage space
    B. you doubt that proper room security can be permanently provided
    C. there might be a temptation to store items other than tables and chairs
    D. it is unlawful to use electric meter rooms for storage

11. A recommendation to terminate tenancy may be made because of alcoholism where it   11.____
    results in

    A. related medical conditions of a chronic nature
    B. family estrangement leading to divorce proceedings

C. interference with the proper operations of the project
D. substantial reduction in total family income

12. A guide to tenants furnished by a project may NOT give information concerning the address of the local

    A. medicaid alert office
    B. city hospital
    C. Department of Health clinic
    D. drugstore

13. From time to time, employees have been accused of improper actions or behavior while working in apartments. Therefore, when there is someone in the apartment, it is important that certain rules of conduct be observed.
    The one of the following which is NOT such a rule is for employees to

    A. place the official *door knob notice* on the door on entering an apartment
    B. avoid any discussion with children
    C. leave the apartment if anyone appears to be under the influence of liquor
    D. discuss the reason for leaving the door open while working

14. The CHIEF function of the housing manager in dealing with a tenants' association is to

    A. listen to their requests and to advise them on Authority policies
    B. provide leadership in conducting their affairs
    C. attend meetings solely to report their activities to the chief manager
    D. attend meetings to identify certain undesirable militants

15. Certain tenants may keep animals within certain limitations.
    The one of the following which is NOT a specific category of such tenants is

    A. mute   B. blind
    C. elderly   D. severely handicapped

16. The project office is being picketed by a number of tenants protesting a recent Authority-wide rent increase. The one of the following that the housing manager is LEAST likely to notify is the

    A. public information division
    B. office of the chief of the administration division
    C. chief manager
    D. department of social and community services

17. As manager of a site clearance project, you learn that a tenant of record had just vacated, leaving in possession persons who have been in occupancy for more than six months.
    Consistent with the policy on sharing families, you should

    A. consider the remaining persons as tenants
    B. institute summary holdover proceedings
    C. request a notarized certificate of necessity from the occupants
    D. refer the matter to the legal department for disposition

18. On a site you manage, a residential tenant on firm rent refuses to pay the approved scheduled rent.
    Of the following actions, the one you should take IMMEDIATELY is to

    A. determine whether a rent reduction is justified
    B. institute summary proceedings for non-payment
    C. notify the tenant of the commencement of the one-month penalty period
    D. refer the matter to the chief of site management

19. Referral of the tenant to the social services division is advisable in all of the following situations EXCEPT that of a(n)

    A. elderly tenant disturbing her neighbors by irrational behavior
    B. young mother separated from her husband complaining that her worker is not responsive to her needs
    C. tenant admitting that she cannot control the disruptive behavior of her ten-year-old twins
    D. young mother separated from her husband being the subject of frequent complaints by several neighbors in reference to unreasonably noisy parties

20. Submission of a tenant's record to the office of the tenancy administrator for termination review is mandatory when a

    A. tenant's son is arrested for selling narcotics off-project
    B. tenant is arrested for assaulting his wife with his fists
    C. tenant's brother is arrested for possession of marijuana in a neighborhood youth center
    D. tenant is arrested for forgery of his sister's signature

21. A housing police patrolman requests supper money because he worked a tour of 8:00 M. to 8:00 P.M. The overtime was a result of his arresting a suspect caught leaving an apartment with the tenant's television set.
    You are obliged to REJECT the request because

    A. the housing police are not granted supper money in any circumstances
    B. the management petty cash funds cannot be used for police work
    C. the officer was off duty at 8:00 P.M., and it was unreasonable to expect supper money
    D. only his sergeant may authorize such supper money

22. The housing police have submitted an incident report to you involving a tenant of a neighboring project. It is a minor incident which took place in your project and which also involved several of your tenants.
    Of the following actions, you are REQUIRED to

    A. request an interview with the non-tenant at his convenience
    B. write a letter to the non-tenant warning of penalties if the incident recurs
    C. notify the other manager and send a copy of the incident report
    D. arrange with the other manager for a joint conference

6 (#1)

23. The housing police apprehend a 12-year-old boy, living in the project, chipping away at the elevator buttons in the lobby and defacing the wall tiles. The damage is thereafter repaired at a cost of $75. The responsible tenant refuses to pay for this damage.
In order to recover the expense of this unlawful destruction, the housing manager may

   A. institute a civil damage suit in small claims court
   B. ask the chief manager to evaluate whether a civil damage suit should be brought
   C. include the charge in a dispossession for non-payment of rent
   D. refer the responsible tenant to the social services division for consultation

23._____

24. Assume that the housing police advise you that a tenant has been found murdered in his apartment.
The FIRST action you should take is to

   A. call the local police precinct
   B. notify the president of the tenants' association
   C. call the public relations division
   D. notify the legal division

24._____

25. Data show a relationship between felony rates in housing projects and certain other factors. This data showed that, in projects with well-structured moderate-income families, the felony rate per 1,000 families

   A. *falls* as the density of dwelling units per acre increases
   B. *rises* as the density of dwelling units per acre decreases
   C. *falls* as the height of buildings increases
   D. *rises* as the height of buildings increases

25._____

KEY (CORRECT ANSWERS)

1.	A	11.	C
2.	C	12.	D
3.	B	13.	D
4.	D	14.	A
5.	A	15.	C
6.	D	16.	D
7.	D	17.	A
8.	C	18.	B
9.	B	19.	B
10.	D	20.	A

21.	A
22.	C
23.	B
24.	C
25.	D

TEST 2

DIRECTIONS: Each question or incomplete statement is followed by several suggested answers or completions. Select the one that BEST answers the question or completes the statement. *PRINT THE LETTER OF THE CORRECT ANSWER IN THE SPACE AT THE RIGHT.*

1. Assume that a housing manager of a large subsidized project advised her senior teller to have the petty cash fund available for inspection on the afternoon of the third Wednesday of the month.
   This practice is considered to be

   A. *desirable* because such an inspection will not interfere with the bookkeeping office when rent is being collected
   B. *undesirable* because an audit of the petty cash fund should be unannounced
   C. *desirable* because it will encourage a better relationship between the manager and the teller
   D. *undesirable* because the third Wednesday may be a welfare check day

   1.____

2. The Authority carries insurance policies for indemnification against certain losses or damages.
   The one of the following for which the Authority is NOT insured is

   A. damage caused by a strike
   B. claims by persons other than employees, including damages for care and loss of services
   C. coverage for alteration of any check, draft, or promissory note
   D. protection against claims by tenants for damage to personal property by employees

   2.____

3. Assume that, as housing manager, you are presented with contract papers which require your signature before payment can be made. The papers are for partial payment for roofing work at a total cost of $50,000. The superintendent and the plant services inspector have already signed, indicating that work has been satisfactorily completed to date.
   Of the following, the BEST reason for you to sign the papers is that

   A. the signatures of the superintendent and the inspector assure that payment is in order
   B. the superintendent has requested you to sign the papers immediately to insure prompt payment
   C. you are satisfied that the work to date complies with the contract
   D. the rules of the Authority requires that the manager sign that he is aware of the progress of the work

   3.____

4. You have posted on the bulletin board in the bookkeeping office information issued by the Treasury Department giving descriptions of counterfeit $20 bills in circulation. The branch bank handling the project account advises you that the previous night's deposit contained a counterfeit $20 bill.
   The one of the following actions you should take is to

   A. request the cashier who accepted the bill to make restitution
   B. request the cashier who accepted the bill to process a shortage adjustment report and sign it

   4.____

C. call the U.S. Treasury Department to report the matter
D. call the housing police for assistance in tracing the passer

5. An aged tenant of the project requests that the teller cash a city payroll check for $287.50 made out to his wife. The check bears the wife's endorsement and the tenant endorses the check in front of the teller. He does not wish to pay his rent at this time. The teller cashes the check.
   The teller's action is

   A. *correct;* city payroll checks in any amount should be cashed for tenants
   B. *correct;* this tenant was entitled to have this check cashed
   C. *incorrect;* the tenant should have presented his wife's authorization on a consent to second-party payee form
   D. *incorrect;* the check was payable only to the tenant's spouse

5.____

6. Assume that, at the project, a stalled elevator is brought down to floor level. None of the passengers has suffered injury, appear to be in shock or request medical attention. They leave the elevator in a normal manner. One of the passengers is carrying a sleeping infant in her arms.
   In this situation, you should GENERALLY

   A. refer adult passengers to the legal department
   B. refrain from submitting a report of the incident
   C. submit a report of accident, public liability
   D. telephone the insurance adjuster for specific instructions

6.____

7. A charge may PROPERLY be imposed on tenants for

   A. certain instances of repainting
   B. minor repairs when a tenant is vacating
   C. a transfer to an apartment of a different size to conform to occupancy standards
   D. repair of two leaking faucets

7.____

8. A project audit by the audit section of the control department reveals a large number of discrepancies between the E.D.P. listings of tools, equipment, and material and the physical inventory.
   Of the following, the LEAST desirable action to take in this situation is to

   A. review all procedures relating to issuing tools and withdrawals from the storeroom
   B. call the housing police detective squad to investigate
   C. institute a semi-annual internal audit covering all accountable items
   D. review storage security

8.____

9. The one of the following which is CONSISTENT with the policies and procedures for prevention and elimination of pest and rodent infestation is that

   A. all vacated apartments should be treated for roach infestation
   B. the foreman of pest control operators must inspect the personal property of all intra-project transfer tenants for infestation
   C. in cases of serious infestation the tenant may be required to empty all closets
   D. if no infestation is found in a routine inspection, the premises are not treated

9.____

10. You have learned that the maintenance men refuse to make a repair in an apartment because of what they consider filthy housekeeping.
    Of the following actions, the one which would be BEST for you to take FIRST is to

    A. write a letter to the tenant explaining the reason the repair has not been made
    B. send a work order to the superintendent, asking that it be returned showing when the work was completed
    C. inform the superintendent of the situation, and advise him of management's responsibility to make the repair
    D. direct the maintenance men to follow up on the housekeeping problem to insure compliance before the work is done

11. Tenants who wish to install their own refrigerators in place of refrigerators provided by the Authority may do so subject to certain regulation.
    The one of the following statements which is such a regulation is that

    A. requests for installation of tenant-owned refrigerators must be submitted to the superintendent for approval
    B. refrigerators with dual temperature controls are not permitted
    C. only extension cords bearing U.L. approval may be used between refrigerators and wall outlets
    D. tenant-owned refrigerators may be installed only in kitchens

12. A tenant complains to you that the painter shattered a $50 mirror. The tenant requests payment for the mirror. The painter is an employee of the contractor and not of the Authority.
    The one of the following actions that you should take in handling this complaint is to

    A. approve a property damage claim for 90% of the loss
    B. refer the tenant to the contractor to whom she should present her claim
    C. advise the contractor of the claim and request that the tenant be paid
    D. prepare and submit to the legal department a notice of claim

13. In the event of fire in the boiler plant, the FIRST step to take is to

    A. fight the fire with the prescribed fire extinguisher
    B. ask the first person passing by to call the Fire Department
    C. activate the nearest Fire Department alarm box
    D. pull the remote control switch

14. Assume that a boiler explosion has occurred. The resulting damage is less than $700.
    Of the following actions, the one which the manager should take FIRST is to

    A. consult with the chief of insurance
    B. proceed through the superintendent to repair or restore the premises
    C. request a performance bond from a designated outside contractor
    D. report the problem to the state division of housing and community renewal

15. Top priority in snow removal must be given to

    A. clearing ramps and interior secondary sidewalks
    B. providing access to fuel lines and fire hydrants
    C. building entrance steps and entrance landings
    D. interior sidewalks leading from buildings directly to perimeter sidewalks

4 (#2)

16. A housing manager may approve a request for an inter-project transfer when the tenant

    A. who is the principal wage-earner was transferred two months ago to a new work location requiring two hours' traveling time
    B. who has a chronic illness or a physical handicap requires specialized care or facilities not available near the project
    C. is in an overcrowded apartment because a daughter who was an original member of the family has returned home with her husband
    D. in a middle-income project requests a transfer to a subsidized project because he has been on strike for two months

17. The assistant housing manager requests your advice, as housing manager, about an unauthorized occupancy. A daughter and her two children have moved into a tenant's apartment. The tenant family consists of husband, wife, and teenage son. The tenant is receiving aid from the department of social services and produces evidence that the three additional family members have also been budgeted since their unauthorized move-in about a year ago. Therefore, the tenant should be advised

    A. to seek special permission from the housing consultant for this occupancy arrangement
    B. to tell the three additional occupants to move out and then apply for approval to move into this apartment
    C. that since there has been no change in rent you will approve a change in status
    D. that the Authority considers the family composition to be in violation of occupancy standards

18. Assume that in the course of a regular call to an apartment by an employee a serious quarrel arises among several adults who are in the apartment.
    Of the following, the MOST important rule for the employee to follow is to

    A. observe these persons carefully to determine possible signs of intoxication or of substance abuse
    B. attempt to mediate the dispute so that he may proceed to complete his assigned tasks without interruption
    C. instruct the tenants and their guests, if any, as to their privileges and responsibilities relative to the premises
    D. avoid involvement and, if necessary, leave the apartment

19. For a residual single person to remain in occupancy, he is required to

    A. have reached age 30
    B. be ambulatory
    C. accept immediate transfer to a smaller apartment
    D. pass a monthly apartment inspection for six consecutive months

20. You have evicted a tenant whose entire furnishings have been placed on the street on the order of the marshal, who has given you possession of the apartment.
    Of the following, it would be CORRECT for you to

    A. have the department of sanitation dispose of the street encumbrance
    B. have project personnel dispose of the encumbrance by commercial storage
    C. charge the tenant's account for the cost of removing the encumbrance
    D. charge the tenant on a time basis for removal from the street by project staff

5 (#2)

21. Assume that you have decided to recommend termination of tenancy based on non-desirability.
The way in which you should treat the facts or incidents and their sources upon which you relied for your decision should be to

    A. *withhold* the facts, although the source may be revealed to the tenant
    B. *reveal* the facts, although the source need not be revealed to the tenant
    C. *reveal* the facts and the source to the tenant
    D. *withhold* the facts and the source from the tenant

21.____

22. A single elderly occupant is found dead in his apartment. You have been unable to locate any relatives or references appearing in the tenant record, despite diligent efforts.
You may, therefore, take possession of the apartment ONLY if

    A. you receive a release from the public administrator's office
    B. there is more than one month's rent in arrears
    C. the furnishings are considered worthless
    D. the police find the keys in the apartment and turn them over to you

22.____

23. When a manager decides that a tenant's shades are in such condition that replacement is required, and he provides the tenant with used shades, there shall be _____ charge.

    A. a charge of 3/4 of the scheduled
    B. a charge of 1/2 of the scheduled
    C. a charge of 1/4 of the scheduled
    D. no

23.____

24. Certain public agencies are entitled to full disclosure of confidential information concerning tenants or applicants.
One such agency is the State

    A. Crime Victims Compensation Board
    B. Department of Audit and Control
    C. Division of Housing and Community Renewal
    D. Division of Municipal Affairs

24.____

25. Assume that you are asked by a local community organization to serve on a special committee which is to select an executive director for the organization. You accept the invitation and subsequently interview several candidates.
Which of the following is the LEAST important consideration in reaching a valid decision about the suitability of each candidate for the position?

    A. Amount and sequence of experience in the candidate's work history
    B. Candidate's behavior during the interview
    C. Inferences concerning the candidate's underlying motives for seeking the position
    D. General qualifications needed for satisfactory job performance by a candidate

25.____

KEY (CORRECT ANSWERS)

1. B
2. A
3. C
4. B
5. B

6. B
7. A
8. B
9. C
10. C

11. D
12. B
13. D
14. B
15. B

16. B
17. D
18. D
19. B
20. C

21. B
22. A
23. D
24. C
25. C

TEST 3

DIRECTIONS: Each question or incomplete statement is followed by several suggested answers or completions. Select the one that BEST answers the question or completes the statement. *PRINT THE LETTER OF THE CORRECT ANSWER IN THE SPACE AT THE RIGHT.*

1. Authority officials have stressed that crime reported in public housing is proportionately much less than crime reported in the city as a whole. Some critics, however, hold such a comparison to mean little.
Which of the following statements BEST supports the view of these critics?

   A. In compiling its data, the Authority uses a method different from the uniform crime reporting system of the city's Police Department.
   B. Many crime victims do not report crimes because they fear retaliation by criminals or believe that the police can do nothing.
   C. Recent sharp drops in reported crime have resulted from a temporary increase in security measures in the project.
   D. There are generally more commercial establishments and other inviting targets for criminals outside, rather than inside, housing projects.

1.____

2. The Authority police consider a major impediment to the performance of their duties to be an unacceptably large number of defects in

   A. locks   B. radios
   C. handcuffs   D. ammunition

2.____

3. MOST disagreements between the Authority police and the city police are caused by

   A. differences in salaries
   B. jurisdictional disputes
   C. conflicts concerning peace officer and police officer status
   D. unequal advancement opportunities

3.____

4. Designated employee union representatives are permitted to be released with pay by the housing manager for several purposes.
For which of the following activities would released time be WITHOUT pay?

   A. Investigation of grievances
   B. Participating in meetings of departmental joint labor relations committees
   C. Negotiating with and appearing before departmental and other city officials and agencies
   D. Attendance at union meetings or conventions

4.____

5. Assume that you are the trial officer in a local disciplinary trial of a maintenance man based on charges by the superintendent that he demanded $2.00 from each tenant for whom he had installed a door-lock chain provided by the tenant. At the hearing, it develops that much more serious wrongdoing appears to have occurred.
As trial officer, you believe that maximum penalties available to you are inadequate in this case. Of the following action, it would be MOST appropriate for you to

   A. advise the maintenance man to seek competent counsel
   B. impose a separate maximum penalty for each instance of wrongdoing

5.____

C. postpone the trial and present the information to the District Attorney
D. suspend the trial and consult with the Authority's general counsel

6. Monthly toll telephone charges reveal a number of costly personal calls in the sum of $50 traced to an employee. Despite the evidence, the employee denies the accusation and refuses to pay the charges. You decide to hold a local disciplinary hearing.
The one of the following actions you are REQUIRED to take is to

   A. discuss the problem with the chief manager before taking any other action
   B. advise the employee you will be the hearing officer
   C. give the employee a notice of disciplinary charges indicating the charges and time and place of hearing
   D. advise the employee that the technical rules of evidence will be adhered to at the hearing

7. The housing manager has authority to write off claims in favor of or against the Authority within specified amounts. In accordance with this policy, the housing manager may

   A. dispose of any claim by a tenant or former tenant provided the amount of the payment does not exceed $50
   B. dispose of any claim by a tenant or former tenant provided the amount of the payment does not exceed $25
   C. write off any claim against a tenant in residence if the amount does not exceed $25
   D. write off any claim against a former tenant if the amount does not exceed $75

8. The one of the following statements which is CORRECT in reference to assets and eligibility for continued occupancy is that

   A. any tenant whose assets exceed three times the continued occupancy limit for his size apartment is ineligible
   B. a tenant who owns a building which contains a suitable dwelling unit in which he can live is ineligible if his equity in the building exceeds three times the occupancy limit
   C. a tenant whose earning capacity is limited or nonexistent is exempted from any limitation on excess assets for eligibility for continued occupancy provided that the district chief manager approves such exemption
   D. assets are defined to include cash on hand and in banks and the initial purchase value of real property, stocks, and bonds, and other forms of capital investment

9. Families determined as falling within certain categories may be declared ineligible for admission to public housing projects in the absence of extenuating circumstances. The one of the following which is SUCH a category is a family in which a(n)

   A. member of the family was involved in the sale of narcotics more than five years before the rental interview
   B. member of the family is a confirmed addict and is not undergoing follow-up treatment by a professional agency after discharge from an institution
   C. member of the family under the age of sixteen was involved as an offender in a crime of a sexual nature such as rape, carnal abuse, or impairing the morals of a minor
   D. adult member of the family was involved in an act of violence not of a serious criminal nature

10. The TOTAL proportion of apartments painted which the housing manager and the superintendent should inspect, or have inspected, is usually about

    A. 10% B. 20% C. 30% D. 40%

11. Because of the great demand for housing in the city, some developments have been constructed on landfill on reclaimed river edges.
    One such project is

    A. Roosevelt Island
    B. Brooklyn Bridge Southwest
    C. Battery Park City
    D. Twin Parks

12. The issue raised by the plaintiffs in the recent legal suit against the Authority regarding the public housing in the Seward Park Extension Urban Renewal Area was the granting of preference in tenant selection to

    A. large families
    B. families from outside the area
    C. families of war veterans
    D. non-welfare families

13. *Exclusionary zoning* leads to residential segregation by social class or race.
    The one of the following MOST likely to lead to exclusionary zoning is for a state to permit

    A. apartment units to be of various sizes
    B. low-income housing to be built on private land
    C. municipalities to control building permits
    D. unrelated persons to live together

14. The portion of the Administrative Code that sets minimum standards for decent, safe, and sanitary dwellings is known as the _____ Code.

    A. General Construction   B. Multiple Dwelling
    C. Housing Maintenance   D. Building Standards

15. Of the following, which is the MOST accurate general description of the book, DEFENSIBLE SPACE, by Oscar Newman?
    The book

    A. is a detailed study of the architectural design of public housing projects in the city for the purpose of achieving greater economy of materials
    B. advocates using architectural design to create an environment for the enhancement of inhabitants' lives while also providing security for their families, neighbors, and friends
    C. concludes that a large police force is the major protection against most ordinary kinds of crime in public housing
    D. proposes high-rise developments as the rational remedy for chronic housing shortages and the most effective use of urban space

16. In recent years, a number of cities have emphasized the construction of low-rise vest-pocket public housing projects.
    The one of the following which is the MAJOR disadvantage of this type of public housing, compared to larger-scale public housing projects, is that it

    A. has relatively higher tenant-borne operating and maintenance costs
    B. is more likely to encourage criminal activity
    C. inhibits community activities among tenants
    D. must be located at considerable distance from the central city

16.____

17. The one of the following which is usually LEAST significant in predicting whether a particular building located in a disadvantaged area of the city will be abandoned is

    A. its condition in comparison to low-income housing in other parts of the city
    B. the cost of maintaining it in good repair
    C. the extent of the drug addiction problem and criminal activity in the immediate neighborhood
    D. the attitude and behavior of the tenants of the particular building

17.____

18. The one of the following which is the MOST important cause of the low vacancy rate in public housing in the city in comparison to vacancy rates in other cities is the

    A. similarity in architectural design between public housing and middle-income housing in the city
    B. stringent enforcement in the city of relevant housing codes
    C. greater proximity of public housing in the city to unskilled job markets
    D. relatively large number of households in the city public housing which consist of the working poor

18.____

19. Housing experts who advocate the construction of public housing, rental supplements, and similar direct subsidies usually attribute the shortage of adequate housing for low-income families PRIMARILY to

    A. racial discrimination which has resulted in a destructive attitude toward housing on the part of minority group members
    B. the absence of mass production techniques in the building industry
    C. the recurrent lack of mortgage credit
    D. the ability of major cities to mount effective housing programs

19.____

20. A federally-funded program of free legal service, serving persons with poverty-level income, represents many residents of public housing.
    In the city, the program is known as

    A. the Bar Association of the City
    B. the Council Against Poverty
    C. Community Action for Legal Services
    D. the Community Service Society

20.____

21. The federal government has recently proposed reducing the rent of newly constructed subsidized units for low-income households and, instead, assisting such households through cash housing allowances.
    This proposed program lacks a provision to

21.____

A. give low-income persons freedom to choose where and how to live
B. pay the difference between what low-income persons can afford and the fair rent value of the quarters
C. prohibit landlords from raising rents unduly
D. provide special grants for cities with low vacancy rates

22. The Federal housing policies of the 1960s were LEAST successful in

A. generating increased housing production
B. improving conditions in deteriorating neighborhoods
C. promoting economic stabilization of the housing industry
D. encouraging home ownership for moderate-income households

23. The following sentences, when put in correct order, constitute a complete paragraph. Select from among the choices listed below, the one in which the CORRECT order is shown.
    I. Project residents had first claim to this use, followed by surrounding neighborhood children.
    II. By contrast, recreation space within the project's interior was found to be used more often by both groups.
    III. Studies of the use of project grounds in many cities showed grounds left open for public use were neglected and unused, both by residents and by members of the surrounding community.
    IV. Project residents had clearly laid claim to the play spaces, setting up and enforcing unwritten rules for use.
    V. Each group, by experience, found their activities easily disrupted by other groups, and their claim to the use of space for recreation difficult to enforce.
    The CORRECT answer is:

    A. IV, V, I, II, III
    B. V, II, IV, III, I
    C. I, IV, III, II, V
    D. III, V, II, IV, I

24. The following sentences, when put in correct order, constitute a complete paragraph. Select from among the choices listed below the one in which the CORRECT order is shown.
    I. They do not consider the problems correctable within the existing subsidy formula and social policy of accepting all eligible applicants regardless of social behavior and life style.
    II. A recent survey, however, indicated that tenants believe these problems correctable by local housing authorities and management within the existing financial formula.
    III. Many of the problems and complaints concerning public housing management and design have created resentment between the tenant and the landlord.
    IV. This same survey indicated that administrators and managers do not agree with the tenants.
    The CORRECT answer is:

    A. II, I, III, IV
    B. I, III, IV, II
    C. III, II, IV, I
    D. IV, II, I, III

25. The following sentences, when put in correct order, constitute a complete paragraph. Select from among the choices listed below the one in which the CORRECT order is shown.

   I. In single family residences, there is usually enough distance between tenants to prevent occupants from annoying one another.
   II. For example, a certain small percentage of tenant families has one or more members addicted to alcohol.
   III. While managers believe in the right of individuals to live as they choose, the manager becomes concerned when the pattern of living jeopardizes others' rights.
   IV. Still others turn night into day, staging lusty entertainments which carry on into the hours when most tenants are trying to sleep.
   V. In apartment buildings, however, tenants live so closely together that any misbehavior can result in unpleasant living conditions.
   VI. Other families engage in violent argument.

The CORRECT answer is:

A. III, II, V, IV, VI, I
B. I, V, II, VI, IV, III
C. II, V, IV, I, III, VI
D. IV, II, V, VI, III, I

KEY (CORRECT ANSWERS)

1. D
2. B
3. B
4. D
5. D

6. C
7. B
8. C
9. B
10. B

11. C
12. B
13. C
14. C
15. B

16. A
17. A
18. D
19. C
20. C

21. C
22. B
23. D
24. C
25. B

EXAMINATION SECTION
TEST 1

DIRECTIONS: Each question or incomplete statement is followed by several suggested answers or completions. Select the one that BEST answers the question or completes the statement. *PRINT THE LETTER OF THE CORRECT ANSWER IN THE SPACE AT THE RIGHT.*

1. During an interview with a tenant at your office, he confides to you that he would rather find his own apartment for his family than move into public housing. He asks for your advice in this matter.
   The BEST thing you can do is

   A. advise that he look only to public housing since these are the best apartments
   B. tell him that you cannot advise him in such personal matters and then refer him to Social Services
   C. discuss with him the different ways he might find an apartment, including one in public housing
   D. suggest that he talk over his decision more carefully with his family

2. While inspecting conditions around a site, you notice that some of the garbage cans are not covered.
   Which of the following BEST explains why this condition should be corrected? To

   A. prevent the garbage cans from getting lost
   B. prevent garbage from cans spreading onto the street
   C. allow sanitation men to handle the cans without spillage
   D. keep dogs and cats from knocking garbage cans over

3. While interviewing tenants, an assistant may find that a tenant will be silent for a short time before answering questions.
   In order to get the required information from the tenant when this happens, the assistant should GENERALLY

   A. repeat the same question to make the tenant stop hesitating
   B. ask the tenant to write out his answer
   C. ask the tenant to answer quickly because other tenants are waiting to see you
   D. wait patiently and not pressure the tenant into quick, undeveloped answers

4. A tenant that you have been trying to encourage to apply for public housing comes to your desk at the site office. He is talking in a very angry and excited way about the lack of heat in his apartment. He says he will not pay his rent until there is heat.
   The BEST thing for you to do at this time is to

   A. tell him that he should have applied for public housing as you suggested
   B. immediately let your supervisor know that he is refusing to pay his rent
   C. let him talk until he finishes and then discuss his problem with him
   D. tell him that you will not talk to him until he stops yelling

5. You have been informed that no determination has yet been made on the eligibility of a certain tenant for public housing. The decision will depend upon further checking. When you see the tenant, he seems to be quite worried, and he asks you whether his application has been accepted.
What would be BEST for you to do under these circumstances? Tell him

   A. you can't talk to him because there is no definite information and you are very busy
   B. to put his question in writing and send it to your manager so that it will be on record
   C. you don't know yet but that he should not worry since you are quite sure he will be accepted
   D. his application is being checked, and you will let him know the final result

6. An assistant is interviewing a high priority applicant who, contrary to usual experience, is extremely well-prepared and supplied with all the information the assistant is seeking. Which of the following possible actions by the assistant is MOST suitable under these circumstances?

   A. Directly showing a willingness to review the information carefully and promptly
   B. Exercising extreme caution about the credibility of the facts presented
   C. Showing his awareness that the applicant is trying to trick him with false information
   D. Accepting all of the candidate's information because of his obviously high level of intelligence

7. One of the tenants to be relocated is an extremely alert but elderly man who resists your every attempt to discuss with him the necessity for moving. He has lived in this building for almost thirty years, and he states flatly that he will NOT move.
Of the following, the MOST acceptable action for you to take is to

   A. tell him he is being unreasonable and selfish
   B. forcibly have him removed from the premises
   C. refer his case to a social worker
   D. advise him to take his case to the Legal Aid Society

8. Suppose you telephone to set up an important appointment with a tenant for a specific day on your calendar. He refuses to meet with you on that day because he claims the day is his religious holiday.
What is the BEST way of handling this situation?

   A. Tell him it is against his interest not to meet with you on that day
   B. Give up any idea now of meeting with him and go on to arranging your next appointment
   C. Ask when he will be able to meet with you and indicate to him what the subject is
   D. Indicate to him that you know the holiday cannot be important since city employees do not officially have that day off

9. In a building slated for demolition but still inhabited by tenants, an assistant sees some children of tenants pulling on a pipe in the hall. He tells them to stop but they say that the building is being torn down anyway. What should the assistant do FIRST?

   A. Explain to the children that although this is true, they are causing danger to tenants still in the building.

B. Go immediately to the parents and tell them to punish their children for their misbehavior.
C. Say nothing else to the children but go to the site office and report the problem to his supervisor.
D. Go outside and call a policeman but tell the policeman to treat the children gently.

10. When interviewing a tenant who is to be relocated, the FIRST of the following actions for you to take is to

    A. inform the tenant that your office will help only if he cooperates
    B. advise the tenant that you must see proof for all statements he makes
    C. assure the tenant that every effort will be made to find suitable housing
    D. tell the tenant he will have no trouble finding new housing facilities

11. During interviews, people give information about themselves in several ways. Of the following, which would usually give the LEAST amount of information about the person being questioned? His

    A. spoken words
    B. tone of voice
    C. facial expression
    D. body position

12. Suppose that while you are interviewing a tenant about the condition of his apartment, he becomes angered by your questioning and begins to use abusive language. Which of the following is the BEST way for you to react to him?

    A. Use the same kind of language as he does to show him that you are neither impressed nor upset by his speech.
    B. Interrupt him and tell him that you are not required to listen to such language.
    C. Lower your voice and speak more slowly in an attempt to set an example that will calm him.
    D. Let him continue to use abusive language but insist that he answer your questions at once.

13. Of the following characteristics, the one which would be MOST helpful for an assistant when helping an angry applicant understand why he has been turned down for public housing would be the ability to

    A. state the rules exactly as they are written
    B. show examples of other cases where the same thing happened
    C. remain patient and understanding of the person's position
    D. remain uninvolved and cold to individual personal problems

Questions 14-19.

DIRECTIONS: Answer Questions 14 through 19 on the basis of the information given in the paragraphs below.

Three year's ago, a city introduced a program of reduced transit rates for the elderly. It was hoped that this program would increase the travel of the elderly and help them maintain a greater measure of independence. About 600,000 of the 800,000 eligible residents are currently enrolled in the program. To be eligible, a person must be 65 years of age or older and not employed full-time. Riding for reduced fare is permitted between 10:00 M. and 4:00 P.M. and between 7:00 P.M. and midnight on weekdays and 24 hours a day on Saturdays, Sundays, and holidays.

In a city university study based on a sampling of 728 enrollees interviewed, it was learned that 51 percent are able to travel more, and 30.8 percent had been able to save enough money to make a noticeable difference in their budgets as a result of the reduced-fare program.

It has been recommended that reduced-fare programs be extended to encourage the use of transit Lines in off-hours by other groups such as the poor, the very young, housewives, and the physically handicapped. To implement this recommendation, it would be necessary for the Federal government to increase transit subsidies.

14. Which one of the following would be the BEST title for the passage above?

    A. A Program of Reduced Transit Rates for the Elderly
    B. Recommendations for Extending Programs for the Elderly
    C. City University Study on the Relationship of Age and Travel
    D. Eligibility Requirements for the Reduced Rate Program

15. *Approximately* what percentage of the eligible residents is currently enrolled in the reduced-fare program?

    A. 25%   B. 50%   C. 65%   D. 75%

16. Which one of the following persons is NOT eligible for the reduced-fare program? A

    A. Woman, age 67, employed part-time as a stenographer
    B. Handicapped man, age 62
    C. Blind man, age 66, employed part-time as a transcribing typist
    D. Housewife, age 70

17. At which one of the following times would the reduced-fare NOT be permitted for an eligible elderly person?

    A. Sunday, 6:00 P.M.   B. Christmas Day, 2:00 M.
    C. Tuesday, 9:00 M.   D. Thursday, 8:00 P.M.

18. Of the 728 enrollees interviewed in a city university study of the reduced-fare program, it was found that

    A. the majority traveled more and saved money at the same time
    B. more than half traveled less and therefore saved money
    C. about half traveled more and. about one-third saved money
    D. the majority saved money but traveled the same rate as before

19. According to the passage above, what would be necessary to extend the reduced-fare program to other groups of people?

   A. Increasing the eligible age to 68
   B. Reducing the hours when half-fare is permitted
   C. Increasing the fare for other riders
   D. Increasing the transit subsidies by the Federal government

20. Reports are made MOST often in order to

   A. suggest new ideas
   B. give information
   C. issue orders to workers
   D. show that work is being done

21. An assistant is reporting a loose floor board in a certain apartment building on the site. The MOST important thing he should report in order to get immediate repairs is

   A. how the floor board became loose
   B. when the floor board became loose
   C. the type of material and the number of men needed to make the repair
   D. in which apartment the loose floor board is located

22. Suppose you receive a phone call from a tenant about a problem that requires you to look up the information and call her back. Although the tenant had given you her name earlier and you can say the name, you are not sure that you can spell it correctly. Which of the following would be MOST likely to insure that you spell the name correctly?

   A. Say the name slowly and ask her if you are saying it correctly.
   B. Spell her name as you have been saying it.
   C. Ask her to spell the name so that you can write it.
   D. Look through your files for a similar name and copy the spelling.

23. When tenants relocate, a report is made. This report is in the form of a standard form instead of a fully written report.
   The MOST important advantage of using a standard form for certain information is that

   A. one can be sure that the report will be sent in as soon as possible
   B. anyone can write out the report without directions from a supervisor
   C. needed information is less likely to be left out of the report
   D. information that is written up this way is less likely to be false

24. Suppose you are filling out a section of a form to describe an incident which will be read by a social worker but you run out of space before finishing. It would be BEST for you to

   A. leave out whatever information you consider unimportant
   B. write what you can on the form and attach another sheet with the rest of the information
   C. cross out what you wrote on the form and write on a separate sheet of paper which you attach to the form
   D. write what you can on the form and tell your supervisor or the social worker the rest of it

25. It is part of an assistant's job to help a manager enter various items of information on a monthly report. This information may be, for example, the number of tenants relocated to different types of housing and the number of tenants left on the site.
    The assistant must be careful NOT to make mistakes on his entries about tenants because

    A. mistakes will show his supervisor that his work is poor
    B. records must not be too difficult to read
    C. these mistakes are hard to notice and correct
    D. correct records are needed for the department to operate smoothly

    25.____

26. For tenants who are not eligible for public housing and who are unable to find a new apartment, the relocation agency

    A. refers the case to the Human Rights Commission
    B. seeks to obtain private housing for the family
    C. advises the family to move in with relatives and friends
    D. arranges sleeping quarters at the site office

    26.____

27. The MAXIMUM amount of money a relocated family can receive for moving expenses is

    A. under $500
    B. $500 - 750
    C. $751 - 1000
    D. $1001 - 1500

    27.____

28. Of the following conditions that are often present in slum buildings, the one which is MOST likely to cause lead poisoning in children is

    A. exposed rusty nails in floors
    B. uncovered garbage cans containing old pencils
    C. paint flaking off walls and window sills
    D. the escape of fumes from faulty oil burners

    28.____

29. An assistant would be correct to advise a tenant that it is ILLEGAL to throw which of the following into an incinerator?

    A. Compactly wrapped bundles
    B. Empty plastic bags
    C. Loose vacuum or carpet sweepings
    D. Soapy rags

    29.____

30. A housing project is being built on Site X.
    Of the following, the people who are given priority for apartments in the project if they meet eligibility requirements are

    A. former tenants of Site X
    B. welfare recipients
    C. minority groups with the lowest income
    D. families with the most children

    30.____

31. A family which occupied a 4 1/2 room apartment at an urban renewal site moved to an off-site 5-room apartment. They were eligible for a 6-room apartment, but it was unavailable.
    The family is now entitled to reimbursement for moving expenses based on

    31.____

A. a 4-room apartment
B. a 5-room apartment
C. a 6-room apartment
D. actual cost of the move in an unlimited amount

32. During inspection of a tenant's apartment, you observe that the grids and burners of the stove are greasy and heavily caked with spilled food. Because of this, the burners do not produce an even flame from all the gas openings.
Of the following, the BEST thing to tell the tenant FIRST is that she should

   A. scrape off the caked-on drippings and then poke open all the clogged openings so the gas will burn evenly
   B. remove the soiled parts of the burner and soak them in hot water with a mild cleaner to remove the dirt
   C. learn how to use the stove properly so that her food does not boil over or splatter onto the grids
   D. stop using the range until someone from the management office comes to adjust the flame

33. While inspecting a tenant's apartment, one of the things you should check is the drainage of the sinks. In testing the kitchen sink, you observe that there are coffee grinds and a film of grease in the drain basket.
Of the following, the BEST instructions to give the tenant are to

   A. throw coffee grinds in the garbage and wash oils down the drain
   B. collect oil in a can and put it in the garbage, but wash coffee grinds down with cold water
   C. avoid clogging, wash both coffee grinds and oil down the sink with hot, soapy water
   D. collect and dispose of coffee grinds and oils by putting them in the garbage and not in the sink

34. Mrs. Mary Jones and her family live in a 5-room apartment in a building on an urban renewal site. A public housing development is planned for this site. You are interviewing her with regard to relocation. During the interview, you learn that Mrs. Jones is divorced, unemployed, and receiving public assistance. Her four children are all under eight years of age, she is from a small town in North Carolina, and she has lived in the city for over 2 1/2 years.
From your questions, what should you *immediately* know regarding relocation possibilities?
She is

   A. *eligible* for high priority in a public housing development
   B. *eligible* for public housing but not for another two months
   C. *not eligible* for public housing
   D. *not eligible* for public housing for another six months

35. You are about to visit a tenant to encourage him to move from the site when a neighbor tells you that for the last week the tenant has been quarreling loudly and constantly with his wife and children. When you knock on his door, he tells you to go away. You try several times to visit this apartment, but with no success.
What is the BEST thing to do in an effort to solve this problem?

A. Ask the neighbor to encourage him to let you in since he probably has confidence in the neighbor
B. Report the problem to your supervisor since the services of a social worker may be needed
C. Leave a note in the door telling the tenant to come to the site office
D. Call the police and tell them of the unusual difficulty you are having with this man

36. Which one of the following is the BEST kind of evidence presented by a tenant to prove that he actually lives at his current address?

    A. change-of-address form that the tenant has filled out for a creditor
    B. letter with the tenant's name and present address on it
    C. library card
    D. receipt

37. As an assistant, you could be asked to make a recommendation regarding the type of lighting fixtures a tenant should use.
If you were concerned with not overburdening the present electrical circuits, a recommendation to use fluorescent lights rather than incandescent lights would be

    A. *good,* because fluorescent lights flicker less than , incandescent bulbs
    B. *good,* because fluorescent lights draw less current than incandescent bulbs
    C. *poor,* because fluorescent lights are very hard to install in a system designed for incandescent lights
    D. *poor,* because incandescent lights use less current than fluorescent lights

38. If a tenant had to move more than one time, moving expenses would be paid for all of the following combinations of moves EXCEPT

    A. an intrasite move and a subsequent move to a tenant-found apartment
    B. a move to another site and a subsequent move to public housing
    C. two moves to another site and a subsequent move to a tenant-found apartment
    D. a move-out to a tenant-found apartment and a subsequent move to public housing

39. The step of eviction of an on-site tenant is *generally* considered

    A. when a tenant has failed to pay a month's rent
    B. only when a tenant has refused to move into public housing
    C. as a last step in solving any housing problems of a tenant
    D. as a warning to an on-site tenant who is allowing more relatives to live with him than is noted on the S.O.R. card

40. Suppose that a tenant tells you her moving expenses will come to more than the amount she is eligible to receive. You WOULD tell her to

    A. pay the extra expense herself
    B. ask the Social Service Department for help
    C. submit a moving bill from the mover
    D. leave behind all broken furniture

KEY (CORRECT ANSWERS)

1. C	11. D	21. D	31. A
2. B	12. C	22. C	32. B
3. D	13. C	23. C	33. D
4. C	14. A	24. D	34. A
5. D	15. D	25. B	35. B
6. A	16. B	26. B	36. D
7. C	17. C	27. A	37. B
8. C	18. C	28. C	38. D
9. A	19. D	29. C	39. C
10. C	20. B	30. A	40. C

TEST 2

DIRECTIONS: Each question or incomplete statement is followed by several suggested answers or completions. Select the one that BEST answers the question or completes the statement. *PRINT THE LETTER OF THE CORRECT ANSWER IN THE SPACE AT THE RIGHT.*

1. Housing officials and experts have long suggested changing slum tenements into cooperatives.
   The PROBABLE reason that the advocates of tenement cooperatives feel that tenant-owners would be more likely than absentee landlords to keep buildings in good condition is that

   A. the tenant-owners would be living there while an absentee landlord would not
   B. the tenants in cooperatives want to demonstrate the advantages of cooperative living
   C. absentee landlords do not understand inner city problems
   D. absentee landlords have no reason to provide good maintenance

   1._____

2. A three-part plan to control the loss of an estimated sixty million dollars a year in welfare monies has been proposed.
   Which one of the following proposals would LEAST likely be part of this plan?

   A. Identification cards with photographs of the welfare client
   B. Face-to-face interviews with the welfare clients
   C. Computerized processing of welfare money records
   D. Individual cash payments to each member of a family

   2._____

3. Which one of the following statements describes the purpose of the Equal Rights Amendment which was passed by Congress but was not ratified by the required number of states?
   To

   A. eliminate state-enforced racial discrimination in public schools through extensive use of busing
   B. guarantee to aliens living in the United States the right to hold Civil Service jobs
   C. prohibit sex discrimination by any law or action of the government
   D. extend the right to vote to those previously ineligible by requiring only thirty days residency in a state

   3._____

4. In dealing with members of different ethnic groups in the area he serves, the assistant should give

   A. individuals the services required by his agency
   B. less service to those he judges to be more advantaged
   C. better service to groups with which he sympathizes most
   D. better service to groups with political *muscle*

   4._____

5. The MAJOR reason for joining a professional group such as The National Association of Housing and Redevelopment Officials, The Citizens Housing and Planning Council, or The National Housing Conference is to

   5._____

A. keep yourself informed about current ideas and
B. directions in the housing field · put it on your resume
C. get promoted
D. gain respect from fellow workers

6. Suppose you are interviewing a tenant whose clothing is sloppy, strange, or out of fashion.
Which of the following is MOST certain to be an appropriate action taken toward this tenant?

   A. Tell him he will get better service when he dresses better.
   B. Refer him to the Department of Social Services for help.
   C. Refer his children to the Bureau of Child Welfare.
   D. Treat him as respectfully as you treat other tenants.

6._____

7. An assistant may initiate an order that a tenant's welfare check be *rent-restricted* if that tenant has mismanaged his welfare check and not paid his rent.
Taking this action assures that

   A. all of the tenant's next welfare checks will be sent to the Urban Renewal Site as payment on account
   B. the Urban Renewal Site will receive a certain portion of the tenant's next welfare check and the tenant will receive the remainder
   C. the welfare center will send the Urban Renewal Site full payment for the rent and will require that the tenant repay this amount
   D. the welfare center will hold payment of checks from the tenant until they are notified by the assistant that the rent has been paid

7._____

8. For six months, a family lived in a 4-room apartment where they paid $376 a month. They made an intrasite move to a 4-room apartment where they paid $92 per room a month for six months.
Comparing the two six-month periods, the TOTAL amount of money the family saved by making the intrasite move was

   A. $48   B. $58   C. $86   D. $118

8._____

9. To calculate a tenant's usable income, you should make tax deductions of 4.4 percent on salary up to a maximum of $9,000 and state disability deductions of .5 percent on salary up to $3,000.
What does a tenant's COMBINED deduction amount to if his annual salary is $6,700?

   A. $228.00   B. $284.30   C. $309.80   D. $350.00

9._____

10. If the temporary relocation expenses for housing are set at $27 per day for one adult and $15 per day for each additional person in a room, how much money is allowed for a woman and four children temporarily relocated in one room for a period of six days?

    A. $252   B. $522   C. $567   D. $777

10._____

11. According to relocation policy, a family relocating to private housing from federally-aided or certain other sites will be granted a relocation payment. This payment equals the difference between 1/5 of the family's yearly income and the scheduled yearly rent for a standard apartment for their size family.
    Suppose a two-person family whose yearly income is $6,450 has been unable to obtain public housing and so finds a one-bedroom private apartment. The scheduled rent for a one-bedroom apartment appropriate for their occupancy is $120 a month. What payment will they receive?

    A. $120   B. $144   C. $150   D. $205

12. A family on a housing relocation site is paying $240 per month for rent. This represents 25% of their gross monthly income.
    If the husband earns 4/5 of their total combined monthly income, how much does the WIFE earn per month?

    A. $192   B. $324   C. $768   D. $960

13. In a nearly vacant building, there are only a few tenants left who are waiting to move into public housing. When you visit them to check their present conditions, you notice that some of the *tinned-up* apartments have the sheet metal partly pulled off the doors. The tenants tell you that they think that the many men who come and go frequently are drug addicts.
    The BEST action for you to take is to

    A. ignore the incident since all tenants will be moving out soon
    B. visit the site when you think someone might actually be selling drugs
    C. put up a sign warning these men that the building will be knocked down shortly
    D. report all your observations and the reports of the tenants to your supervisor

Questions 14-19.

DIRECTIONS: Answer Questions 14 through 19 on the basis of the information given in the passage below.

The City of X has set up a Maximum Base Rent Program for all rent-controlled apartments. The objective is to insure that the landlord will get a fair, but not excessive, profit on his building to stem the great tide of buildings being abandoned by their owners and to encourage landlords to continue the upkeep of their property. The Maximum Base Rent Program permits the landlord to raise rents under carefully devised standards, while practically no raises in rents in this City were permitted under previous guidelines.

Under this plan, the City determines a Maximum Ease Rent amount by means of a formula which takes into account the age of the building, the number of apartments, total rents received from the building, the amount of expenses, and labor costs. The Maximum Base Rent amount is to be recomputed every two years to allow for increases or decreases in building costs.

The Maximum Base Rent, which will allow the landlord to make a "fair return" on his investment, may not be collected immediately, however, since no rent increases over 7.5 percent will be permitted in any one year. The highest actual rent for each apartment during a given year will be called the Maximum Collectible Rent. This will be computed so that the increase over the present rent is not more . than 7.5 percent ($7.50 on every $100.00). Sometimes it may be less. Therefore, collectible rents will increase each year until the Maximum Base Rent is reached.

14. According to the above passage, the Maximum Base Rent is determined by the 14.____

    A. landlord
    B. Mayor
    C. Rent Commissioner
    D. City

15. Which of the following, according to the passage, permits a *fair return* on the landlord's investment? 15.____
    The _____ Rent Program.

    A. Minimum Base
    B. Maximum Base
    C. Minimum Collectible
    D. Maximum Collectible

16. It may be concluded from the passage that the City of X hopes that insuring fair profits for landlords will be followed by 16.____

    A. good upkeep of apartment buildings
    B. decreased interest rates on home mortgages
    C. lower rents in the future
    D. a better formula for determining rents

17. According to the passage, guidelines for determining rents previous to the Maximum Base Rent Program resulted in 17.____

    A. practically no raises in rents being made
    B. rent increases of approximately 10 percent a year
    C. a *fair return* to landlords from most rents
    D. landlords making too much money on their property

18. Based on the above passage, which is the MOST correct description of the kinds of facts that are taken into consideration when determining the Maximum Base Rent? Facts about 18.____

    A. labor costs and politics
    B. the landlord and labor costs
    C. the building and labor costs
    D. the building and the landlord

19. According to the above passage, the MAXIMUM annual increase in rent for a tenant in rent-controlled housing under the Maximum Base Rent Program is 19.____

    A. 7.5 percent each year for ten years
    B. 7.5 percent each year until the Maximum Base Rent is reached
    C. always under 7.5 percent a year
    D. $7.50 each year until it reaches $100.00

Questions 20-25.

DIRECTIONS: Answer Questions 20 through 25 on the basis of the information in the following form.

METROPOLITAN CITY		
Last Name Smith	First Name John	Middle Initial G.
Street 758 Reason Street		Apartment 1C
Borough or Town Bronx	State New York	Zip Code 10403
Monthly Rent $110.00	Number of Rooms 5	

E.

FAMILY COMPOSITION				
Name	Relation to Head	Birth Date Mo./Yr.	Annual Income	Employer or School
1. Smith, John G.	Head	7/58	$10,400	Harris Chemical
2. Smith, Ethel S.	Wife	3/61	0	
3. Smith, Lucy M.	Daughter	4/81	0	P.S. 172
4. Smith, John G., Jr.	Son	8/83	0	P.S. 172
5. Smith, Susan F.	Daughter	1/88	0	
6. Simmons, Sylvia T.	Mother-in-law	4/40	$4,680	F.W. Woolworth (part-time)
7.				

Total Annual Income	$15,080
Total Assets: Small Savings Accounts. Mr. Smith.	$5,000 life insurance on
Additional Information	

20. The occupants of the Smith apartment are Mr. Smith, Mrs. Smith, _____ mother, their _____ and _____. 20._____

    A. her; son; daughters
    B. his; son; daughters
    C. her; sons; daughter
    D. her; sons; daughters

21. The income of the Smith household comes from the earnings of the father, the 21._____

    A. mother, the mother-in-law, and the children
    B. mother, and the children, but not the mother-in-law
    C. mother-in-law, and the children, but not the mother
    D. mother-in-law, but not the mother and children

22. From the information given about the Smith family, their apartment seems to be 22._____

    A. too small
    B. the right size
    C. a little large
    D. much too large

23. If an assistant goes to the Smiths' apartment to discuss their relocation and everyone is home except Mr. Smith, with whom should the assistant talk about relocation? 23._____

    A. John Jr. and Ethel Smith
    B. Ethel Smith and Sylvia Simmons
    C. Lucy and Ethel Smith
    D. John Smith, Jr. and Sylvia Simmons

24. The reason why the last column was left blank for Susan Smith is PROBABLY that 24._____

    A. the assistant forgot to ask for this information
    B. Susan's parents would not give this information
    C. Susan is too young to go to school
    D. Susan does not live at home

25. The section for Additional Information was left blank MOST probably because 25._____

    A. the assistant did not have time to ask for more information
    B. the Smith family is sufficiently well-described by the other information on the form
    C. the Additional Information section is not an important part of the form
    D. unfavorable facts have been purposely left out

26. Whenever a tenant moves into a private apartment for which a finder's fee is to be paid, this fee is payable to the 26._____

    A. landlord or broker
    B. tenant
    C. local site office
    D. Housing and Development Administration

27. When a relocated tenant moves into public housing in the city, all rents must be paid DIRECTLY to the 27._____

    A. Relocation and Management Services Office
    B. Housing and Redevelopment Administration

C. Model Cities Administration
D. City Housing Authority

28. According to relocation rules and regulations, in order for an apartment to be considered *standard,* it is LEAST important that the apartment

   A. not be overcrowded
   B. have a bathroom with a shower
   C. have hot and cold running water
   D. be free of hazardous violations

29. The PRIMARY purpose of the Finder's Fee Program is to

   A. provide a listing of private home owners willing to take in tenants during emergencies
   B. establish a link between private contractors and public housing
   C. arrange housing for those forced to vacate because of boiler breakdowns
   D. provide a listing of housing facilities in private housing

30. Which one of the following would MOST likely cause the GREATEST amount of damage to the asphalt tiles on apartment floors?

   A. Protective furniture casters
   B. Wet mopping
   C. Liquid wax
   D. Grease

31. The rents for three families in a relocation site come to a total of $0,720 per year. If Family A pays $3,480 per year and Family B pays $2,400 per year, how much does Family C pay?

   A. $2,760   B. $3,840   C. $4,200   D. $5,800

32. Of 180 families that relocated in a given month, one-fifth moved into Finder's Fee apartments, one-quarter moved into tenant-found apartments, one-third moved into public housing, and the rest moved out of the city.
How many moved out of the city?

   A. 36   B. 39   C. 45   D. 60

33. If a tenant earns $5,280 a year and his rent is 25% of his annual income, the amount of rent he pays each month is

   A. $110   B. $115   C. $120   D. $135

34. The word *recycling* has become a popular one as used by those who are concerned with saving the environment. This word USUALLY refers to an interest in

   A. using bicycles again instead of automobiles for transportation
   B. the chemical treatment of rain water for drinking purposes
   C. collecting used bottles, cans, and newspaper which will be sold, treated, and re-used
   D. reorganizing public transportation routes in the city so that noise and traffic will be reduced

35. Recent accusations of fraud involving FHA-insured mortgages in various American cities   35.____
have brought to light the fact that
   A. blockbusting has become the favorite tactic of real estate brokers
   B. families with incomes of $16,000 - $20,000 have been prevented from obtaining mortgages
   C. homes bought through false credit ratings at inflated prices were quickly lost by low income owners
   D. the bad design of homes involved has helped pollute the urban environment

KEY (CORRECT ANSWERS)

1. A		16. A
2. D		17. A
3. C		18. C
4. A		19. B
5. A		20. A
6. D		21. D
7. B		22. A
8. A		23. B
9. C		24. C
10. B		25. B
11. C		26. A
12. A		27. D
13. D		28. B
14. D		29. D
15. B		30. D

31. B
32. B
33. A
34. C
35. C

EXAMINATION SECTION

TEST 1

DIRECTIONS: Each question or incomplete statement is followed by several suggested answers or completions. Select the one that BEST answers the question or completes the statement. *PRINT THE LETTER OF THE CORRECT ANSWER IN THE SPACE AT THE RIGHT.*

1. Good procedure in handling complaints from the public may be divided into the following four principal stages:
   I. Investigation of the complaint
   II. Receipt of the complaint
   III. Assignment of responsibility for investigation and correction
   IV. Notification of correction

   The ORDER in which these stages ordinarily come is:
   A. III, II, I, IV   B. II, III, I, IV   C. II, III, IV, I   D. II, IV, III, I

   1.____

2. The department may expect the MOST severe public criticism if
   A. it asks for an increase in its annual budget
   B. it purchases new and costly street cleaning equipment
   C. sanitation officers and men are reclassified to higher salary grades
   D. there is delay in cleaning streets of snow

   2.____

3. The MOST important function of public relations in the department should be to
   A. develop cooperation on the part of the public in keeping streets clean
   B. get stricter penalties enacted for health code violations
   C. recruit candidates for entrance positions who ca be developed into supervisors
   D. train career personnel so that they can advance in the department

   3.____

4. The one of the following which has MOST frequently elicited unfavorable public comment has been
   A. dirty sidewalks or streets   B. dumping on lot
   C. failure to curb dogs   D. overflowing garbage cans

   4.____

5. It has been suggested that, as a public relations measure, sections hold *open house* for the public.
   The MOST effective time for this would be
   A. during the summer when children are not in school and can accompany their parents
   B. during the winter when show is likely to fall and the public can see snow removal preparations
   C. immediately after a heavy snow storm when department snow removal operations are in full progress
   D. when street sanitation is receiving general attention as during *Keep City Clean* week

   5.____

129

6. When a public agency conducts a public relations program, it is MOST likely to find that each recipient of its message will
   A. disagree with the basic purpose of the message if the officials are not well known to him
   B. accept the message if it is presented by someone perceived as having a definite intention to persuade
   C. ignore the message unless it is presented in a literate and clever manner
   D. give greater attention to certain portions of the message as a result of his individual and cultural differences

7. Following are three statements about public relations and communications:
   I. A person who seeks to influence public opinion can speed up a trend
   II. Mass communications is the exposure of a mass audience to an idea
   III. All media are equally effective in reaching opinion leaders
   Which of the following choices CORRECTLY classifies the above statements into those which are correct and those which are not?
   A. I and II are correct, but III is not.
   B. II and III are correct, but I is not.
   C. I and III are correct, but II is not.
   D. III is correct, but I and II are not.

8. Public relations experts say that MAXIMUM effect for a message results from
   A. concentrating in one medium
   B. ignoring mass media and concentrating on *opinion makers*
   C. presenting only those factors which support a given position
   D. using a combination of two or more of the available media

9. To assure credibility and avoid hostility, the public relations man MUST
   A. make certain his message is truthful, not evasive or exaggerated
   B. make sure his message contains some dire consequence if ignored
   C. repeat the message often enough so that it cannot be ignored
   D. try to reach as many people and groups as possible

10. The public relations man MUST be prepared to assume that members of his audience
    A. may have developed attitudes toward his proposals—favorable, neutral, or unfavorable
    B. will be immediately hostile
    C. will consider his proposals with an open mind
    D. will invariably need an introduction to his subject

11. The one of the following statements that is CORRECT is:
    A. When a stupid question is asked of you by the public, it should be disregarded
    B. If you insist on formality between you and the public, the public will not be able to ask stupid questions that cannot be answered
    C. The public should be treated courteously, regardless of how stupid their questions may be
    D. You should explain to the public how stupid their questions are

12. With regard to public relations, the MOST important item which should be emphasized in an employee training program is that
    A. each inspector is a public relations agent
    B. an inspector should give the public all the information it asks for
    C. it is better to make mistakes and give erroneous information than to tell the public that you do not know the correct answer to their problem
    D. public relations is so specialized a field that only persons specially trained in it should consider it

13. Members of the public frequently ask about departmental procedures.
    Of the following, it is BEST to
    A. advise the public to put the question in writing so that he can get a proper formal reply
    B. refuse to answer because this is a confidential matter
    C. explain the procedure as briefly as possible
    D. attempt to avoid the issue by discussing other matters

14. The effectiveness of a public relations program in a public agency such as the authority is BEST indicated by the
    A. amount of mass media publicity favorable to the policies of the authority
    B. morale of those employees who directly serve the patrons of the authority
    C. public's understanding and support of the authority's program and policies
    D. number of complaint received by the authority from patrons using its facilities

15. In an attempt to improve public opinion about a certain idea, the BEST course of action for an agency to take would be to present the
    A. clearest statements of the idea even though the language is somewhat technical
    B. idea as the result of long-term studies
    C. idea in association with something familiar to most people
    D. idea as the viewpoint of the majority leaders

16. The fundamental factor in any agency's community relations program is
    A. an outline of the objectives
    B. relations with the media
    C. the everyday actions of the employees
    D. a well-planned supervisory program

17. The FUNDAMENTAL factor in the success of a community relations program is
    A. true commitment by the community
    B. true commitment by the administration
    C. a well-planned, systematic approach
    D. the actions of individuals in their contacts with the public

4 (#1)

18. The statement below which is LEAST correct is:
    A. Because of selection standards, the supervisor frequently encounters problems resulting from subordinates' inability to express themselves in the language of the profession.
    B. Distortion of the meaning of a communication is usually brought about by a failure to use language that has a precise meaning to others.
    C. The term *filtering* is the distortion or dilution of content of a communication that occurs as information is passed from individual to individual.
    D. The complexity of the *communications net* will directly affect.

18.____

19. Consider the following three statements that may or may not be CORRECT:
    I. In order to prevent the stifling of communications flow, supervisors should insist that employees use the formal communications network.
    II. Two-way communications are faster and more accurate than one-way communications.
    III. There is a direct correlation between the effectiveness of communications and the total setting in which they occur.
    The choice below which MOST accurately describes the above statement is:
    A. All three are correct.
    B. All three are incorrect.
    C. More than one statement is correct.
    D. Only one of the statements is correct.

19.____

20. The statement below which is MOST inaccurate is:
    A. The supervisor's most important tool in learning whether or not he is communicating well is feedback.
    B. Follow-up is essential if useful feedback is to be obtained.
    C. Subordinates are entitled, as a matter of right, to explanations from management concerning the reasons for orders or directives.
    D. A skilled supervisor is often able to use the grapevine to good advantage.

20.____

21. *Since concurrence by those affected is not sought, this kind of communication can be issued with relative ease.*
    The kind of communication being referred to in this quotation is
    A. autocratic   B. democratic   C. directive   D. free-rein

21.____

22. The statement below which is LEAST correct is:
    A. Clarity is more important in oral communicating than in written since the readers of a written communication can read it over again.
    B. Excessive use of abbreviations in written communications should be avoided.
    C. Short sentences with simple words are preferred over complex sentences and difficult words in a written communication.
    D. The *newspaper* style of writing ordinarily simplifies expression and facilitates understanding.

22.____

23. Which one of the following is the MOST important factor for the department to consider in building a good public image?
    A. A good working relationship with the news media
    B. An efficient community relations program
    C. An efficient system for handling citizen complaints
    D. The proper maintenance of facilities and equipment
    E. The behavior of individuals in their contacts with the public.

24. It has been said that the ability to communicate clearly and concisely is the MOST important single skill of the supervisor.
    Consider the following statements:
    I. The adage, *Actions speak louder than words*, has NO application in superior/subordinate communications since good communications are accomplished with words.
    II. The environment in which a communication takes place will *rarely* determine its effect.
    III. Words are symbolic representations which must be associated with past experience or else they are meaningless.
    The choice below which MOST accurately describes the above statements is:
    A. I, II, and III are correct.
    B. I and II are correct, but III is not.
    C. I and III are correct, but II is not.
    D. III is correct, but I and II are not.
    E. I, II, and III are incorrect.

25. According to expert opinion, the effectiveness of an organization is very dependent upon good upward, downward, and lateral communications. Lateral communications are most important to the activity of coordinating the efforts of organizational units. Before real communication can take place at any level, barriers to communication must be recognized, understood, and removed.
    Consider the following three statements:
    I. The *principal* barrier to good communications is a failure to establish empathy between sender and receiver.
    II. The difference in status or rank between the sender and receiver of a communication may be a communications barrier.
    III. Communications are easier if they travel upward from subordinate to superior
    The choice below which MOST accurately describes the above statements is:
    A. I, II and III are incorrect.   B. I and II are incorrect.
    C. I, II, and III are correct.   D. I and II are correct.
    E. I and III are incorrect.

KEY (CORRECT ANSWERS)

1.	B	11.	C
2.	D	12.	A
3.	A	13.	C
4.	A	14.	C
5.	D	15.	C
6.	D	16.	C
7.	A	17.	D
8.	D	18.	A
9.	A	19.	D
10.	A	20.	C

21. A
22. A
23. E
24. D
25. E

EXAMINATION SECTION
TEST 1

DIRECTIONS: Each question or incomplete statement is followed by several suggested answers or completions. Select the one that BEST answers the question or completes the statement. *PRINT THE LETTER OF THE CORRECT ANSWER IN THE SPACE AT THE RIGHT.*

1. Of the following, the one MOST important quality required of a good supervisor is
    A. ambition   B. leadership   C. friendliness   D. popularity

2. It is often said that a supervisor can delegate authority but never responsibility. This means MOST NEARLY that
    A. a supervisor must do his own work if he expects it to be done properly
    B. a supervisor can assign someone else to do his work, but in the last analysis, the supervisor himself must take the blame for any actions followed
    C. authority and responsibility are two separate things that cannot be borne by the same person
    D. it is better for a supervisor never to delegate his authority

3. One of your men who is a habitual complainer asks you to grant him a minor privilege.
    Before granting or denying such a request, you should consider
    A. the merits of the case
    B. that it is good for group morale to grant a request of this nature
    C. the man's seniority
    D. that to deny such a request will lower your standing with the men

4. A supervisory practice on the part of a foreman which is MOST likely to lead to confusion and inefficiency is for him to
    A. give orders verbally directly to the man assigned to the job
    B. issue orders only in writing
    C. follow up his orders after issuing them
    D. relay his orders to the men through co-workers

5. It would be POOR supervision on a foreman's part if he
    A. asked an experienced maintainer for his opinion on the method of doing a special job
    B. make it a policy to avoid criticizing a man in front of his co-workers
    C. consulted his assistant supervisor on unusual problems
    D. allowed a cooling-off period of several days before giving one of his men a deserved reprimand

6. Of the following behavior characteristics of a supervisor, the one that is MOST likely to lower the morale of the men he supervises is
   A. diligence
   B. favoritism
   C. punctuality
   D. thoroughness

7. Of the following, the BEST method of getting an employee who is not working up to his capacity to produce more work is to
   A. have another employee criticize his production
   B. privately criticize his production but encourage him to produce more
   C. criticize his production before his associates
   D. criticize his production and threaten to fire him

8. Of the following, the BEST thing for a supervisor to do when a subordinate has done a very good job is to
   A. tell him to take it easy
   B. praise his work
   C. reduce his workload
   D. say nothing because he may become conceited

9. Your orders to your crew are MOST likely to be followed if you
   A. explain the reasons for these orders
   B. warn that all violators will be punished
   C. promise easy assignments to those who follow these orders best
   D. say that they are for the good of the department

10. In order to be a good supervisor, you should
    A. impress upon your men that you demand perfection in their work at all times
    B. avoid being blamed for your crew's mistakes
    C. impress your superior with your ability
    D. see to it that your men get what they are entitled to

11. In giving instructions to a crew, you should
    A. speak in as loud a tone as possible
    B. speak in a coaxing, persuasive manner
    C. speak quietly, clearly, and courteously
    D. always use the word *please* when giving instructions

12. Of the following factors, the one which is LEAST important in evaluating an employee and his work is his
    A. dependability
    B. quantity of work done
    C. quality of work done
    D. education and training

13. When a District Superintendent first assumes his command, it is LEAST important for him at the beginning to observe
    A. how his equipment is designed and its adaptability
    B. how to reorganize the district for greater efficiency
    C. the capabilities of the men in the district
    D. the methods of operation being employed

14. When making an inspection of one of the buildings under your supervision, the BEST procedure to follow in making a record of the inspection is to
    A. return immediately to the office and write a report from memory
    B. write down all the important facts during or as soon as you complete the inspection
    C. fix in your mind all important facts so that you can repeat them from memory if necessary
    D. fix in your mind all important facts so that you can make out your report at the end of the day

14._____

15. Assume that your superior has directed you to make certain changes in your established procedure. After using this modified procedure on several occasions, you find that the original procedure was distinctly superior and you wish to return to it.
    You should
    A. let your superior find this out for himself
    B. simply change back to the original procedure
    C. compile definite data and information to prove your case to your superior
    D. persuade one of the more experienced workers to take this matter up with your superior

15._____

16. An inspector visited a large building under construction. He inspected the soil lines at 9 A.M., water lines at 10 A.M., fixtures at 11 A.M., and did his office work in the afternoon. He followed the same pattern daily for weeks.
    This procedure was
    A. *good*, because it was methodical and he did not miss anything
    B. *good*, because it gave equal time to all phases of the plumbing
    C. *bad*, because not enough time was devoted to fixtures
    D. *bad*, because the tradesmen knew when the inspection would occur

16._____

17. Assume that one of the foremen in a training course, which you are conducting, proposes a poor solution for a maintenance problem.
    Of the following, the BEST course of action for you to take is to
    A. accept the solution tentatively and correct it during the next class meeting
    B. point out all the defects of this proposed solution and wait until somebody thinks of a better solution
    C. try to get the class to reject this proposed solution and develop a better solution
    D. let the matter pass since somebody will present a better solution as the class work proceeds

17._____

18. As a supervisor, you should be seeking ways to improve the efficiency of shop operations by means such as changing established work procedures.
    The following are offered as possible actions that you should consider in changing established work procedures:
    I. Make changes only when your foremen agree to them
    II. Discuss changes with your supervisor before putting them into practice

18._____

III. Standardize any operation which is performed on a continuing basis
IV. Make changes quickly and quietly in order to avoid dissent
V. Secure expert guidance before instituting unfamiliar procedures
Of the following suggested answers, the one that describes the actions to be taken to change established work procedures is
   A. I, IV, V   B. II, III, V   C. III, IV, V   D. All of the above

19. A supervisor determined that a foreman, without informing his superior, delegated responsibility for checking time cards to a member of his gang. The supervisor then called the foreman into his office where he reprimanded the foreman.
This action of the supervisor in reprimanding the foreman was
   A. *proper*, because the checking of time cards is the foreman's responsibility and should not be delegated
   B. *proper*, because the foreman did not ask the supervisor for permission to delegate responsibility
   C. *improper*, because the foreman may no longer take the initiative in solving future problems
   D. *improper*, because the supervisor is interfering in a function which is not his responsibility

20. A capable supervisor should check all operations under his control.
Of the following, the LEAST important reason for doing this is to make sure that
   A. operations are being performed as scheduled
   B. he personally observes all operations at all times
   C. all the operations are still needed
   D. his manpower is being utilized efficiently

21. A supervisor makes it a practice to apply fair and firm discipline in all cases of rule infractions, including those of a minor nature.
This practice should PRIMARILY be considered
   A. *bad*, since applying discipline for minor violations is a waste of time
   B. *good*, because not applying discipline for minor infractions can lead to a more serious erosion of discipline
   C. *bad*, because employees do not like to be disciplined for minor violations of the rules
   D. *good*, because violating any rule can cause a dangerous situation to occur

22. A maintainer would PROPERLY consider it poor supervisory practice for a foreman to consult with him on
   A. which of several repair jobs should be scheduled first
   B. how to cope with personal problems at home
   C. whether the neatness of his headquarters can be improved
   D. how to express a suggestion which the maintainer plans to submit formally

23. Assume that you have determined that the work of one of your foremen and the men he supervises is consistently behind schedule. When you discuss this situation with the foreman, he tells you that his men are poor workers and then complains that he must spend all of his time checking on their work.
The following actions are offered for your consideration as possible ways of solving the problem of poor performance of the foreman and his men:
   I. Review the work standards with the foreman and determine whether they are realistic.
   II. Tell the foreman that you will recommend him for the foreman's training course for retraining.
   III. Ask the foreman for the names of the maintainers and then replace them as soon as possible.
   IV. Tell the foreman that you expect him to meet a satisfactory level of performance.
   V. Tell the foreman to insist that his men work overtime to catch up to the schedule.
   VI. Tell the foreman to review the type and amount of training he has given the maintainers.
   VII. Tell the foreman that he will be out of a job if he does not produce on schedule.
   VIII. Avoid all criticism of the foreman and his methods.
   Which of the following suggested answers CORRECTLY lists the proper actions to be taken to solve the problem of poor performance of the foreman and his men?
   A. I, II, IV, VI   B. I, III, V, VII   C. II, III, VI, VIII   D. IV, V, VI, VIII

24. When a conference or a group discussion is tending to turn into a *bull session* without constructive purpose, the BEST action to take is to
   A. reprimand the leader of the bull session
   B. redirect the discussion to the business at hand
   C. dismiss the meeting and reschedule it for another day
   D. allow the bull session to continue

25. Assume that you have been assigned responsibility for a program in which a high production rate is mandatory. From past experience, you know that your foremen do not perform equally well in the various types of jobs given to them. Which of the following methods should you use in selecting foremen for the specific types of work involved in the program?
   A. Leave the method of selecting foremen to your supervisor
   B. Assign each foreman to the work he does best
   C. Allow each foreman to choose his own job
   D. Assign each foreman to a job which will permit him to improve his own abilities

KEY (CORRECT ANSWERS)

1.	B		11.	C
2.	B		12.	D
3.	A		13.	B
4.	D		14.	B
5.	D		15.	C
6.	B		16.	D
7.	B		17.	C
8.	B		18.	B
9.	A		19.	A
10.	D		20.	B

21. B
22. A
23. A
24. B
25. B

TEST 2

DIRECTIONS: Each question or incomplete statement is followed by several suggested answers or completions. Select the one that BEST answers the question or completes the statement. *PRINT THE LETTER OF THE CORRECT ANSWER IN THE SPACE AT THE RIGHT.*

1. A foreman who is familiar with modern management principles should know that the one of the following requirements of an administrator which is LEAST important is his ability to
   A. coordinate work
   B. plan, organize, and direct the work under his control
   C. cooperate with others
   D. perform the duties of the employees under his jurisdiction

   1.____

2. When subordinates request his advice in solving problems encountered in their work, a certain chief occasionally answers the request by first asking the subordinate what he thinks should be done.
   This action by the chief is, on the whole,
   A. *desirable*, because it stimulates subordinates to give more thought to the solution of problems encountered
   B. *undesirable*, because it discourages subordinates from asking questions
   C. *desirable*, because it discourages subordinates from asking questions
   D. *undesirable*, because it undermines the confidence of subordinates in the ability of their supervisor

   2.____

3. Of the following factors that may be considered by a unit head in dealing with the tardy subordinate, the one which should be given LEAST consideration is the
   A. frequency with which the employee is tardy
   B. effect of the employee's tardiness upon the work of other employees
   C. willingness of the employee to work overtime when necessary
   D. cause of the employee's tardiness

   3.____

4. The MOST important requirement of a good inspectional report is that it should be
   A. properly addressed   B. lengthy
   C. clear and brief   D. spelled correctly

   4.____

5. Building superintendents frequently inquire about departmental inspectional procedures.
   Of the following, it is BEST to
   A. advise them to write to the department for an official reply
   B. refuse as the inspectional procedure is a restricted matter
   C. briefly explain the procedure to them
   D. avoid the inquiry by changing the subject

   5.____

6. Reprimanding a crew member before other workers is a
    A. *good* practice; the reprimand serves as a warning to the other workers
    B. *bad* practice; people usually resent criticism made in public
    C. *good* practice; the other workers will realize that the supervisor is fair
    D. *bad* practice; the other workers will take sides in the dispute

7. Of the following actions, the one which is LEAST likely to promote good work is for the group leader to
    A. praise workers for doing a good job
    B. call attention to the opportunities for promotion for better workers
    C. threaten to recommend discharge of workers who are below standard
    D. put into practice any good suggestion made by crew members

8. A supervisor notices that a member of his crew has skipped a routine step in his job.
   Of the following, the BEST action for the supervisor to take is to
    A. promptly question the worker about the incident
    B. immediately assign another man to complete the job
    C. bring up the incident the next time the worker asks for a favor
    D. say nothing about the incident but watch the worker carefully in the future

9. Assume you have been told to show a new worker how to operate a piece of equipment.
   Your FIRST step should be to
    A. ask the worker if he has any questions about the equipment
    B. permit the worker to operate the equipment himself while you carefully watch to prevent damage
    C. demonstrate the operation of the equipment for the worker
    D. have the worker read an instruction booklet on the maintenance of the equipment

10. Whenever a new man was assigned to his crew, the supervisor would introduce him to all other crew members, take him on a tour of the plant, tell him about bus schedules and places to eat.
    This practice is
     A. *good*; the new man is made to feel welcome
     B. *bad*; supervisors should not interfere in personal matters
     C. *good*; the new man knows that he can bring his personal problems to the supervisor
     D. *bad*; work time should not be spent on personal matters

11. The MOST important factor in successful leadership is the ability to
     A. obtain instant obedience to all orders
     B. establish friendly personal relations with crew members
     C. avoid disciplining crew members
     D. make crew members want to do what should be done

12. Explaining the reasons for departmental procedure to workers tends to
    A. waste time which should be used for productive purposes
    B. increase their interest in their work
    C. make them more critical of departmental procedures
    D. confuse them

    12.____

13. If you want a job done well do it yourself.
    For a supervisor to follow this advice would be
    A. *good*; a supervisor is responsible for the work of his crew
    B. *bad*; a supervisor should train his men, not do their work
    C. *good*; a supervisor should be skilled in all jobs assigned to his crew
    D. *bad*; a supervisor loses respect when he works with his hands

    13.____

14. When a supervisor discovers a mistake in one of the jobs for which his crew is responsible, it is MOST important for him to find out
    A. whether anybody else knows about the mistake
    B. who was to blame for the mistake
    C. how to prevent similar mistakes in the future
    D. whether similar mistakes occurred in the past

    14.____

15. A supervisor who has to explain a new procedure to his crew should realize that questions from the crew USUALLY show that they
    A. are opposed to the new practice
    B. are completely confused by the explanation
    C. need more training in the new procedure
    D. are interested in the explanation

    15.____

16. A good way for a supervisor to retain the confidence of his or her employees is to
    A. say as little as possible
    B. check work frequently
    C. make no promises unless they will be fulfilled
    D. never hesitate in giving an answer to any question

    16.____

17. Good supervision is ESSENTIALLY a matter of
    A. patience in supervising workers   B. care in selecting workers
    C. skill in human relations   D. fairness in disciplining workers

    17.____

18. It is MOST important for an employee who has been assigned a monotonous task to
    A. perform this task before doing other work
    B. ask another employee to help
    C. perform this task only after all other work has been completed
    D. take measures to prevent mistakes in performing the task

    18.____

19. One of your employees has violated a minor agency regulation.
    The FIRST thing you should do is
    A. warn the employee that you will have to take disciplinary action if it should happen again
    B. ask the employee to explain his or her actions
    C. inform your supervisor and wait for advice
    D. write a memo describing the incident and place it in the employee's personnel file

    19.____

20. One of your employees tells you that he feels you give him much more work than the other employees, and he is having trouble meeting your deadlines.
    You should
    A. ask if he has been under a lot of non-work related stress lately
    B. review his recent assignments to determine if he is correct
    C. explain that this is a busy time, but you are dividing the work equally
    D. tell him that he is the most competent employee and that is why he receives more work

    20.____

21. A supervisor assigns one of his crew to complete a portion of a job. A short time later, the supervisor notices that the portion has not been completed.
    Of the following, the BEST way for the supervisor to handle this is to
    A. ask the crew member why he has not completed the assignment
    B. reprimand the crew member for not obeying orders
    C. assign another crew member to complete the assignment
    D. complete the assignment himself

    21.____

22. Supposes that a member of your crew complains that you are *playing favorites* in assigning work.
    Of the following, the BEST method of handling the complaint is to
    A. deny it and refuse to discuss the matter with the worker
    B. take the opportunity to tell the worker what is wrong with his work
    C. ask the worker for examples to prove his point and try to clear up any misunderstanding
    D. promise to be more careful in making assignments in the future

    22.____

23. A member of your crew comes to you with a complaint. After discussing the matter with him, it is clear that you have convinced him that his complaint was not justified.
    At this point, you should
    A. permit him to drop the matter
    B. make him admit his error
    C. pretend to see some justification in his complaint
    D. warn him against making unjustified complaints

    23.____

24. Suppose that a supervisor has in his crew an older man who works rather slowly. In other respects, this man is a good worker; he is seldom absent, works carefully, never loafs, and is cooperative.

    24.____

The BEST way for the supervisor to handle this worker is to
   A. try to get him to work faster and less carefully
   B. give him the most disagreeable job
   C. request that he be given special training
   D. permit him to work at his own speed

25. Suppose that a member of your crew comes to you with a suggestion he thinks will save time in doing a job. You realize immediately that it won't work.
Under these circumstances, your BEST action would be to
   A. thank the worker for the suggestion and forget about it
   B. explain to the worker why you think it won't work
   C. tell the worker to put the suggestion in writing
   D. ask the other members of your crew to criticize the suggestion

25.____

KEY (CORRECT ANSWERS)

1.	D		11.	D
2.	A		12.	B
3.	C		13.	B
4.	C		14.	C
5.	C		15.	D
6.	B		16.	C
7.	C		17.	C
8.	A		18.	D
9.	C		19.	B
10.	A		20.	B

21. A
22. C
23. A
24. D
25. B

EXAMINATION SECTION
TEST 1

DIRECTIONS: Each question or incomplete statement is followed by several suggested answers or completions. Select the one that BEST answers the question or completes the statement. *PRINT THE LETTER OF THE CORRECT ANSWER IN THE SPACE AT THE RIGHT.*

1. Which one of the following is LEAST likely to be an area or cause of trouble in the use of staff personnel?

    A. Misunderstanding of the role the staff personnel are supposed to play as a result of vagueness of definition of their duties and authority
    B. Tendency of staff personnel almost always to be older than line personnel at comparable salary levels with whom they must deal
    C. Selection of staff personnel who fail to have simultaneously both competence in their specialities and skill in staff work
    D. The staff person fails to understand mixed staff and operating duties

2. Which of the following is generally NOT a valid statement with respect to the supervisory process?

    A. General supervision is more effective than close supervision.
    B. Employee-centered supervisors lead more effectively than do production-centered supervisors.
    C. Employee satisfaction is directly related to productivity.
    D. Low-producing supervisors use techniques that are different from high-producing supervisors.

3. Which of the following is the MOST essential element for proper evaluation of the performance of subordinate supervisors?

    A. Careful definition of each supervisor's specific job responsibilities and of his progress in meeting mutually agreed upon work goals
    B. System of rewards and penalties based on each supervisor's progress in meeting clearly defined performance standards
    C. Definition of personality traits, such as industry, initiative, dependability, and cooperativeness, required for effective job performance
    D. Breakdown of each supervisor's job into separate components and a rating of his performance on each individual task

4. The PRINCIPAL advantage of specialization for the operating efficiency of a public service agency is that specialization

    A. reduces the amount of red tape in coordinating the activities of mutually dependent departments
    B. simplifies the problem of developing adequate job controls
    C. provides employees with a clear understanding of the relationship of their activities to the overall objectives of the agency
    D. reduces destructive competition for power between departments

5. A list of conditions which encourages good morale inside a work group would NOT include a

   A. high rate of agreement among group members on values and objectives
   B. tight control system to minimize the risk of individual error
   C. good possibility that joint action will accomplish goals
   D. past history of successful group accomplishment

6. Of the following, the MOST important factor to be considered in selecting a training strategy or program is the

   A. requirements of the job to be performed by the trainees
   B. educational level or prior training of the trainees
   C. size of the training group
   D. quality and competence of available training specialists

7. Of the following, the one which is considered to be LEAST characteristic of the higher ranks of management is

   A. that higher levels of management benefit from modern technology
   B. that success is measured by the extent to which objectives are achieved
   C. the number of subordinates that directly report to a manager
   D. the de-emphasis of individual and specialized performance

8. Assume that a manager is preparing a training syllabus to be used in training members of her staff.
   Which of the following would NOT be a valid principle of the learning process to consider when preparing this training syllabus?

   A. When a person has thoroughly learned a task, it takes a lot of effort to create a little more improvement.
   B. In complicated learning situations, there is a period in which an additional period of practice produces an equal amount of improvement in learning.
   C. The less a person knows about the task, the slower the initial progress.
   D. The more a person knows about the task, the slower the initial progress.

9. Which statement BEST illustrates when collective bargaining agreements are working well?

   A. Executives strongly support subordinate managers.
   B. The management rights clause in the contract is clear and enforced.
   C. Contract provisions are competently interpreted.
   D. The provisions of the agreement are properly interpreted, communicated, and observed.

10. An executive who wishes to encourage subordinates to communicate freely with him about a job-related problem should FIRST

   A. state his own position on the problem before listening to the subordinates' ideas
   B. invite subordinates to give their own opinions on the problem
   C. ask subordinates for their reactions to his own ideas about the problem
   D. guard the confidentiality of management information about the problem

11. The ability to deal constructively with intra-organizational conflict is an essential attribute of the successful manager.
The one of the following types of conflict which would be LEAST difficult to handle constructively is a situation in which there is

   A. agreement on objectives, but disagreement as to the probable results of adopting the various alternatives
   B. agreement on objectives, disagreement on alternative courses of action, and relative certainty as to the outcome of one of the alternatives
   C. disagreement on objectives and on alternative courses of action, and relative certainty as to the outcome of one of the alternatives
   D. disagreement on objectives and on alternative courses of action, but uncertainty as to the outcome of the alternatives

12. Which of the following actions does NOT belong in a properly conducted grievance handling process?

   A. Gathering relevant information on why the grievance arose
   B. Formulating a personal judgment about the fairness or unfairness of the grievance at the time the grievance is presented
   C. Establishing tentative answers to the grievance
   D. Following up to see whether the solution has eliminated the difficulty

13. Grievances are generally defined as complaints expressed over work-related matters.
Which one of the following is MOST important for managers to be aware of in connection with this definition?
The

   A. fact that the definition fails to separate the subject of the grievance from the attitude of the grievant
   B. fact that anything in the organization may be the source of the grievance
   C. need to assume that dissatisfied people have adverse effects on productivity
   D. implication that management should be concerned about expressed grievances and unconcerned about unexpressed grievances

14. In carrying out disciplinary action, the MOST important procedure for all managers to follow is to

    A. convince all levels of management on the need for discipline from the organization's viewpoint
    B. follow up on a disciplinary action and not assume that the action has been effective
    C. convince all executives that proper discipline is a legitimate tool for their use
    D. convince all executives that they need to display confidence in the organization's rules

15. Assume that an employee under your supervision is acquitted in court of criminal charges arising out of his employment.
    Of the following statements concerning disciplinary action, which is MOST NEARLY correct?

    A. Disciplinary proceedings against the employee may not be held for the same offenses on which he was tried and acquitted.
    B. In a disciplinary action, the acquittal dispenses with the requirement that the employee be advised as to his constitutional rights.
    C. Civil Rights Law Section 79 prohibits the taking of any further punitive action by an employer if the offense did not involve official corruption.
    D. It is possible for the employee to be found guilty of the same offense when tried in a departmental hearing.

16. Work rules can be an effective tool in the process of personnel management.
    The BEST practical definition for work rules is that they are

    A. minimum standards of conduct or performance that apply to individuals or groups at work in an organization
    B. prescriptions that serve to specialize employee behavior
    C. predetermined decisions about disciplinary action
    D. the major determinant of an organization's climate and the morale of its workforce

Questions 17-18

DIRECTIONS: Questions 17 and 18 pertain to identification of words that are incorrectly used because they are not in keeping with the meaning of the quotation. In answering each question, the first step is to read the passage and identify the incorrectly used word, and then select the word which, when substituted, BEST serves to convey the meaning of the quotation.

5 (#1)

17. Among the Housing Manager's overall responsibilities in administering a project is the prevention of the development of conditions which might lead to termination of tenancy and eviction of a tenant. Where there appears to be doubt that a tenant is fully aware of his responsibilities and is thus jeopardizing his tenancy, the Housing Manager should acquaint him with these responsibilities. Where a situation involves behavior of a tenant or a member of his family, the Housing Manager should confirm, through discussions and referrals to social agencies, correction of the conditions before they reach a state where there is no alternative but termination proceedings.   17._____

    A. Coordinate   B. Identify
    C. Assert   D. Attempt

18. The one universal administrative complaint is that the budget is inadequate. Between adequacy and inadequacy lie all degrees of adequacy. Further, human wants are modest in relation to human resources. From these two facts we may conclude that the fundamental criterion of administrative decision must be a criterion of efficiency (the degree to which the goals have been reached relative to the available resources) rather than a criterion of adequacy (the degree to which its goals have been reached). The task of the manager is to maximize social values relative to limited resources.   18._____

    A. Improve   B. Simple
    C. Limitless   D. Optimize

Questions 19-21.
DIRECTIONS: Questions 19 through 21 are to be answered SOLELY on the basis of the following situation.

John Foley, a top administrator, is responsible for output in his organization. Because productivity had been lagging for two periods in a row, Foley decided to establish a committee of his subordinate managers to investigate the reasons for the poor performance and to make recommendations for improvements. After two meetings, the committee came to the conclusions and made the recommendations that follow.

Output forecasts had been handed down from the top without prior consultation with middle management and first level supervision. Lines of authority and responsibility had been unclear. The planning and control process should be decentralized.

After receiving the committee's recommendations, Foley proceeded to take the following actions. Foley decided he would retain final authority to establish quotas but would delegate to the middle managers the responsibility for meeting quotas.

After receiving Foley's decision, the middle managers proceeded to delegate to the first-line supervisors the authority to establish their own quotas. The middle managers eventually received and combined the first-line supervisors' quotas so that these conformed to Foley's.

19. Foley's decision to delegate responsibility for meeting quotas to the middle managers is inconsistent with sound management principles because

    A. Foley should not have involved himself in the first place
    B. middle managers do not have the necessary skills
    C. quotas should be established by the chief executive
    D. responsibility should not be delegated

19._____

20. The principle of co-extensiveness of responsibility and authority bears on Foley's decision.
    In this case, it implies that

    A. authority should exceed responsibility
    B. authority should be delegated to match the degree of responsibility
    C. both authority and responsibility should be retained and not delegated
    D. responsibility should be delegated, but authority should be retained

20._____

21. The middle managers' decision to delegate to the first-line supervisors the authority to establish quotas was INCORRECTLY reasoned because

    A. delegation and control must go together
    B. first-line supervisors are in no position to establish quotas
    C. one cannot delegate authority that one does not possess
    D. the meeting of quotas should not be delegated

21._____

22. If one attempts to list the advantages of the management-by-exception principle as it is used in connection with the budgeting process, several distinct advantages could be cited.
    Which of the following is NOT an advantage of this principle as it applies to the budgeting process?
    Management-by-exception

    A. saves time
    B. identifies critical problem areas
    C. focuses attention and concentrates effort
    D. escalates the frequency and importance of budget-related decisions

22._____

23. The MOST accurate description of a budget is that

    A. a budget is made up by an organization to plan its future activities
    B. a budget specifies in dollars and cents how much is spent in a particular time period
    C. a budget specifies how much the organization to which it relates estimates it will spend over a certain period of time
    D. all plans dealing with money are budgets

23._____

24. Of the following, the one which is NOT a contribution that a budget makes to organizational programming is that a budget

    A. enables a comparison of what actually happened with what was expected
    B. stresses the need to forecast specific goals and eliminates the need to focus on tasks needed to accomplish goals
    C. may illustrate duplication of effort between interdependent activities
    D. shows the relationship between various organizational segments

25. A line-item budget is a good control budget because

    A. it clearly specifies how the items being purchased will be used
    B. expenditures can be shown primarily for contractual services
    C. it clearly specifies what the money is buying
    D. it clearly specifies the services to be provided

KEY (CORRECT ANSWERS)

1.	B	11.	B
2.	C	12.	B
3.	A	13.	C
4.	B	14.	B
5.	B	15.	D
6.	A	16.	A
7.	A	17.	D
8.	D	18.	C
9.	D	19.	D
10.	B	20.	B

21. C
22. D
23. C
24. B
25. C

TEST 2

DIRECTIONS: Each question or incomplete statement is followed by several suggested answers or completions. Select the one that BEST answers the question or completes the statement. *PRINT THE LETTER OF THE CORRECT ANSWER IN THE SPACE AT THE RIGHT.*

1. The insights of Chester I. Barnard have influenced the development of management thought in significant ways. He is MOST closely identified with a position that has become known as the

    A. acceptance theory of authority
    B. principle of the manager's or executive's span of control
    C. *Theory X* and *Theory Y* dichotomy
    D. unit of command principle

    1._____

2. Certain conditions should exist to insure that a subordinate will decide to accept a communication as being authoritative.
   Which of the following is LEAST valid as a condition which should exist?

    A. The subordinate understands the communication.
    B. At the time of the subordinate's decision, he views the communication as consistent with the organization's purpose and his personal interest.
    C. At the time of the subordinate's decision, he views the communication as more consistent with his personal purposes than with the organization's interest.
    D. The subordinate is mentally and physically able to comply with the communication.

    2._____

3. In exploring the effects that employee participation has on implementing changes in work methods, certain relationships have been established between participation and productivity.
   It has MOST generally been found that highest productivity occurs in groups provided with

    A. participation in the process of change only through representatives of their group
    B. no participation in the change process
    C. full participation in the change process
    D. intermittent participation in the process of change

    3._____

4. The trend LEAST likely to occur in the area of employee-management relations is that

    A. employees will exert more influence on decisions affecting their interests
    B. technological change will have a stronger impact on organizations' human resources
    C. labor will judge management according to company profits
    D. government will play a larger role in balancing the interests of the parties in labor-management affairs

    4._____

5. Members of an organization must satisfy several fundamental psychological needs in order to be happy and productive.
   The BROADEST and MOST basic needs are

   A. achievement, recognition, and acceptance
   B. competition, recognition, and accomplishment
   C. salary increments and recognition
   D. acceptance of competition and economic award

   5._____

6. Morale has been defined as the capacity of a group of people to pull together steadily for a common purpose.
   Morale thus defined is MOST generally dependent on

   A. job security
   B. group and individual self-confidence
   C. organizational efficiency
   D. physical health of the individuals

   6._____

7. Which is the CORRECT order of steps to follow when revising office procedure?
   To

   I. develop the improved method as determined by time and motion studies and effective workplace layout
   II. find out how the task is now performed
   III. apply the new method
   IV. analyze the current method

   The CORRECT answer is:
   A. IV, II, I, III
   B. II, I, III, IV
   C. I, II, IV, III
   D. II, IV, I, III

   7._____

8. In contrast to broad spans of control, narrow spans of control are MOST likely to

   A. provide opportunity for more personal contact between superior and subordinate
   B. encourage decentralization
   C. stress individual initiative
   D. foster group of team effort

   8._____

9. A manager is coaching a subordinate on the nature of decision-making. She could BEST define decision-making as

   A. choosing between alternatives
   B. making diagnoses of feasible ends
   C. making diagnoses of feasible means
   D. comparing alternatives

   9._____

10. Of the following, the LEAST valid purpose of an organizational policy statement is to

    A. keep personnel from performing improper actions and functions on routine matters
    B. prevent the mishandling of non-routine matters
    C. provide management personnel with a tool that precludes the need for their use of judgment
    D. provide standard decisions and approaches in handling problems of a recurrent nature

11. Current thinking on bureaucratic organizations is that

    A. bureaucracy is on the way out
    B. bureaucracy, though not perfect, is unlikely to be replaced
    C. bureaucratic organizations are most effective in dealing with constant change
    D. bureaucratic organizations are most effective when dealing with sophisticated customers or clients

12. The development of alternate plans as a major step in planning will normally result in the planner's having several possible course of action available. GENERALLY, this is

    A. *desirable* since such development helps to determine the most suitable alternative and to provide for the unexpected
    B. *desirable* since such development makes the use of planning premises and constraints unnecessary
    C. *undesirable* since the planners should formulate only one way of achieving given goals at a given time
    D. *undesirable* since such action restricts efforts to modify the planning to take advantage of opportunities

13. Assume a manager carries out his responsibilities to his staff according to what is now known about managerial leadership.
    Which of the following statements would MOST accurately reflect his assumptions about proper management?

    A. Efficiency in operations results from allowing the human element to participate in a minimal way.
    B. Efficient operation results from balancing work considerations with personnel considerations.
    C. Efficient operation results from a work force committed to its self-interest.
    D. Efficient operation results from staff relationships that produce a friendly work climate.

14. Assume that a manager is called upon to conduct a management audit. To do this properly, he would have to take certain steps in a specific sequence. Which step should this manager take FIRST?

    A. Managerial performance must be surveyed.
    B. A method of reporting must be established.
    C. Management auditing procedures and documentation must be developed.
    D. Criteria for the audit must be established.

    14._____

15. If a manager is required to conduct a scientific investigation of an organizational problem, the FIRST step he should take is to

    A. state his assumptions about the problem
    B. carry out a search for background information
    C. choose the right approach to investigate the validity of his assumptions
    D. define and state the problem

    15._____

16. A manager would be correct to assert that the principle of delegation states that decisions should be made PRIMARILY

    A. by persons in an executive capacity qualified to make them
    B. by persons in a non-executive capacity
    C. at as low an organizational level of authority as practicable
    D. by the next lower level of authority

    16._____

17. Of the following, which one is NOT regarded by management authorities as a fundamental characteristic of an ideal bureaucracy?

    A. Division of labor and specialization
    B. An established hierarchy
    C. Decentralization of authority
    D. A set of operating rules and regulations

    17._____

18. As the number of subordinates in a manager's span of control increases, the actual number of possible relationships

    A. increases disproportionately to the number of subordinates
    B. increases in equal number to the number of subordinates
    C. reaches a stable level
    D. will first increase, then slowly decrease

    18._____

19. Management experts generally believe that computer-based management information systems (MIS) have greater potential for improving the process of management than any other development in recent decades.
The one of the following which MOST accurately describes the objectives of MIS is to

    A. provide information for decision-making on planning, initiating, and controlling the operations of the various units of the organization
    B. establish mechanization of routine functions such as clerical records, payroll, inventory, and accounts receivable in order to promote economy and efficiency
    C. computerize decision-making on planning, initiating, organizing, and controlling the operations of an organization
    D. provide accurate facts and figures on the various programs of the organization to be used for purposes of planning and research

19.____

20. The one of the following which is the BEST application of the *management-by-exception* principle is that this principle

    A. stimulates communication and aids in management of crisis situations, thus reducing the frequency of decision-making
    B. saves time and reserves top management decisions only for crisis situations, thus reducing the frequency of decision-making
    C. stimulates communication, saves time, and reduces the frequency of decision-making
    D. is limited to crisis-management situations

20.____

21. Generally, each organization is dependent upon the availability of qualified personnel.
Of the following, the MOST important factor affecting the availability of qualified people to each organization is

    A. availability of public transportation
    B. the general rise in the educational levels of our population
    C. the rise of sentiment against racial discrimination
    D. pressure by organized community groups

21.____

22. A fundamental responsibility of all managers is to decide what physical facilities and equipment are needed to help attain basic goals.
Good planning for the purchase and use of equipment is seldom easy to do and is complicated most by the fact that

    A. organizations rarely have stable sources of supply
    B. nearly all managers tend to be better at personnel planning than at equipment planning
    C. decisions concerning physical resources are made too often on an emergency basis rather than under carefully prepared policies
    D. legal rulings relative to depreciation fluctuate very frequently

22.____

23. In attempting to reconcile managerial objectives and an individual employee's goals, it is generally LEAST desirable for management to

    A. recognize the capacity of the individual to contribute toward realization of managerial goals
    B. encourage self-development of the employee to exceed minimum job performance
    C. consider an individual employee's work separately from other employees
    D. demonstrate that an employee advances only to the extent that he contributes directly to the accomplishment of stated goals

23._____

24. As a management tool for discovering individual training needs, a job analysis would generally be of LEAST assistance in determining

    A. the performance requirements of individual jobs
    B. actual employee performance on the job
    C. acceptable standards of performance
    D. training needs for individual jobs

24._____

25. One of the major concerns of organizational managers today is how the spread of automation will affect them and the status of their positions. Realistically speaking, one can say that the MOST likely effect of our newer forms of highly automated technology on managers will be to

    A. make most top-level positions superfluous or obsolete
    B. reduce the importance of managerial work in general
    C. replace the work of managers with the work of technicians
    D. increase the importance of and demand for top managerial personnel

25._____

KEY (CORRECT ANSWERS)

1. A		11. B	
2. C		12. A	
3. C		13. B	
4. C		14. D	
5. A		15. D	
6. B		16. C	
7. D		17. C	
8. A		18. A	
9. A		19. A	
10. C		20. C	

21. B
22. C
23. C
24. B
25. D

INTERVIEWING EXAMINATION SECTION
TEST 1

DIRECTIONS: Each question or incomplete statement is followed by several suggested answers or completions. Select the one that BEST answers the question or completes the statement. *PRINT THE LETTER OF THE CORRECT ANSWER IN THE SPACE AT THE RIGHT.*

1. Of the following, the BEST way for an interviewer to calm a person who seems to have become emotionally upset as a result of a question asked is for the interviewer to

    A. talk to the person about other things for a short time
    B. ask that the person control himself
    C. probe for the cause of his emotional upset
    D. finish the questioning as quickly as possible

    1.____

2. You find that an applicant is hesitant about showing you some required personal material and documents. Your *initial* reaction to this situation should be to

    A. quietly insist that he give you the required materials
    B. make an exception in his case to avoid making him uncomfortable
    C. suspect that he may be trying to withhold evidence
    D. understand that he is in a stressful situation and may feel ashamed to reveal such information

    2.____

3. An applicant has just given you a response which does not seem clear.
Of the following, the BEST course of action for you to take in order to check your understanding of the applicant's response is for you to

    A. ask the question again during a subsequent interview with this applicant
    B. repeat the applicant's answer in the applicant's own words and ask if that is what the applicant meant
    C. later in the interview, repeat the question that led to this response
    D. repeat the question that led to this response, but say it more forcefully

    3.____

4. While speaking with applicants, you may find that there are times when an applicant will be silent for a short while before answering questions.
In order to gather the best information from the applicant, the interviewer should *generally* treat these silences by

    A. repeating the same question to make the applicant stop hesitating
    B. rephrasing the question in a way that the applicant can answer it faster
    C. directing an easier question to the applicant so that he can gain confidence in answering
    D. waiting patiently and not pressuring the applicant into quick, undeveloped answers

    4.____

5. In dealing with members of *different* ethnic and religious groups among the applicants you interview, you should give

    A. individuals the services to which they are entitled
    B. less service to those you judge to be more advantaged

    5.____

C. better service to groups with which you sympathize most
D. better service to groups with political "muscle"

6. You must be sure that, when interviewing an applicant, you phrase each question carefully.
   Of the following, the MOST important reason for this is to insure that

   A. the applicant will phrase each of his responses carefully
   B. you use correct grammar
   C. it is clear to the applicant what information you are seeking
   D. you do not word the same question differently for different applicants

7. When given a form to complete, a client hesitates, tells you that he cannot fill out forms too well and that he is afraid he will do a poor job. He asks you to do it for him. You are quite sure, however, that he is able to do it himself.
   In this case, it would be MOST advisable for you to

   A. encourage him to try filling out the application as well as he can
   B. fill out the application for him
   C. explain to him that he must learn to accept responsibility
   D. tell him that, if others can fill out an application, he can too

8. Assume that an applicant whom you are interviewing has made a statement that is obviously not true.
   Of the following, the BEST course of action for you to take at this point in the interview is to

   A. ask the applicant if he is sure about his statement
   B. tell the applicant that his statement is incorrect
   C. question the applicant further to clarify his response
   D. assume that the statement is correct

9. Assume that you are conducting an *initial* interview with an applicant.
   Of the following, the MOST advisable questions for you to ask at the beginning of this interview are those that

   A. can be answered in one or two sentences
   B. have nothing to do with the subject matter of the interview
   C. are most likely to reveal any hostility on the part of the applicant
   D. the applicant is most likely to be willing and able to answer

10. When interviewing a particularly nervous and upset applicant, the one of the following actions which you should take FIRST is to

    A. inform the applicant that, to be helped, he must cooperate
    B. advise the applicant that proof must be provided for statements he makes
    C. assure the applicant that every effort will be made to provide him with whatever assistance he is entitled to
    D. tell the applicant he will have no trouble so long as he is truthful

11. Assume that it is part of your job to prepare a monthly report for your unit head that eventually goes to the director. The report contains information on the number of applicants you have interviewed that have been approved and the number of applicants you have interviewed that have been turned down. Errors on such reports are *serious* because

    A. you are expected to be able to prove how many applicants you have interviewed each month
    B. accurate statistics are needed for effective management of the department
    C. they may not be discovered before the report is transmitted to the director
    D. they may result in a loss to the applicants left out of the report

11.____

12. During interviews, people give information about themselves in several ways. Which of the following *usually* gives the LEAST amount of information about the person being questioned? His

    A. spoken words
    B. tone of voice
    C. facial expression
    D. body position

12.____

13. Suppose an applicant, while being interviewed, becomes angered by your questioning and begins to use sharp, uncontrolled language.
    Which of the following is the BEST way for you to react to him?

    A. Speak in his style to show him that you are neither impressed nor upset by his speech
    B. Interrupt him and tell him that you are not required to listen to this kind of speech
    C. Lower your voice and slow the rate of your speech in an attempt to set an example that will calm him
    D. Let him continue in his way but insist that he answer your questions directly

13.____

14. You have been informed that no determination has yet been made on the eligibility of an applicant whom you have interviewed. The decision depends on further checking. His situation, however, is similar to that of many other applicants whose eligibility has been approved. The applicant, *quite worried,* calls you, and asks whether his application has been accepted.
    What would be BEST for you to do under these circumstances? Tell him

    A. his application is being checked and you will let him know the final result as soon as possible
    B. that a written request addressed to your supervisor will probably get faster action for his case
    C. not to worry since other applicants with similar backgrounds have already been accepted
    D. since there is no definite information and you are very busy, you will call him back

14.____

15. Suppose that you have been talking with an applicant. You have the feeling from the latest things the applicant has said that some of his answers to earlier questions were not totally correct. You guess that he might have been afraid or confused earlier but that your conversation has now put him in a more comfortable frame of mind.
    In order to test the reliability of information received from the earlier questions, the BEST thing for you to do *now* is to ask new questions that

15.____

A. allow the applicant to explain why he deliberately gave false information to you
B. ask for the same information, although worded differently from the original questions
C. put pressure on the applicant so that he personally wants to clear up the facts in his earlier answers
D. indicate to the applicant that you are aware of his deceptiveness

16. While providing you with required information, an applicant whom you are interviewing, informs you that she does not know certain facts.
Of the following, the MOST advisable action for you to take is to

    A. ask her to explain further
    B. advise her about research facilities
    C. express your sympathy for the situation
    D. go on to the next item of information

16.____

17. If, in an interview, you wish to determine a client's usual occupation, which one of the following questions is MOST likely to elicit the *most* useful information?

    A. Did you ever work in a factory?
    B. Do you know how to do office work?
    C. What kind of work do you do?
    D. Where are you working now?

17.____

18. Assume that you are approached by a clerk from another office who starts questioning you about one of the clients you have just interviewed. The clerk says that she is a relative of the client. According to departmental policy, all matters discussed with clients are to be kept confidential.
Of the following, the BEST course of action for you to take in this situation would be to

    A. check to see whether the clerk is really a relative before you make any further decisions
    B. explain to the clerk why you cannot divulge the information
    C. tell the clerk that you do not know the answers to her questions
    D. tell the clerk that she can get from the client any information the client wishes to give

18.____

19. Which of the following is usually the BEST technique for you, as an interviewer, to use to bring an applicant back to subject matter from which the applicant has strayed?

    A. Ask the applicant a question that is related to the subject of the interview
    B. Show the applicant that his response is unrelated to the question
    C. Discreetly reind the applicant that there is a time allotment for the interview
    D. Tell the applicant that you will be happy to discuss the extraneous matters at a future interview

19.____

20. Assume that you are interviewing a witness who is telling a story crucial to your investigation. It is important that you get all the facts being related by this witness. In order to secure this vital information, the BEST of the following techniques is to

    A. quietly interrupt the witness's story and request him to speak with deliberation so that you can record his statement
    B. guide the witness during his recital so that all important points are validated

20.____

C. confine your activities during the story to brief note-taking, and, after the information has been secured, request a full written statement
D. inform the witness that he must relate all the facts as truthfully and concisely as possible

21. The statement of any witness obtained in an interview should GENERALLY be considered

    A. as a lead requiring substantiation by additional evidence
    B. accurate if the witness appears honest and is cooperative
    C. unreliable if the witness has been involved in similar investigations
    D. as a fact admissible under the rules of evidence

22. During an important interview, an interviewer takes notes from time to time but very rarely looks at the subject being questioned.
    Such action on the part of the interviewer is

    A. *unacceptable,* chiefly because during the actual interview an interviewer should pay more attention to the witness's manner of giving the information rather than to the content of his statements
    B. *acceptable,* chiefly because data should be recorded at the earliest opportunity and important data should be noted meticulously
    C. *unacceptable,* chiefly because it inhibits the person being interviewed and is not conducive to a give-and-take discussion
    D. *unacceptable,* chiefly because focusing attention on note-taking and not on the person being interviewed creates an impression of professional objectivity

23. Since he must interview persons with various personalities and attitudes, an interviewer should, *generally,* adopt a method of interviewing that

    A. is uniformly applicable to all types so that discrepancies in the accounts of individuals may be readily detected
    B. can be adjusted to the persons whom he interviews
    C. is based on the premise that most interviewees tend to be uncooperative
    D. requires the interviewer to spend as little time as possible in questioning applicants

24. One of the more difficult tasks facing an interviewer is to control the tendency of witnesses to ramble when giving information.
    Of the following, the BEST technique for keeping a witness's comments pertinent is to

    A. ask questions which indicate the desired answer
    B. insist on "yes" and "no" answers to his questions
    C. construct questions that restrict the range of information which the witness can give in response
    D. ask precise questions so that the answers of the witness will necessarily be brief

25. During interviews, a certain interviewer phrases follow-up questions mentally during pauses while the subject is still answering the previous question. This practice is, *generally,* 25.____

   A. *desirable,* chiefly because it gives the impression that the interviewer is well acquainted with all the facts
   B. *undesirable,* chiefly because the interviewer cannot know whether such questions will be appropriate
   C. *desirable,* chiefly because it enables the interviewer to pose new questions without significant breaks in the discussion
   D. *undesirable,* chiefly because it subjects the person being interviewed to a barrage of questions

KEY (CORRECT ANSWERS)

1. A	11. B
2. D	12. D
3. B	13. C
4. D	14. A
5. A	15. B
6. C	16. D
7. A	17. C
8. C	18. B
9. D	19. A
10. C	20. C

21. A
22. C
23. B
24. C
25. C

TEST 2

DIRECTIONS: Each question or incomplete statement is followed by several suggested answers or completions. Select the one that BEST answers the question or completes the statement. *PRINT THE LETTER OF THE CORRECT ANSWER IN THE SPACE AT THE RIGHT.*

1. The one of the following which is the BEST description of a *properly* objective interviewer is one who

    A. is friendly and sensitive to the client's feelings, without becoming emotionally involved
    B. is distant and impersonal, remaining unaffected by what the client says
    C. lets personal emotions enter as far as the client's situation calls for them
    D. becomes emotionally involved with the client's situation, but without showing this involvement

    1.____

2. The one of the following which is MOST necessary for successfully intefviewing a person who belongs to a culture different from that of the interviewer is for the interviewer to

    A. have some appreciation of the other culture
    B. ignore those cultural differences which lead to bias
    C. stay away from sensitive, "touchy" issues
    D. assume the mannerisms of people in the other culture

    2.____

3. In fact-finding interviews, it is generally assumed that the smaller the lumber of interviewees, the greater the increase of reliability with the addition of others.
The PROPER number of interviewees needed to insure the accuracy of information obtained *generally* depends upon the

    A. educational level of those interviewed
    B. number of people who have the required information
    C. directness of the questions asked
    D. variability of the information received

    3.____

4. The one of the following which is generally MOST likely to be *accurately* described in an interview by an interviewee is

    A. the presence of a large painting in the interviewer's office
    B. the number of people in the interviewer's waiting room
    C. space relations
    D. duration of time

    4.____

5. The one of the following which is *generally* the BEST course of action for an interviewer to take when interviewing a person who is reluctant to tell what he knows about a matter under investigation is to

    A. be curt and abrupt, and threaten the person with the consequences of his withholding information
    B. be firm and severe, and pressure the person into telling the needed information

    5.____

167

C. be patient and candid with the person being questioned about the investigation since doing otherwise is not ethical
D. give the person false information about the investigation so he will give the needed information without realizing its importance

6. It is often recommended that an interviewer prepare in advance a list of questions or topics to be covered in an interview.
The MAIN reason for using such a checklist is to

   A. allow investigations to be assigned to less efficient interviewers
   B. eliminate a large amount of follow-up paper work
   C. aid the interviewer in remembering to cover all important topics
   D. aid the interviewer in maintaining an objective distance from the person interviewed

6.____

7. *Usually*, the CHIEF advantage of a directive approach in an interview is that the

   A. interviewer maintains control over the course of the interview
   B. person interviewed is more likely to be put at ease
   C. person interviewed is generally left free to direct the interview
   D. interviewer will not suggest answers to the person interviewed

7.____

8. *Usually*, the CHIEF advantage of a non-directive approach in conducting an interview is that the

   A. interviewer generally conceals what he is looking for in the interview
   B. person interviewed is more likely to express his true feelings about the topic under discussion
   C. person interviewed is more likely to follow an idea introduced by the interviewer
   D. interviewer can keep the discussion limited to topics he believes to be relevant

8.____

9. The one of the following which is generally the LEAST likely to be *accurate* in a description of an event given to an interviewer is a statement about

   A. the presence of an object
   B. the number of people, when their number is small
   C. locations of people
   D. duration of time

9.____

10. Assume that you, an interviewer, are conducting a character investigation.
In an interview, the one of the following character traits of the person being interviewed which can *usually* be determined with a GOOD degree of reliability is

    A. honesty   B. dependability
    C. forcefulness   D. perseverance

10.____

11. You have been assigned the task of obtaining a family's social history.
The BEST place for you to interview members of the family while obtaining this social history would, *generally*, be in

    A. the family's home
    B. your agency's general offices
    C. the home of a friend of the family
    D. your own private office

11.____

12. If an interviewer obtains testimony from persons in interviews by means of interrogation or asking questions rather than by letting the person freely relate the testimony, what is said will, *generally*, be

    A. *greater* in range and *less* accurate
    B. *greater* in range and *more* accurate
    C. about the *same* in range and *less* accurate
    D. about the *same* in range and *more* accurate

13. Experienced interviewers have learned to phrase their questions carefully in order to obtain the desired response. Of the following, the question which would *usually* elicit the MOST accurate answer is:

    A. "How old are you?"
    B. "What is your income?"
    C. "How are you today?"
    D. "What is your date of birth?"

14. The one of the following questions which would *generally* lead to the LEAST reliable answer is:

    A. "Did you see a wallet?"
    B. "Was the German Shepherd gray?"
    C. "Didn't you see the stop sign?"
    D. "Did you see the guard on duty?"

15. Some interviewers may make a practice of observing details of the surroundings when interviewing in someone's home or office.
    Such a practice is, *generally*, considered

    A. *undesirable*, mainly because such snooping is an unwarranted, unethical invasion of privacy
    B. *undesirable*, mainly because useful information is rarely, if ever, gained this way
    C. *desirable*, mainly because useful insights into the character of the person interviewed may be gained
    D. *desirable*, mainly because it is impossible to evaluate a person adequately without such observation of his environment

KEY (CORRECT ANSWERS)

1. A
2. A
3. D
4. A
5. C
6. C
7. A
8. B
9. D
10. C
11. A
12. A
13. D
14. B
15. C

INTERPRETING STATISTICAL DATA GRAPHS, CHARTS AND TABLES
EXAMINATION SECTION
TEST 1

DIRECTIONS: Each question or incomplete statement is followed by several suggested answers or completions. Select the one that BEST answers the question or completes the statement. *PRINT THE LETTER OF THE CORRECT ANSWER IN THE SPACE AT THE RIGHT.*

Questions 1-10.

DIRECTIONS: Questions 1 through 10 are to be answered SOLELY on the basis of the following tables, which contain data concerning the Green Valley Region, a fictional area.

HOUSING PATTERNS, GREEN VALLEY REGION 2010-2020

TABLE I

TYPE OF HOUSING	SUBURBS 2010	SUBURBS 2020	TOWNS 2010	TOWNS 2020	REGION TOTAL* 2010	REGION TOTAL* 2020
Multi-unit Dwellings	2,600	5,200	9,300	10,900	13,700	18,800
Single-unit Dwellings	15,100	17,700	11,000	11,400	43,700	46,900
Mobile Dwellings	300	?	900	1,800	14,700	31,400
TOTAL	18,000	23,600	21,200	24,100	72,100	97,100

*NOTE: Region totals include other categories in addition to suburbs and towns.

TABLE II
SUBSTANDARD HOUSING, GREEN VALLEY REGION
(INCLUDED IN FIGURES IN TABLE I, ABOVE)

	2010-800 UNITS	2020-1,200 UNITS
Multi-unit	64%	54%
Single-unit	33%	28%
Mobile	3%	18%

1. If the single-unit dwellings in towns in 2010 each contained an average of 5.1 rooms, the total number of rooms in this category was MOST NEARLY

    A. 56,000   B. 61,000   C. 561,000   D. 651,000

2. The number of mobile dwellings in the suburbs in 2020 was

    A. 500   B. 600   C. 700   D. 800

3. From 2010 to 2020, the total number of all Green Valley Region housing units increased by MOST NEARLY

    A. 31%   B. 34%   C. 37%   D. 40%

4. For 2020, what was the TOTAL number of substandard multi-unit dwellings? 4.____

   A. 548   B. 573   C. 623   D. 648

5. In the towns from 2010 to 2020, the type of housing having the LARGEST proportionate increase was 5.____

   A. mobile   B. multi-unit
   C. single-unit   D. substandard

6. In 2020, the TOTAL number of dwellings which were NOT substandard was 6.____

   A. 95,300   B. 95,900   C. 96,200   D. 96,500

7. Assume that in 2010, 3.5 persons was the average occupancy in the towns in each kind of dwelling. 7.____
   Thus, the population of the towns in the Green Valley Region in 2010 was

   A. 73,600   B. 73,800   C. 74,000   D. 74,200

8. Which of the following statements concerning mobile dwellings is CORRECT? 8.____
   In

   A. 2020, mobile dwellings were the largest category of substandard dwellings
   B. 2010, the number of mobile dwellings in suburbs was greater by 30% than the number in towns
   C. the Green Valley Region during the period 2010-20, the number of mobile dwellings increased by 50%
   D. 2010, the total number of mobile dwellings in the Green Valley Region was less than 25% of the total number of all dwellings

9. Assume that of the single-unit dwellings not in suburbs and towns in 2010, 20% were in villages. 9.____
   Therefore, the number of single-unit dwellings in villages in 2010 was

   A. 2,480   B. 3,070   C. 3,520   D. 4,110

10. Assume that in the Green Valley Region the following changes were expected in 2024 as compared to 2020: the number of suburban dwellings was increased by 30%; the number of town dwellings was decreased by 15%. 10.____
    Therefore, the ratio of suburban dwellings to town dwellings expected for 2024 was MOST NEARLY

    A. 3:2   B. 4:3   C. 5:4   D. 6:5

KEY (CORRECT ANSWERS)

1. A
2. C
3. B
4. D
5. A
6. B
7. D
8. D
9. C
10. A

TEST 2

Questions 1-6.

DIRECTIONS: Questions 1 through 6 are to be answered SOLELY on the basis of the graph below which presents data on two demographic characteristics and the rate of new home construction in Empire State during the period 2005 through 2016.

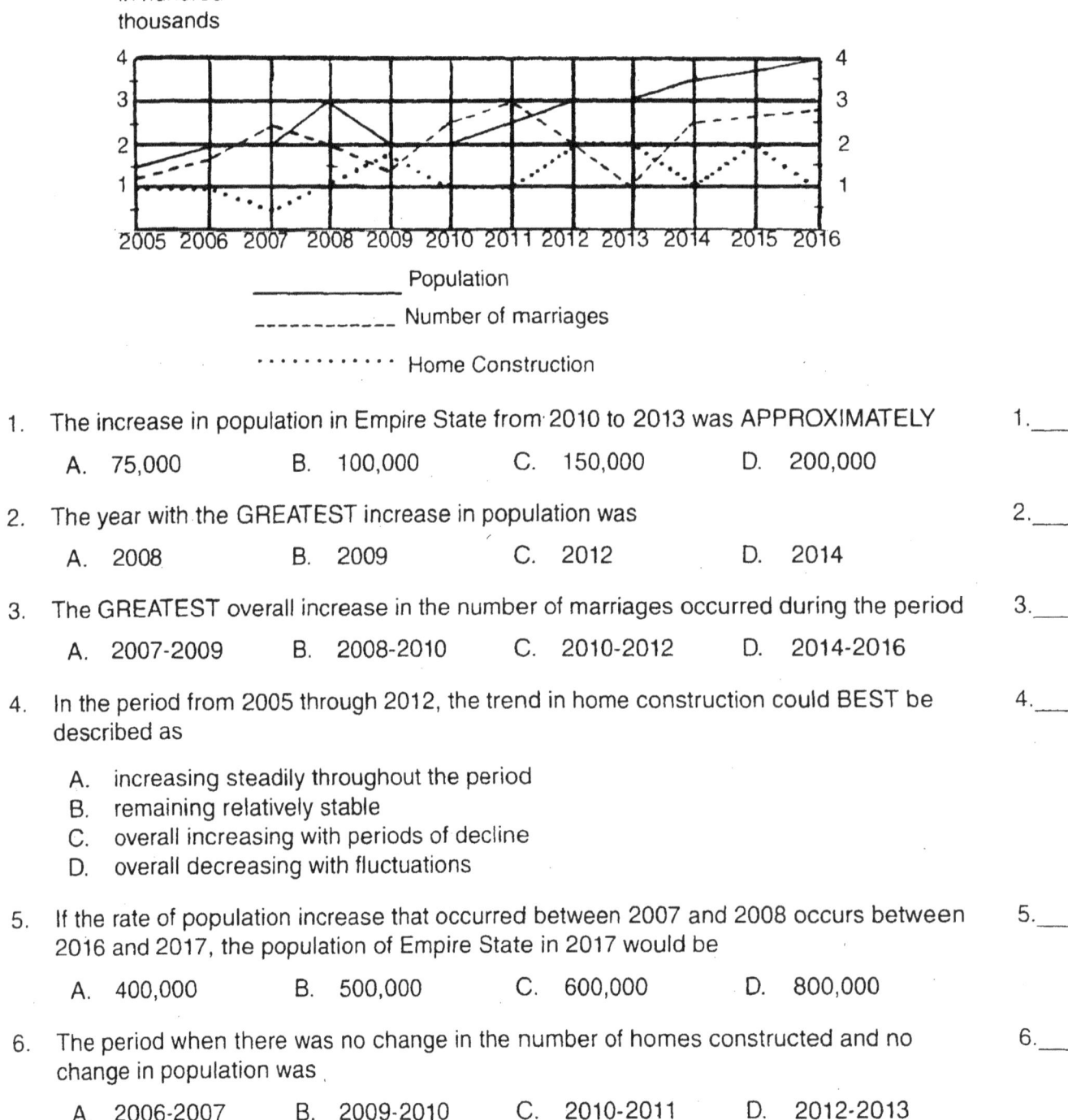

1. The increase in population in Empire State from 2010 to 2013 was APPROXIMATELY

   A. 75,000 B. 100,000 C. 150,000 D. 200,000

2. The year with the GREATEST increase in population was

   A. 2008 B. 2009 C. 2012 D. 2014

3. The GREATEST overall increase in the number of marriages occurred during the period

   A. 2007-2009 B. 2008-2010 C. 2010-2012 D. 2014-2016

4. In the period from 2005 through 2012, the trend in home construction could BEST be described as

   A. increasing steadily throughout the period
   B. remaining relatively stable
   C. overall increasing with periods of decline
   D. overall decreasing with fluctuations

5. If the rate of population increase that occurred between 2007 and 2008 occurs between 2016 and 2017, the population of Empire State in 2017 would be

   A. 400,000 B. 500,000 C. 600,000 D. 800,000

6. The period when there was no change in the number of homes constructed and no change in population was

   A. 2006-2007 B. 2009-2010 C. 2010-2011 D. 2012-2013

KEY (CORRECT ANSWERS)

1. B
2. A
3. B
4. C
5. C
6. D

TEST 3

Questions 1-6.

DIRECTIONS: Questions 1 through 6 are to be answered SOLELY on the basis of the information given in the graph below, which presents data on the rate of new office construction in the uptown, midtown, and downtown areas of Gotham City for the period from 2003 through 2016.

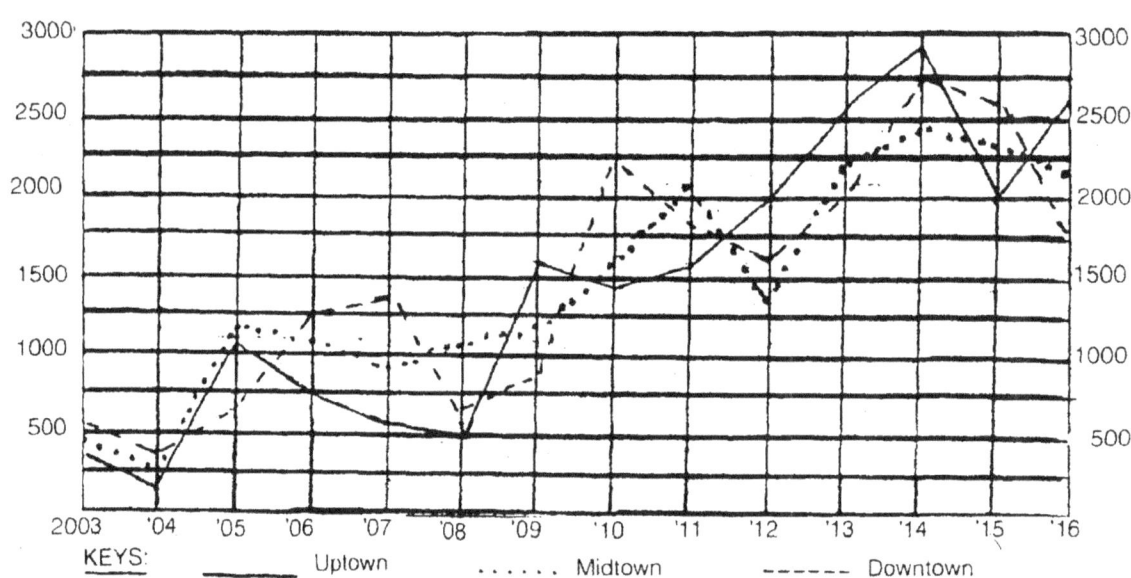

1. The amount of office space which was constructed in Gotham City in the year 2012 is MOST NEARLY _____ square feet.

    A. 2,100,000
    B. 3,500,000
    C. 4,900,000
    D. 5,700,000

2. In which of the following years was the LEAST amount of office space constructed in the downtown area?

    A. 2003　　B. 2006　　C. 2008　　D. 2010

3. The year with the GREATEST amount of new office construction was

    A. 2005　　B. 2009　　C. 2014　　D. 2016

4. In the years 2010 through 2014, the overall trend in new uptown office space construction could BEST be described as

    A. generally stable
    B. steadily increasing with small annual fluctuations
    C. generally increasing with large annual fluctuations
    D. steadily decreasing with major annual fluctuations

5. The GREATEST increase in percentage of new office space construction occurred in the year

    A. 2003　　B. 2010　　C. 2007　　D. 2005

2 (#3)

6. Consider the relationship between the amount of midtown office construction in 2005 and 2009.
   If the same relationship exists in 2016 and 2020, the amount of midtown office construction in 2020 would be _____ square feet.   6._____

   A. 1,300,000
   B. 1,600,000
   C. 2,100,000
   D. 2,500,000

KEY (CORRECT ANSWERS)

1. C
2. A
3. C
4. B
5. D
6. C

TEST 4

Questions 1-7.

DIRECTIONS: Questions 1 through 7 are to be answered SOLELY on the basis of the information and the table below which lists the minimum and average monthly rents paid for various kinds of apartments in 3 groups of housing projects in City Z.

MINIMUM AND AVERAGE MONTHLY RENTS FOR VARIOUS KINDS OF APARTMENTS IN HOUSING PROJECTS IN CITY Z

Size of Apartment	Group I Projects Minimum	Group I Projects Average	Group II Projects Minimum	Group II Projects Average	Group III Projects Minimum	Group III Projects Average
2 rooms	$167.00	$178.00	$196.00	$216.60	$212.60	$229.00
3 rooms	$208.00	$223.20	$232.60	$253.00	$245.00	$260.60
4 rooms	$237.00	$248.00	$285.00	$315.00	$299.00	$329.80
5 rooms	$278.00	$296.60	$338.00	$355.00	$358.00	$387.00
6 rooms or more	$321.00	$344.40	$380.00	$418.00	$421.00	$462.00

Names of Group I Projects: Allen, Belton, Carlton, Grand, Ramsey, Redwood, Sandford, Trent

Names of Group II Projects: Alden, Berton, Carry, Gerrard, Long, Randall, Tallwood, Tenth St., Thomas Ave.

Names of Group III Projects: Astor Lane, Edgewood, Kennelly, Lange, Roosevelt, Summerset, Turner, Westgate

Each of Questions 1 through 7 gives the name of a housing project, the monthly rent paid by a tenant in that project, and the size of the tenant's apartment. You are to compare the information in each question with the table and lists of projects, and then mark A, B, C, or D in the answer space at the right in accordance with the following instructions:

A. If the rent in the question is the minimum for this size apartment in this project, mark your answer A.
B. If the rent in the question is higher than the minimum rent for this size apartment in this project but lower than the average rent, mark your answer B.
C. If the rent in the question is exactly the same as the average rent for this size apartment in this project, mark your answer C.
D. If the rent in the question is higher than the average rent for this size apartment in this project, mark your answer D.

SAMPLE QUESTION: Astor Lane Project, 2 rooms, $217.00

According to the lists of projects, the Astor Lane Project is in Group III. In the table above, under Group III Projects and across the line reading *2 rooms,* the minimum rent is $212.60 and the

178

average rent is $229.00. Thus, the rent paid by this tenant is higher than the minimum rent but lower than the average rent. Therefore, the answer is B.

1. Randall Project, 4 rooms, $285.00 1.____
2. Trent Project, 6 rooms, $328.20 2.____
3. Lange Project, 3 rooms, $264.60 3.____
4. Alden Project, 5 rooms, $355.00 4.____
5. Summerset Project, 4 rooms, $337.00 5.____
6. Grand Project, 2 rooms, $181.60 6.____
7. Carry Project, 6 rooms, $407.00 7.____

KEY (CORRECT ANSWERS)

1. A
2. B
3. D
4. C
5. D
6. D
7. B

TEST 5

Questions 1-8.

DIRECTIONS: Questions 1 through 8 are to be answered SOLELY on the basis of the information given below. Assume that apartments of the sizes indicated in the questions exist in the projects named. In each question, the title of the Resident Employee, the size of the apartment he occupies, and the project he lives in are given. Choose from the options at the right in each question the monthly rental the Resident Employee pays.

MONTHLY RENTALS FOR RESIDENT EMPLOYEES IN STATE PROJECTS				
	Group I Projects		Group II Projects	
	Supt. & Asst. Supt	All Other Employees	Supt. & Asst. Supt	All Other Employees
2 rooms	$186	$170	$188	$172
3 rooms	$194	$182	$200	$188
4 rooms	$206	$194	$224	$212
5 rooms	$228	$212	$254	$238
6 rooms	$240	$228	$262	$250
7 rooms or more	$252	$236	$272	$256

Names of Group I Projects: Amsterdam, Astoria, Bland, Bronx River, Brownsville, Carver, Cypress Hills, Farragut, Forest, Gowanus, Ingersoll, Johnson, King, Lincoln, Marcy, Melrose, Patterson, Redfern, Smith, Soundview, Wald, Whitman.

Names of Group II Projects: Albany, Audubon, Baychester, Bronx River Add., Bushwick, Butler, Castle Hill, Chelsea, Douglass, Douglass Add., Drew-Hamilton, Edgemere, Haber, Howard, Independence, Manhattanville, Marlboro, Mill Brook, Murphy, Rutgers, Stapleton, Sumner, White, Williams, Plaza, Wilson, Wise Towers

1. Maintenance Man
   2-room apartment
   Manhattanville Project

   A. $170 B. $172 C. $186 D. $188

2. Housing Caretaker
   3-room apartment
   Baychester Project

   A. $172 B. $182 C. $188 D. $200

3. Maintenance Man
   6-room apartment
   Redfern Project

   A. $228 B. $238 C. $240 D. $250

1.___

2.___

3.___

180

4. Assistant Superintendent
   3-room apartment
   Lincoln Project
   A. $182   B. $188   C. $194   D. $200

5. Housing Caretaker
   4-room apartment
   Stapleton Project
   A. $182   B. $194   C. $206   D. $212

6. Assistant Superintendent
   5-room apartment
   Drew-Hamilton Project
   A. $212   B. $228   C. $238   D. $254

7. Housing Fireman
   8-room apartment
   Gowanus Project
   A. $238   B. $252   C. $256   D. $292

8. Superintendent
   6-room apartment
   Whitman Project
   A. $238   B. $240   C. $252   D. $262

KEY (CORRECT ANSWERS)

1. B
2. C
3. A
4. C
5. D
6. D
7. A
8. B

PREPARING WRITTEN MATERIAL

PARAGRAPH REARRANGEMENT
COMMENTARY

The sentences that follow are in scrambled order. You are to rearrange them in proper order and indicate the letter choice containing the correct answer at the space at the right.

Each group of sentences in this section is actually a paragraph presented in scrambled order. Each sentence in the group has a place in that paragraph; no sentence is to be left out. You are to read each group of sentences and decide upon the best order in which to put the sentences so as to form a well-organized paragraph.

The questions in this section measure the ability to solve a problem when all the facts relevant to its solution are not given.

More specifically, certain positions of responsibility and authority require the employee to discover connection between events sometimes, apparently, unrelated. In order to do this, the employee will find it necessary to correctly infer that unspecified events have probably occurred or are likely to occur. This ability becomes especially important when action must be taken on incomplete information.

Accordingly, these questions require competitors to choose among several suggested alternatives, each of which presents a different sequential arrangement of the events. Competitors must choose the MOST logical of the suggested sequences.

In order to do so, they may be required to draw on general knowledge to infer missing concepts or events that are essential to sequencing the given events. Competitors should be careful to infer only what is essential to the sequence. The plausibility of the wrong alternatives will always require the inclusion of unlikely events or of additional chains of events which are NOT essential to sequencing the given events.

It's very important to remember that you are looking for the best of the four possible choices, and that the best choice of all may not even be one of the answers you're given to choose from.

There is no one right way to solve these problems. Many people have found it helpful to first write out the order of the sentences, as they would have arranged them, on their scrap paper before looking at the possible answers. If their optimum answer is there, this can save them some time. If it isn't, this method can still give insight into solving the problem. Others find it most helpful to just go through each of the possible choices, contrasting each as they go along. You should use whatever method feels comfortable and works for you.

While most of these types of questions are not that difficult, we've added a higher percentage of the difficult type, just to give you more practice. Usually there are only one or two questions on this section that contain such subtle distinctions that you're unable to answer confidently. And you then may find yourself stuck deciding between two possible choices, neither of which you're sure about.

EXAMINATION SECTION
TEST 1

DIRECTIONS: The sentences that follow are in scrambled order. You are to rearrange them in proper order and indicate the letter choice containing the correct answer. *PRINT THE LETTER OF THE CORRECT ANSWER IN THE SPACE AT THE RIGHT.*

1. Below are four statements labeled W, X, Y and Z.
   W. He was a strict and fanatic drillmaster.
   X. The word is always used in a derogatory sense and generally shows resentment and anger on the part of the user.
   Y. It is from the name of this Frenchman that we derive our English word, martinet.
   Z. Jean Martinet was the Inspector-General of Infantry during the reign of King Louis XIV.
   The PROPER order in which these sentences should be placed in a paragraph is:
   A. X, Z, W, Y   B. X, Z, Y, W   C. Z, W, Y, X   D. Z, Y, W, X

   1.____

2. In the following paragraph, the sentences, which are numbered, have been jumbled.
   I. Since then it has undergone changes.
   II. It was incorporated in 1955 under the laws of the State of New York.
   III. Its primary purposes, a cleaner city, has, however, remained the same.
   IV. The Citizens Committee works in cooperation with the Mayor's Inter-departmental Committee for a Clean City.
   The order in which these sentences should be arranged to form a well-organized paragraph is:
   A. II, IV, I, III   B. III, IV, I, II   C. IV, II, I, III   D. IV, III, II, I

   2.____

   3.____

Questions 3-5.

DIRECTIONS: The sentences listed below are part of a meaningful paragraph but they are not given in their proper order. You are to decide what would be the BEST order in which to put the sentences so as to form a well-organized paragraph. Each sentence has a place in the paragraph; there are no extra sentences. You are then to answer Questions 3 through 5 inclusive on the basis of your rearrangements of these scrambled sentences into a properly organized paragraph.

In 1887 some insurance companies organized an Inspection Department to advise their clients on all phases of fire prevention and protection. Probably this has been due to the smaller annual fire losses in Great Britain than in the United States. It tests various fire prevention devices and appliances and determines manufacturing hazards and their safeguards. Fire research began earlier in the United States and is more advanced than in Great Britain. Later they established a laboratory specializing in electrical, mechanical, hydraulic, and chemical fields.

2 (#1)

3. When the five sentences are arranged in proper order, the paragraph starts with the sentence which begins
    A. "In 1887..."   B. "Probably this..."   C. "It tests..."
    D. "Fire research..."   E. "Later they..."

3.____

4. In the last sentence listed above, "they" refers to
    A. the insurance companies   B. the United States and Great Britain
    C. the Inspection Department   D. clients
    E. technicians

4.____

5. When the above paragraph is properly arranged, it ends with the words
    A. "...and protection."   B. "...the United States."
    C. "...their safeguards."   D. "...in Great Britain."
    E. "...chemical fields."

5.____

KEY (CORRECT ANSWERS)

1. C
2. C
3. D
4. A
5. C

TEST 2

DIRECTIONS: In each of the questions numbered I through V, several sentences are given. For each question, choose as your answer the group of number that represents the MOST logical order of these sentences if they were arranged in paragraph form. *PRINT THE LETTER OF THE CORRECT ANSWER IN THE SPACE AT THE RIGHT.*

1.   I. It is established when one shows that the landlord has prevented the tenant's enjoyment of his interest in the property leased.
   II. Constructive eviction is the result of a breach of the covenant of quiet enjoyment implied in all leases.
   III. In some parts of the United States, it is not complete until the tenant vacates within a reasonable time.
   IV. Generally, the acts must be of such serious and permanent character as to deny the tenant the enjoyment of his possessing rights.
   V. In this event, upon abandonment of the premises, the tenant's liability for that ceases.
The CORRECT answer is:
  A. II, I, IV, III, V   B. V, II, III, I, IV
  C. IV, III, I, II, V   D. I, III, V, IV, II

1.____

2.   I. The powerlessness before private and public authorities that is the typical experience of the slum tenant is reminiscent of the situation of blue-collar workers all through the nineteenth century.
   II. Similarly, in recent years, this chapter of history has been reopened by anti-poverty groups which have attempted to organize slum tenants to enable them to bargain collectively with their landlords about the conditions of their tenancies.
   III. It is familiar history that many of the worker remedied their condition by joining together and presenting their demands collectively.
   IV. Like the workers, tenants are forced by the conditions of modern life into substantial dependence on these who possess great political aid and economic power.
   V. What's more, the very fact of dependence coupled with an absence of education and self-confidence makes them hesitant and unable to stand up for what they need from those in power.
The CORRECT answer is:
  A. V, IV, I, II, III   B. II, III, I, V, IV
  C. III, I, V, IV, II   D. I, IV, V, III, II

2.____

3.   I. A railroad, for example, when not acting as a common carrier may contract away responsibility for its own negligence.
   II. As to a landlord, however, no decision has been found relating to the legal effect of a clause shifting the statutory duty of repair to the tenant.
   III. The courts have not passed on the validity of clauses relieving the landlord of this duty and liability.
   IV. They have, however, upheld the validity of exculpatory clauses in other types of contracts.

3.____

187

V. Housing regulations impose a duty upon the landlord to maintain leased premises in safe condition.
VI. As another example, a bailee may limit his liability except for gross negligence, willful acts, or fraud.

The CORRECT answer is:
A. II, I, VI, IV, III, V
B. I, III, IV, V, VI, II
C. III, V, I, IV, II, VI
D. V, III, IV, I, VI, II

4.
I. Since there are only samples in the building, retail or consumer sales are generally eschewed by mart occupants, and in some instances, rigid controls are maintained to limit entrance to the mart only to those persons engaged in retailing.
II. Since World War I, in many larger cities, there has developed a new type of property, called the mart building.
III. It can, therefore, be used by wholesalers and jobbers for the display of sample merchandise.
IV. This type of building is most frequently a multi-storied, finished interior property which is a cross between a retail arcade and a loft building.
V. This limitation enables the mart occupants to ship the orders from another location after the retailer or dealer makes his selection from the samples.

The CORRECT answer is:
A. II, IV, III, I, V
B. IV, III, V, I, II
C. I, III, II, IV, V
D. I, IV, II, III, V

5.
I. In general, staff-line friction reduces the distinctive contribution of staff personnel.
II. The conflicts, however, introduce an uncontrolled element into the managerial system.
III. On the other hand, the natural resistance of the line to staff innovations probably usefully restrains over-eager efforts to apply untested procedures on a large scale.
IV. Under such conditions, it is difficult to know when valuable ideas are being sacrificed.
V. The relatively weak position of staff, requiring accommodation to the line, tends to restrict their ability to engage in free, experimental innovation.

The CORRECT answer is:
A. IV, II, III, I, V
B. I, V, III, II, IV
C. V, III, I, II, IV
D. II, I, IV, V, III

KEY (CORRECT ANSWERS)

1. A
2. D
3. D
4. A
5. B

TEST 3

DIRECTIONS: Questions 1 through 4 consist of six sentences which can be arranged in a logical sequence. For each question, select the choice which places the numbered sentences in the MOST logical sequent. *PRINT THE LETTER OF THE CORRECT ANSWER IN THE SPACE AT THE RIGHT.*

1.
   I. The burden of proof as to each issue is determined before trial and remains upon the same party throughout the trial.
   II. The jury is at liberty to believe one witness' testimony as against a number of contradictory witnesses.
   III. In a civil case, the party bearing the burden of proof is required to prove his contention by a fair preponderance of the evidence.
   IV. However, it must be noted that a fair preponderance of evidence does not necessarily mean a greater number of witnesses.
   V. The burden of proof is the burden which rests upon one of the parties to an action to persuade the trier of the facts, generally the jury, that a proposition he asserts is true.
   VI. If the evidence is equally balanced, or if it leaves the jury in such doubt as to be unable to decide the controversy either way, judgment must be given against the party upon whom the burden of proof rests.
   The CORRECT answer is:
   A. III, II, V, IV, I, VI
   B. I, II, VI, V, III, IV
   C. III, IV, V, I, II, VI
   D. V, I, III, VI, IV, II

   1.____

2.
   I. If a parent is without assets and is unemployed, he cannot be convicted of the crime of non-support of a child.
   II. The term "sufficient ability" has been held to mean sufficient financial ability.
   III. It does not matter if his unemployment is by choice or unavoidable circumstances.
   IV. If he fails to take any steps at all, he may be liable to prosecution for endangering the welfare of a child.
   V. Under the penal law, a parent is responsible for the support of his minor child only if the parent is "of sufficient ability."
   VI. An indigent parent may meet his obligation by borrowing money or by seeking aid under the provisions of the Social Welfare Law.
   The CORRECT answer is:
   A. VI, I, V, III, II, IV
   B. I, III, V, II, IV, VI
   C. V, II, I, III, VI, IV
   D. I, VI, IV, V, II, III

   2.____

3.
   I. Consider, for example, the case of a rabble rouser who urges a group of twenty people to go out and break the windows of a nearby factory.
   II. Therefore, the law fills the indicated gap with the crime of inciting to riot.
   III. A person is considered guilty of inciting to riot when he urges ten or more persons to engage in tumultuous and violent conduct of a kind likely to create public alarm.
   IV. However, if he has not obtained the cooperation of at least four people, he cannot be charged with unlawful assembly.

   3.____

189

V. The charge of inciting to riot was added to the law to cover types of conduct which cannot be classified as either the crime of "riot" or the crime of "unlawful assembly."
VI. If he acquires the acquiescence of at least four of them, he is guilty of unlawful assembly even if the project does not materialize.

The CORRECT answer is:
A. III, V, I, VI, IV, II
B. V, I, IV, VI, II, III
C. III, IV, I, V, II, VI
D. V, I, IV, VI, III, II

4. I. If, however, the rebuttal evidence presents an issue of credibility, it is for the jury to determine whether the presumption has, in fact, been destroyed.
    II. Once sufficient evidence to the contrary is introduced, the presumption disappears from the trial.
    III. The effect of a presumption is to place the burden upon the adversary to come forward with evidence to rebut the presumption.
    IV. When a presumption is overcome and ceases to exist in the case, the fact or facts which gave rise to the presumption still remain.
    V. Whether a presumption has been overcome is ordinarily a question for the court.
    VI. Such information may furnish a basis for a logical inference.

    The CORRECT answer is:
    A. IV, VI, II, V, I, III
    B. III, II, V, I, IV, VI
    C. V, III, VI, IV, II, I
    D. V, IV, I, II, VI, III

KEY (CORRECT ANSWERS)

1. D
2. C
3. A
4. B

EXAMINATION SECTION
TEST 1

DIRECTIONS: In each of the following questions, only one of the four sentences conforms to standards of correct usage. The other three contain errors in grammar, diction, or punctuation. Select the choice in each question which BEST conforms to standards of correct usage. Consider a choice correct if it contains none of the errors mentioned above, even though there may be other ways of expressing the same thought. *PRINT THE LETTER OF THE CORRECT ANSWER IN THE SPACE AT THE RIGHT.*

1. A. Because he was ill was no excuse for his behavior
   B. I insist that he see a lawyer before he goes to trial.
   C. He said "that he had not intended to go."
   D. He wasn't out of the office only three days.

   1.____

2. A. He came to the station and pays a porter to carry his bags into the train.
   B. I should have liked to live in medieval times.
   C. My father was born in Linville. A little country town where everybody knows everyone else.
   D. The car, which is parked across the street, is disabled.

   2.____

3. A. He asked the desk clerk for a clean, quiet, room.
   B. I expected James to be lonesome and that he would want to go home.
   C. I have stopped worrying because I have heard nothing further on the subject.
   D. If the board of directors controls the company, they may take actions which are disapproved by the stockholders.

   3.____

4. A. Each of the players knew their place.
   B. He whom you saw on the stage is the son of an actor.
   C. Susan is the smartest of the twin sisters.
   D. Who ever thought of him winning both prizes?

   4.____

5. A. An outstanding trait of early man was their reliance on omens.
   B. Because I had never been there before.
   C. Neither Mr. Jones nor Mr. Smith has completed his work.
   D. While eating my dinner, a dog came to the window.

   5.____

6. A. A copy of the lease, in addition to the Rules and Regulations, are to be given to each tenant.
   B. The Rules and Regulations and a copy of the lease is being given to each tenant.
   C. A copy of the lease, in addition to the Rules and Regulations, is to be given to each tenant.
   D. A copy of the lease, in addition to the Rules and Regulations, are being given to each tenant.

   6.____

7. A. Although we understood that for him music was a passion, we were disturbed by the fact that he was addicted to sing along with the soloists.
    B. Do you believe that Steven is liable to win a scholarship?
    C. Give the picture to whomever is a connoisseur of art.
    D. Whom do you believe to be the most efficient worker in the office?

7.____

8. A. Each adult who is sure they know all the answers will some day realize their mistake.
    B. Even the most hardhearted villain would have to feel bad about so horrible a tragedy.
    C. Neither being licensed teachers, both aspirants had to pass rigorous tests before being appointed.
    D. The principal reason why he wanted to be designated was because he had never before been to a convention.

8.____

9. A. Being that the weather was so inclement, the party has been postponed for at least a month.
    B. He is in New York City only three weeks and he has already seen all the thrilling sights in Manhattan and in the other four boroughs.
    C. If you will look it up in the official directory, which can be consulted in the library during specified hours, you will discover that the chairman and director are Mr. T. Henry Long.
    D. Working hard at college during the day and at the post office during the night, he appeared to his family to be indefatigable.

9.____

10. A. I would have been happy to oblige you if you only asked me to do it.
    B. The cold weather, as well as the unceasing wind and rain, have made us decide to spend the winter in Florida.
    C. The politician would have been more successful in winning office if he would have been less dogmatic.
    D. These trousers are expensive; however, they will wear well.

10.____

11. A. All except him wore formal attire at the reception for the ambassador.
    B. If that chair were to be blown off of the balcony, it might injure someone below.
    C. Not a passenger, who was in the crash, survived the impact.
    D. To borrow money off friends is the best way to lose them.

11.____

12. A. Approaching Manhattan on the ferry boat from Staten Island, an unforgettable sight of the skyscrapers is seen.
    B. Did you see the exhibit of modernistic paintings as yet?
    C. Gesticulating wildly and ranting in stentorian tones, the speaker was the sinecure of all eyes.
    D. The airplane with crew and passengers was lost somewhere in the Pacific Ocean.

12.____

13. A. If one has consistently had that kind of training, it is certainly too late to change your entire method of swimming long distances.
    B. The captain would have been more impressed if you would have been more conscientious in evacuation drills.
    C. The passengers on the stricken ship were all ready to abandon it at the signal.
    D. The villainous shark lashed at the lifeboat with it's tail, trying to upset the rocking boat in order to partake of it's contents.

    13.____

14. A. As one whose been certified as a professional engineer, I believe that the decision to build a bridge over that harbor is unsound.
    B. Between you and me, this project ought to be completed long before winter arrives.
    C. He fervently hoped that the men would be back at camp and to find them busy at their usual chores.
    D. Much to his surprise, he discovered that the climate of Korea was like his home town.

    14.____

15. A. An industrious executive is aided, not impeded, by having a hobby which gives him a fresh point of view on life and its problems.
    B. Frequent absence during the calendar year will surely mitigate against the chances of promotion.
    C. He was unable to go to the committee meeting because he was very ill.
    D. Mr. Brown expressed his disapproval so emphatically that his associates were embarassed

    15.____

16. A. At our next session, the office manager will have told you something about his duties and responsibilities.
    B. In general, the book is absorbing and original and have no hesitation about recommending it.
    C. The procedures followed by private industry in dealing with lateness and absence are different from ours.
    D We shall treat confidentially any information about Mr. Doe, to whom we understand you have sent reports to for many years.

    16.____

17. A. I talked to one official, whom I knew was fully impartial.
    B. Everyone signed the petition but him.
    C. He proved not only to be a good student but also a good athlete.
    D. All are incorrect.

    17.____

18. A. Every year a large amount of tenants are admitted to housing projects.
    B. Henry Ford owned around a billion dollars in industrial equipment.
    C. He was aggravated by the child's poor behavior.
    D. All are incorrect.

    18.____

19. A. Before he was committed to the asylum he suffered from the illusion that he was Napoleon.
    B. Besides stocks, there were also bonds in the safe.
    C. We bet the other team easily.
    D. All are incorrect.

    19.____

20. A. Bring this report to your supervisory.
    B. He set the chair down near the table.
    C. The capitol of New York is Albany.
    D. All are incorrect.

    20.____

21. A. He was chosen to arbitrate the dispute because everyone knew he would be disinterested.
    B. It is advisable to obtain the best council before making an important decision.
    C. Less college students are interested in teaching than ever before.
    D. All are incorrect.

    21.____

22. A. She, hearing a signal, the source lamp flashed.
    B. While hearing a signal, the source lamp flashed.
    C. In hearing a signal, the source lamp flashed.
    D. As she heard a signal, the source lamp flashed.

    22.____

23. A. Every one of the time records have been initialed in the designated spaces.
    B. All of the time records has been initialed in the designated spaces.
    C. Each one of the time records was initialed in the designated spaces.
    D. The time records all been initialed in the designated spaces.

    23.____

24. A. If there is no one else to answer the phone, you will have to answer it.
    B. You will have to answer it yourself if no one else answers the phone.
    C. If no one else is not around to pick up the phone, you will have to do it.
    D. You will have to answer the phone when nobodys here to do it.

    24.____

25. A. Dr. Barnes not in his office. What could I do for you?
    B. Dr. Barnes is not in his office. Is there something I can do for you?
    C. Since Dr. Barnes is not in his office, might there be something I may do for you?
    D. Is there any ways I can assist you since Dr. Barnes is not in his office?

    25.____

26. A. She do not understand how the new console works.
    B. The way the new console works, she doesn't understand.
    C. She doesn't understand how the new console works.
    D. The new console works, so that she doesn't understand.

    26.____

27. A. Certain changes in my family income must be reported as they occur.
    B. When certain changes in family income occur, it must be reported.
    C. Certain family income change must be reported as they occur.
    D. Certain changes in family income must be reported as they have been occurring.

    27.____

28. A. Each tenant has to complete the application themselves. 28._____
    B. Each of the tenants have to complete the application by himself.
    C. Each of the tenants has to complete the application himself.
    D. Each of the tenants has to complete the application by themselves.

29. A. Yours is the only building that the construction will effect. 29._____
    B. Your's is the only building affected by the construction.
    C. The construction will only effect your building.
    D. Yours is the only building that will be affected by the construction.

30. A. There is four tests left. 30._____
    B. The number of tests left are four.
    C. There are four tests left.
    D. Four of the tests remains.

31. A. Each of the applicants takes a test. 31._____
    B. Each of the applicant take a test.
    C. Each of the applicants take tests.
    D. Each of the applicants have taken tests.

32. A. The applicant, not the examiners, are ready. 32._____
    B. The applicants, not the examiners, is ready.
    C. The applicants, not the examiner, are ready.
    D. The applicant, not the examiner, are ready

33. A. You will not progress except you practice. 33._____
    B. You will not progress without you practicing.
    C. You will not progress unless you practice.
    D. You will not progress provided you do not practice.

34. A. Neither the director or the employees will be at the office tomorrow. 34._____
    B. Neither the director nor the employees will be at the office tomorrow.
    C. Neither the director, or the secretary nor the other employees will be at the office tomorrow.
    D. Neither the director, the secretary or the other employees will be at the office tomorrow.

35. A. In my absence, he and her will have to finish the assignment. 35._____
    B. In my absence he and she will have to finish the assignment.
    C. In my absence she and him, they will have to finish the assignment.
    D. In my absence he and her both will have to finish the assignment.

KEY (CORRECT ANSWERS)

1.	B	11.	A	21.	A	31.	A
2.	B	12.	D	22.	D	32.	C
3.	C	13.	C	23.	C	33.	C
4.	B	14.	B	24.	A	34.	B
5.	C	15.	A	25.	B	35.	B
6.	C	16.	C	26.	C		
7.	D	17.	B	27.	A		
8.	B	18.	D	28.	C		
9.	D	19.	B	29.	D		
10.	D	20.	B	30.	C		

TEST 2

DIRECTIONS: Each question or incomplete statement is followed by several suggested answers or completions. Select the one that BEST answers the question or completes the statement. *PRINT THE LETTER OF THE CORRECT ANSWER IN THE SPACE AT THE RIGHT.*

Questions 1-4.

DIRECTIONS: Questions 1 through 4 consist of three sentences each. For each question, select the sentence which contains NO error in grammar or usage.

1. A. Be sure that everybody brings his notes to the conference.
   B. He looked like he meant to hit the boy.
   C. Mr. Jones is one of the clients who was chosen to represent the district.
   D. All are incorrect.

2. A. He is taller than I.
   B. I'll have nothing to do with these kind of people.
   C. The reason why he will not buy the house is because it is too expensive.
   D. All are incorrect.

3. A. Aren't I eligible for this apartment.
   B. Have you seen him anywheres?
   C. He should of come earlier.
   D. All are incorrect.

4. A. He graduated college in 2022.
   B. He hadn't but one more line to write.
   C. Who do you think is the author of this report?
   D. All are incorrect.

Questions 5-35.

DIRECTIONS: In each of the following questions, only one of the four sentences conforms to standards of correct usage. The other three contain errors in grammar, diction, or punctuation. Select the choice in each question which BEST conforms to standards of correct usage. Consider a choice correct if it contains none of the errors mentioned above, even though there may be other ways of expressing the same thought.

5. A. It is obvious that no one wants to be a kill-joy if they can help it.
   B. It is not always possible, and perhaps it never ispossible, to judge a person's character by just looking at him.
   C. When Yogi Berra of the New York Yankees hit an immortal grandslam home run, everybody in the huge stadium including Pittsburgh fans, rose to his feet.
   D. Every one of us students must pay tuition today.

6. A. The physician told the young mother that if the baby is not able to digest its milk, it should be boiled.
    B. There is no doubt whatsoever that he felt deeply hurt because John Smith had betrayed the trust.
    C. Having partaken of a most delicious repast prepared by Tessie Breen, the hostess, the horses were driven home immediately thereafter.
    D. The attorney asked my wife and myself several questions.

7. A. Despite all denials, there is no doubt in my mind that
    B. At this time everyone must deprecate the demogogic attack made by one of our Senators on one of our most revered statesmen.
    C. In the first game of a crucial two-game series, Ted Williams, got two singles, both of them driving in a run.
    D. Our visitor brought good news to John and I.

8. A. If he would have told me, I should have been glad to help him in his dire financial emergency.
    B. Newspaper men have often asserted that diplomats or so-called official spokesmen sometimes employ equivocation in attempts to deceive.
    C. I think someones coming to collect money for the Red Cross.
    D. In a masterly summation, the young attorney expressed his belief that the facts clearly militate against this opinion.

9. A. We have seen most all the exhibits.
    B. Without in the least underestimating your advice, in my opinion the situation has grown immeasurably worse in the past few days.
    C. I wrote to the box office treasurer of the hit show that a pair of orchestra seats would be preferable.
    D. As the grim story of Pearl Harbor was broadcast on that fateful December 7, it was the general opinion that war was inevitable.

10. A. Without a moment's hesitation, Casey Stengel said that Larry Berra works harder than any player on the team.
    B. There is ample evidence to indicate that many animals can run faster than any human being.
    C. No one saw the accident but I.
    D. Example of courage is the heroic defense put up by the paratroopers against overwhelming odds.

11. A. If you prefer these kind, Mrs. Grey, we shall be more than willing to let you have them reasonably.
    B. If you like these here, Mrs. Grey, we shall be more than willing to let you have them reasonably.
    C. If you like these, Mrs. Grey, we shall be more than willing to let you have them.
    D. Who shall we appoint?

12. A. The number of errors are greater in speech than in writing.
    B. The doctor rather than the nurse was to blame for his being neglected.
    C. Because the demand for these books have been so great, we reduced the price.
    D. John Galsworthy, the English novelist, could not have survived a serious illness; had it not been for loving care.

    12.____

13. A. Our activities this year have seldom ever been as interesting as they have been this month.
    B. Our activities this month have been more interesting, or at least as interesting as those of any month this year.
    C. Our activities this month has been more interesting than those of any other month this year.
    D. Neither Jean nor her sister was at home.

    13.____

14. A. George B. Shaw's view of common morality, as well as his wit sparkling with a dash of perverse humor here and there, have led critics to term him "The Incurable Rebel."
    B. The President's program was not always received with the wholehearted endorsement of his own party, which is why the party faces difficulty in drawing up a platform for the coming election.
    C. The reason why they wanted to travel was because they had never been away from home.
    D. Facing a barrage of cameras, the visiting celebrity found it extremely difficult to express his opinions clearly.

    14.____

15. A. When we calmed down, we all agreed that our anger had been kind of unnecessary and had not helped the situation.
    B. Without him going into all the details, he made us realize the horror of the accident.
    C. Like one girl, for example, who applied for two positions.
    D. Do not think that you have to be so talented as he is in order to play in the school orchestra.

    15.____

16. A. He looked very peculiarly to me.
    B. He certainly looked at me peculiar.
    C. Due to the train's being late, we had to wait an hour.
    D. The reason for the poor attendance is that it is raining.

    16.____

17. A. About one out of four own an automobile.
    B. The collapse of the old Mitchell Bridge was caused by defective construction in the central pier.
    C. Brooks Atkinson was well acquainted with the best literature, thus helping him to become an able critic.
    D. He has to stand still until the relief man comes up, thus giving him no chance to move about and keep warm.

    17.____

18. A. He is sensitive to confusion and withdraws from people whom he feels are too noisy.
    B. Do you know whether the data is statistically correct?
    C. Neither the mayor or the aldermen are to blame.
    D. Of those who were graduated from high school, a goodly percentage went to college.

    18.____

19. A. Acting on orders, the offices were searched by a designated committee.
    B. The answer probably is nothing.
    C. I thought it to be all right to excuse them from class.
    D. I think that he is as successful a singer, if not more successful, than Mary.

    19.____

20. A. $360,000 is really very little to pay for such a wellbuilt house.
    B. The creatures looked like they had come from outer space.
    C. It was her, he knew!
    D. Nobody but me knows what to do.

    20.____

21. A. Mrs. Smith looked good in her new suit.
    B. New York may be compared with Chicago.
    C. I will not go to the meeting except you go with me.
    D. I agree with this editorial.

    21.____

22. A. My opinions are different from his.
    B. There will be less students in class now.
    C. Helen was real glad to find her watch.
    D. It had been pushed off of her dresser.

    22.____

23. A. Almost everyone, who has been to California, returns with glowing reports.
    B. George Washington, John Adams, and Thomas Jefferson, were our first presidents.
    C. Mr. Walters, whom we met at the bank yesterday, is the man, who gave me my first job.
    D. One should study his lessons as carefully as he can.

    23.____

24. A. We had such a good time yesterday.
    B. When the bell rang, the boys and girls went in the schoolhouse.
    C. John had the worst headache when he got up this morning.
    D. Today's assignment is somewhat longer than yesterday's.

    24.____

25. A. Neither the mayor nor the city clerk are willing to talk.
    B. Neither the mayor nor the city clerk is willing to talk.
    C. Neither the mayor or the city clerk are willing to talk.
    D Neither the mayor or the city clerk is willing to talk.

    25.____

26. A. Being that he is that kind of boy, cooperation cannot be expected.
    B. He interviewed people who he thought had something to say.
    C. Stop whomever enters the building regardless of rank or office held.
    D. Passing through the countryside, the scenery pleased us.

    26.____

27. A. The childrens' shoes were in their closet.
    B. The children's shoes were in their closet.
    C. The childs' shoes were in their closet.
    D. The childs' shoes were in his closet.

28. A. An agreement was reached between the defendant, the plaintiff, the plaintiff's attorney and the insurance company as to the amount of the settlement.
    B. Everybody was asked to give their versions of the accident.
    C. The consensus of opinion was that the evidence was inconclusive.
    D. The witness stated that if he was rich, he wouldn't have had to loan the money.

29. A. Before beginning the investigation, all the materials related to the case were carefully assembled.
    B. The reason for his inability to keep the appointment is because of his injury in the accident.
    C. This here evidence tends to support the claim of the defendant.
    D. We interviewed all the witnesses who, according to the driver, were still in town.

30. A. Each claimant was allowed the full amount of their medical expenses.
    B. Either of the three witnesses is available.
    C. Every one of the witnesses was asked to tell his story.
    D. Neither of the witnesses are right.

31. A. The commissioner, as well as his deputy and various bureau heads, were present.
    B. A new organization of employers and employees have been formed.
    C. One or the other of these men have been selected.
    D. The number of pages in the book is enough to discourage a reader.

32. A. Between you and me, I think he is the better man.
    B. He was believed to be me.
    C. Is it us that you wish to see?
    D. The winners are him and her.

33. A. Beside the statement to the police, the witness spoke to no one.
    B. He made no statement other than to the police and I.
    C. He made no statement to any one else, aside from the police.
    D. The witness spoke to no one but me.

34. A. The claimant has no one to blame but himself.
    B. The boss sent us, he and I, to deliver the packages.
    C. The lights come from mine and not his car.
    D. There was room on the stairs for him and myself.

35. A. Admission to this clinic is limited to patients' inability to pay for medical care.
    B. Patients who can pay little or nothing for medical care are treated in this clinic.
    C. The patient's ability to pay for medical care is the determining factor in his admission to this clinic.
    D. This clinic is for the patient's that cannot afford to pay or that can pay a little for medical care.

35.____

KEY (CORRECT ANSWERS)

1.	A	11.	C	21.	A	31.	D
2.	A	12.	B	22.	A	32.	A
3.	D	13.	D	23.	D	33.	D
4.	C	14.	D	24.	D	34.	A
5.	D	15.	D	25.	B	35.	B
6.	D	16.	D	26.	B		
7.	B	17.	B	27.	B		
8.	B	18.	D	28.	C		
9.	D	19.	B	29.	D		
10.	B	20.	D	30.	C		

READING COMPREHENSION
UNDERSTANDING AND INTERPRETING WRITTEN MATERIAL
EXAMINATION SECTION
TEST 1

DIRECTIONS: Each question or incomplete statement is followed by several suggested answers or completions. Select the one that BEST answers the question or completes the statement. *PRINT THE LETTER OF THE CORRECT ANSWER IN THE SPACE AT THE RIGHT.*

Questions 1-3.

DIRECTIONS: Questions 1 through 3 are to be answered SOLELY on the basis of the following paragraph.

The aging housing inventory presents a broad spectrum of conditions, from good upkeep to unbelievable deterioration. Buildings, even relatively good buildings, are likely to have numerous minor violations rather than the gross and evident sanitary violations of an earlier age. Except for the serious violations in a relatively small number of slum buildings, the task is to deal with masses of minor violations that, though insignificant in themselves, amount in the aggregate to major deprivations of health and comfort to tenants. Caused by wear and tear, by the abrasions of time, and aggravated by neglect, these conditions do not readily yield to the dramatic *vacate and restore* measures of earlier times. Moreover, the lines between *good* and *bad* housing have become blurred in many parts of our cities; we find a range of *shades of gray* blending into each other. Different kinds of code enforcement efforts may be required to deal with different degrees of deterioration.

1. The above passage suggests that code enforcement efforts may have to be

   A. developed to cope with varying levels of housing dilapidation
   B. aimed primarily at the serious violations in slum buildings
   C. modeled on the *vacate and restore* measures of earlier times
   D. modified to reduce unrealistic penalties for petty violations

   1.____

2. According to the above passage, during former times some buildings had sanitary violations which were

   A. irreparable and minor
   B. blurred and gray
   C. flagrant and obvious
   D. insignificant and numerous

   2.____

3. According to the above passage, the aging housing stock presents a

   A. great number of rent-controlled buildings
   B. serious problem of tenant-caused deterioration
   C. significant increase in buildings without intentional violations
   D. wide range of physical conditions

   3.____

Questions 4-5.

DIRECTIONS: Questions 4 and 5 are to be answered SOLELY on the basis of the following passage.

In general, housing code provisions relating to the safe and sanitary maintenance of dwelling units prescribe the maintenance required for foundations, walls, ceilings, floors, windows, doors, stairways, and also the facilities and equipment required in other sections. The more recent codes have, in addition, extensive provisions designed to ensure that the unit be maintained in a rat-free and rat-proof condition. Also, as an example of new approaches in code provisions, one proposed Federal model housing code prohibits the landlord from terminating vital services and utilities except during temporary emergencies or when actual repairs or maintenance are in process. This provision may be used to prevent a landlord from turning off utility services as a technique of self-help eviction or as a weapon against rent strikes.

4. According to the above passage, the more recent housing codes have extensive provisions designed to

   A. maintain a reasonably fire-proof living unit
   B. prohibit tenants from participating in rent strikes
   C. maintain the unit free from rats
   D. prohibit tenants from using lead-based paints

4.____

5. According to the above passage, one housing code would permit landlords to terminate vital services during

   A. a rent strike
   B. an actual eviction
   C. a temporary emergency
   D. the planning of repairs and maintenance

5.____

Questions 6-8.

DIRECTIONS: Questions 6 through 8 are to be answered SOLELY on the basis of the following passage.

City governments have long had building codes which set minimum standards for building and for human occupancy. The code (or series of codes) makes provisions for standards of lighting and ventilation, sanitation, fire prevention, and protection. As a result of demands from manufacturers, builders, real estate people, tenement owners, and building-trades unions, these codes often have established minimum standards well below those that the contemporary society would accept as a rock-bottom minimum. Codes often become outdated so that meager standards in one era become seriously inadequate a few decades later as society"s concept of a minimum standard of living changes. Out-of-date codes, when still in use, have sometimes prevented the introduction of new devices and modern building techniques. Thus, it is extremely important that building codes keep pace with changes in the accepted concept of a minimum standard of living.

6. According to the above passage, all of the following considerations in building planning would probably be covered in a building code EXCEPT

   A. closet space as a percentage of total floor area
   B. size and number of windows required for rooms of differing sizes
   C. placement of fire escapes in each line of apartments
   D. type of garbage disposal units to be installed

7. According to the above passage, if an ideal building code were to be created, how would the established minimum standards in it compare to the ones that are presently set by city governments?
   They would

   A. be lower than they are at present
   B. be higher than they are at present
   C. be comparable to the present minimum standards
   D. vary according to the economic group that sets them

8. On the basis of the above passage, what is the reason for difficulties in introducing new building techniques?

   A. Builders prefer techniques which represent the rock-bottom minimum desired by society.
   B. Certain manufacturers have obtained patents on various building methods to the exclusion of new techniques.
   C. The government does not want to invest money in techniques that will soon be outdated.
   D. New techniques are not provided for in building codes which are not up-to-date.

Questions 9-11.

DIRECTIONS: Questions 9 through 11 are to be answered SOLELY on the basis of the following paragraph.

When constructed within a multiple dwelling, such storage space shall be equipped with a sprinkler system and also with a system of mechanical ventilation in no way connected with any other ventilating system. Such storage space shall have no opening into any other part of the dwelling except through a fireproof vestibule. Any such vestibule shall have a minimum superficial floor area of fifty square feet, and its maximum area shall not exceed seventy-five square feet. It shall be enclosed with incombustible partitions having a fire-resistive rating of three hours. The floor and ceiling of such vestibule shall also be of incombustible material having a fire-resistive rating of at least three hours. There shall be two doors to provide access from the dwelling to the car storage space. Each such door shall have a fire-resistive rating of one and one-half hours and shall be provided with a device to prevent the opening of one door until the other door is entirely closed.

9. According to the above paragraph, the one of the following that is REQUIRED in order for cars to be permitted to be stored in a multiple dwelling is a(n)

   A. fireproof vestibule
   B. elevator from the garage
   C. approved heating system
   D. sprinkler system

10. According to the above paragraph, the one of the following materials that would NOT be acceptable for the walls of a vestibule connecting a garage to the dwelling portion of a building is   10._____

    A. 3" solid gypsum blocks
    B. 4" brick
    C. 4" hollow gypsum blocks, plastered both sides
    D. 6" solid cinder concrete blocks

11. According to the above paragraph, the one of the following that would be ACCEPTABLE for the width and length of a vestibule connecting a garage that is within a multiple dwelling to the dwelling portion of the building is   11._____

    A. 3'8" x 13'0"   B. 4'6" x 18'6"
    C. 4'9" x 14'6"   D. 4'3" x 19'3"

Questions 12-13.

DIRECTIONS: Questions 12 and 13 are to be answered SOLELY on the basis of the following paragraph.

It shall be unlawful to place, use, or maintain in a condition intended, arranged, or designed for use, any gas-fired cooking appliance, laundry stove, heating stove, range or water heater or combination of such appliances in any room or space used for living or sleeping in any new or existing multiple dwelling unless such room or space has a window opening to the outer air or such gas appliance is vented to the outer air. All automatically operated gas appliances shall be equipped with a device which shall shut off automatically the gas supply to the main burners when the pilot light in such appliance is extinguished. A gas range or the cooking portion of a gas appliance incorporating a room heater shall not be deemed an automatically operated gas appliance. However, burners in gas ovens and broilers which can be turned on and off or ignited by non-manual means shall be equipped with a device which shall shut off automatically the gas supply to those burners when the operation of such non-manual means fails.

12. According to the above paragraph, an automatic shut-off device is NOT required on a gas   12._____

    A. hot water heater   B. laundry dryer
    C. space heater   D. range

13. According to the above paragraph, a gas-fired water heater is permitted   13._____

    A. only in kitchens   B. only in bathrooms
    C. only in living rooms   D. in any type of room

Questions 14-18.

DIRECTIONS: Questions 14 through 18 are to be answered SOLELY on the basis of the information contained in the statement below.

No multiple dwelling shall be erected to a height in excess of one and one-half times the width of the widest street on which it faces, except that above the level of such height, for each one foot that the front wall of such dwelling sets back from the street line, three feet shall be added to the height limit of such dwelling, but such dwelling shall not exceed in maximum height three feet plus one and three-quarter times the width of the widest street on which it faces.

Any such dwelling facing a street more than one hundred feet in width shall be subject to the same height limitations as though such dwelling faced a street one hundred feet in width.

14. The MAXIMUM height of a multiple dwelling set back five feet from the street line and facing a 60 foot wide street is ___ feet.

    A. 60   B. 90   C. 105   D. 165

15. The MAXIMUM height of a multiple dwelling set back six feet from the street line and facing a 120 foot wide street is ___ feet.

    A. 198   B. 168   C. 120   D. 105

16. The MAXIMUM height of a multiple dwelling is

    A. 100 ft. B. 150 ft. C. 178 ft. D. unlimited

17. The MAXIMUM height of a multiple dwelling set back 10 feet from the street line and facing a 110 foot wide street is ___ feet.

    A. 178   B. 180   C. 195   D. 205

18. The MAXIMUM height of a multiple dwelling set back eight feet from the street line and facing a 90 foot wide street is ___ feet.

    A. 135   B. 147   C. 178   D. 159

Questions 19-23.

DIRECTIONS: Questions 19 through 23 are to be answered SOLELY on the basis of the following statement.

The number of persons accommodated on any story in a lodging house shall not be greater than the sum of the following components,

    a. 22 persons for each full multiple of 22 inches in the smallest clear width for each means of egress approved by the department, other than fire escapes
    b. 20 persons for each lawful fire escape accessible from such story.

19. The MAXIMUM number of persons that may be accommodated on a story in a lodging house depends on the

    A. number of lawful fire escapes *only*
    B. number of approved means of egress *only*
    C. smallest clear width in each approved means of egress *only*
    D. number of lawful fire escapes and sum total of smallest clear widths in each approved means of egress

20. The MAXIMUM number of persons that may be accommodated on a story of a lodging house having one lawful fire escape and a sum total of 44 inches in the smallest clear widths of the two approved means of egress is

    A. 20   B. 22   C. 42   D. 64

21. The MAXIMUM number of persons that may be accommodated on a story of a lodging house having two lawful fire escapes and a sum total of 60 inches in the smallest clear width of the approved means of egress is

    A. 64   B. 84   C. 100   D. 106

21.____

22. The MAXIMUM number of persons that may be accommodated on a story of a lodging house having one lawful fire escape and a sum total of 33 inches in the smallest clear width of the approved means of egress is

    A. 42   B. 53   C. 64   D. 73

22.____

23. The MAXIMUM number of persons that may be accommodated on a story of a lodging house having two lawful fire escapes and two approved means of egress, with 40 inches and 44 inches in the smallest clear widths, respectively, is

    A. 84   B. 104   C. 106   D. 108

23.____

Questions 24-25.

DIRECTIONS: Questions 24 and 25 are to be answered SOLELY on the basis of the following paragraph.

Though the recent trend toward apartment construction may appear to be the Region's response to large-lot zoning and centralized industry, it really is not. It is mainly a function of the age of the population. Most of the apartments are occupied by one- and two-person families young people out of school but without a family of their own and older people whose children have grown. Both groups have been increasing in number; and, in this Region, they characteristically live in apartments. It is this increased demand for apartments and the simultaneous decrease in demand for one-family houses that dramatically raised the percentage of building permits issued for multi-family housing units from 36 percent in 1977 to 67 percent in 1981. The fact that three-fourths of the apartments were built in the Core between 1977 and 1981 at the same time as the Core was losing population underscores the failure of the apartment boom to slow the outward spread of the population.

24. According to the above paragraph, one of the reasons for the increase in the number of building permits issued for multi-family construction in the City Metropolitan Region is

    A. that workers in industry want to live close to their jobs
    B. an increase in the number of elderly people living in the Region
    C. the inability of many families to afford the large lots necessary to build private homes
    D. the new zoning ordinance made it easier to build apartments

24.____

25. According to the above paragraph, the apartment construction boom

    A. increased the population density in the Core
    B. spurred a population shift to the suburbs
    C. did not halt the outward flow of the population from the Core
    D. was most significant in the outer areas of the Region

25.____

KEY (CORRECT ANSWERS)

1. A
2. C
3. D
4. C
5. C

6. A
7. B
8. D
9. D
10. B

11. C
12. D
13. D
14. C
15. B

16. C
17. A
18. D
19. D
20. D

21. B
22. A
23. C
24. B
25. C

TEST 2

DIRECTIONS: Each question or incomplete statement is followed by several suggested answers or completions. Select the one that BEST answers the question or completes the statement. *PRINT THE LETTER OF THE CORRECT ANSWER IN THE SPACE AT THE RIGHT.*

Questions 1-4.

DIRECTIONS: Questions 1 through 4 are to be answered SOLELY on the basis of the following paragraph.

Although the suburbs have provided housing and employment for millions of additional families since 1950, many suburban communities have maintained controls over the kinds of families who can live in them. Suburban attitudes have been formed by reaction against a perception of crowded, harassed city life and threatening alien city people. As population, taxable income, and jobs have left the cities for the suburbs, the *urban crisis* of substandard housing, declining levels of education and public services, and decreasing employment opportunities has been created. The crisis, however, is not urban at all, but national, and in part a result of the suburban policy that discourages outward movement by the urban poor.

1. According to the above paragraph, the quality of urban life

    A. is determined by public opinion in the cities
    B. has worsened in recent years
    C. is similar to rural life
    D. can be changed by political means

2. According to the above paragraph, suburban communities have

    A. tried to show that the urban crisis is really a national crisis
    B. avoided taking a position on the urban crisis
    C. been involved in causing the urban crisis
    D. been the innocent victims of the urban crisis

3. According to the above paragraph, the poor have

    A. become increasingly sophisticated in their attempts to move to the suburbs
    B. generally been excluded from the suburbs
    C. lost incentive for betterment of their living conditions
    D. sought improvement of the central cities

4. As used in the above paragraph, the word perception means MOST NEARLY

    A. development   B. impression
    C. opposition   D. uncertainty

Questions 5-8.

DIRECTIONS: Questions 5 through 8 are to be answered SOLELY on the basis of the following paragraph.

The concentration of publicly assisted housing in central cities -- because the suburbs do not want them and effectively bar them -- is usually rationalized by a solicitous regard for keeping intact the city neighborhoods cherished by low-income groups. If one accepted this as valid, the devotion of minorities to blighted city neighborhoods in preference to suburban employment and housing would be an historic first. Certainly no such devotion was visible among the millions who have deserted their city neighborhoods in the last 25 years even if it meant an arduous daily trip from the suburbs to their jobs in the cities.

5. The writer implies that MOST poor people

   A. prefer isolation
   B. fear change
   C. are angry
   D. seek betterment

6. The general tone of the paragraph is BEST characterized as

   A. uncertain   B. skeptical   C. evasive   D. indifferent

7. As used in the above paragraph, the word rationalize means MOST NEARLY

   A. dispute   B. justify   C. deny   D. locate

8. According to the above paragraph, publicly assisted housing is concentrated in the central cities PRIMARILY because

   A. city dwellers are unable to find satisfactory housing
   B. deterioration of older housing has increased in recent years
   C. suburbanites have opposed the movement of the poor to the suburbs
   D. employment opportunities have decreased in the suburbs

Questions 9-11.

DIRECTIONS: Questions 9 through 11 are to be answered SOLELY on the basis of the following paragraph.

In recent years, new and important emphasis has been placed upon the maximum use of conservation and rehabilitation techniques in carrying out programs of urban renewal and revitalization. In urban renewal projects where existing structures are hopelessly deteriorated or land uses are incompatible with the community's overall plans, the entire area may be acquired, cleared, and sold for redevelopment. However, where existing structures are basically sound but have deteriorated to the point where they are a blighting influence on the neighborhood, they may be salvaged through a program of rehabilitation and reconditioning.

9. According to the above paragraph, the one of the following which is MOST likely to cause area-wide razing of the buildings in urban renewal programs is

   A. a program of rehabilitation and reconditioning
   B. concerted insistence by landlords and tenants that certain buildings be bulldozed
   C. an inability of community groups to agree on priorities for staged clearance
   D. land use contrary to the community's general plan

10. According to the above paragraph, rehabilitation of structures may take place if

    A. new conservation and rehabilitation techniques are used
    B. salvaging all the buildings in the entire area is hopeless
    C. the community wishes to preserve historic structures
    D. the existing buildings are structurally sound

11. As used in the above paragraph, the word <u>blighting</u> means MOST NEARLY   11._____

    A. ruining   B. infrequent   C. recurrent   D. traditional

Questions 12-13.

DIRECTIONS: Questions 12 and 13 are to be answered SOLELY on the basis of the following paragraphs.

We must also find better ways to handle the relocation of people uprooted by projects. In the past, many renewal plans have foundered on this problem, and it is still the most difficult part of the community development. Large-scale replacement of low-income residents -- many ineligible for public housing -- has contributed to deterioration of surrounding communities. However, thanks to changes in housing authority procedures, relocation has been accomplished in a far more satisfactory fashion. The step-by-step community development projects we advocate in this plan should bring further improvement.

But additional measures will be necessary. There are going to be more people to be moved; and, with the current shortage of apartments, large ones especially, it is going to be tougher to find places to move them to. The city should have more freedom to buy or lease housing that comes on the market because of normal turnover and make it available to relocatees.

12. According to the above paragraphs, one of the reasons a neighborhood may deteriorate is that   12._____

    A. there is a scarcity of large apartments
    B. step-by-step community development projects have failed
    C. people in the given neighborhood are uprooted from their homes
    D. a nearby renewal project has an inadequate relocation plan

13. From the above paragraphs, one might conclude that the relocation phase of community renewal has been improved.   13._____

    A. by changes in housing authority procedures
    B. by development of step-by-step community development projects
    C. through expanded city powers to buy housing for relocation
    D. by the addition of huge sums of money

Questions 14-15.

DIRECTIONS: Questions 14 and 15 are to be answered SOLELY on the basis of the following paragraphs.

Provision of decent housing for the lower half of the population (by income) was thus taken on as a public responsibility. Public housing was to assist the poorest quarter of urban families while the 221(d)(3) Housing Program would assist the next quarter. But limited funds meant that the supply of subsidized housing could not stretch nearly far enough to help this half of the population. Who were to be left out in the rationing process which was accomplished by the sifting of applicants for housing on the part of public and private authorities?

Discrimination on the grounds of race or color is not allowed under Federal law. In all sections of the country, encouragingly, housing programs are found which follow this law to the letter. Yet, housing programs in some cities still suffer from the residue of racial segregation policies and attitudes that for years were condoned or even encouraged.

Some sifting in the 221(d)(3) Housing Program follows the practice of many public housing authorities, the imposition of requirements with respect to character. This is a delicate matter. To fill a project overwhelmingly with broken families, alcoholics, criminals, delinquents, and other problem tenants would hardly make it a wholesome environment. Yet the total exclusion of such families is hardly an acceptable alternative. To the extent this exclusion is practiced, the very people whose lives are described in order to persuade lawmakers and the public to instigate new programs find the door shut in their faces when such programs come into being. The proper balance is difficult to achieve, but society's neediest families surely should not be totally denied the opportunities for rejuvenation in subsidized housing.

14. From the above paragraphs, it can be assumed that the 221(d)(3) Housing Program

   A. served a population earning more than the median income
   B. served a less affluent population than is served by public housing
   C. excludes all problem families from its projects
   D. is a subsidized housing program

14.____

15. According to this text, the provision of housing for the poor

   A. has not been completely accomplished with public monies
   B. is never influenced by segregationist policies
   C. is limited to providing housing for only the neediest families
   D. is primarily the responsibility of the Federal government

15.____

16. Five hundred persons attended a public hearing at which a proposed public housing project was being considered. Less than half favored the project while the majority opposed the project.
   According to the above statement, it is REASONABLE to conclude that

   A. the proposal stimulated considerable community interest
   B. the public housing project was disapproved by the city because a majority opposed it
   C. those who opposed the project lacked sympathy for needy persons
   D. the supporters of the project were led by militants

16.____

17. A vacant lot close to a polluted creek is for sale. Two buyers compete. One owns an adjacent factory which provides 300 high paying unskilled jobs. He needs to expand or move from the city. If he expands, he will provide 300 additional jobs. The other is a community group in a changing residential area close by. They hope to stabilize the neighborhood by bringing in new housing. They would build an apartment building with 100 dwelling units on the lot.
   According to the above paragraph, it is REASONABLE to conclude that

   A. jobs are more important than housing
   B. there is conflict between the factory owners and the neighborhood group
   C. the neighborhood group will not succeed in stabilizing the area by constructing new housing
   D. the polluted creek should be cleaned up

17.____

18. The housing authority faces every problem of the private developer, and it must also assume responsibilities of which private building is free. The authority must account to the community; it must conform to federal regulations; it must provide durable buildings of good standard at low cost; it must overcome the prejudices against public operations, of contractors, bankers, and prospective tenants. These authorities are being watched by anti-housing enthusiasts for the first error of judgment or the first evidence of high costs, to be torn to bits before a Congressional committee.
On the basis of this statement, it would be MOST correct to state that

   A. private builders do not have the opposition of contractors, bankers, and prospective tenants
   B. Congressional committees impede the progress of public housing by petty investigations
   C. a housing authority must deal with all the difficulties encountered by the private builder
   D. housing authorities are no more immune from errors in judgment than private developers

19. Another factor that has considerably added to the city's housing crisis has been the great influx of low-income workers and their families seeking better employment opportunities during wartime and defense boom periods. The circumstances of these families have forced them to crowd into the worst kind of housing and have produced on a renewed scale the conditions from which slums flourish and grow.
On the basis of this statement, one would be justified in stating that

   A. the influx of low-income workers has aggravated the slum problem
   B. the city has better employment opportunities than other sections of the country
   C. the high wages paid by our defense industries have made many families ineligible for tenancy in public housing projects
   D. the families who settled in the city during wartime and the defense build-up brought with them language and social customs conducive to the growth of slums

20. Much of the city felt the effects of the general postwar increase of vandalism and street crime, and the greatly expanded public housing program was no exception. Projects built in congested slum areas with a high incidence of delinquency and crime were particularly subjected to the depredations of neighborhood gangs. The civil service watchmen who patrolled the projects, unarmed and neither trained nor expected to perform police duties, were unable to cope with the situation.
On the basis of this statement, the MOST accurate of the following statements is:

   A. Neighborhood gangs were particularly responsible for the high incidence of delinquency and crime in congested slum areas having public housing programs
   B. Civil service watchmen who patrolled housing projects failed to carry out their assigned police duties
   C. Housing projects were not spared the effects of the general postwar increase of vandalism and street crime
   D. Delinquency and crime affected housing projects in slum areas to a greater extent than other dwellings in the same area

21. Another peculiar characteristic of real estate is the absence of liquidity. Each parcel is a 21.____
discrete unit as to size, location, rental, physical condition, and financing arrangements.
Each property requires investigation, comparison of rents with other properties, and individualized haggling on price and terms.
On the basis of this statement, the LEAST accurate of the following statements is:

    A. Although the size, location, and rent of parcels vary, comparison with rents of other properties affords an indication of the value of a particular parcel
    B. Bargaining skill is the essential factor in determining the value of a parcel of real estate
    C. Each parcel of real estate has individual peculiarities distinguishing it from any other parcel
    D. Real estate is not easily converted to other types of assets

22. In part, at least, the charges of sameness, monotony, and institutionalism directed at 22.____
public housing projects result from the degree in which they differ from the city's normal housing pattern. They seem alike because their very difference from the usual makes them stand apart.
In many respects, there is considerably more variety between public housing projects than there is between different streets of apartment houses or tenements throughout the city.
On the basis of this statement, it would be LEAST accurate to state that:

    A. There is considerably more variety between public housing projects than there is between different streets of tenements throughout the city
    B. Public housing projects differ from the city's normal housing pattern to the degree that sameness, monotony, and institutionalism are characteristic of public buildings
    C. Public housing projects seem alike because their deviation from the usual dwellings draws attention to them
    D. The variety in structure between public housing projects and other public buildings is related to the period in which they were built

23. The amount of debt that can be charged against the city for public housing is limited by 23.____
law. Part of the city's restricted housing means goes for cash subsidies it may be required to contribute to state-aided projects. Under the provisions of the state law, the city must match the state's contributions in subsidies; and while the value of the partial tax exemption granted by the city is counted for this purpose, it is not always sufficient.
On the basis of this statement, it would be MOST accurate to state that:

    A. The amount of money the city may spend for public housing is limited by annual tax revenues
    B. The value of tax exemptions granted by the city to educational, religious, and charitable institutions may be added to its subsidy contributions to public housing projects
    C. The subsidy contributions for state-aided public housing projects are shared equally by the state and the city under the provisions of the state law
    D. The tax revenues of the city, unless supplemented by state aid, are insufficient to finance public housing projects

24. Maintenance costs can be minimized and the useful life of houses can be extended by building with the best and most permanent materials available. The best and most permanent materials in many cases are, however, much more expensive than materials which require more maintenance. The most economical procedure in home building has been to compromise between the capital costs of high quality and enduring materials and the maintenance costs of less desirable materials.
On the basis of this statement, one would be justified in stating that:

    A. Savings in maintenance costs make the use of less durable and less expensive building materials preferable to high quality materials that would prolong the useful life of houses constructed from them
    B. Financial advantage can be secured by the home builder if he judiciously combines costly but enduring building materials with less desirable materials which, however, require more maintenance
    C. A compromise between the capital costs of high quality materials and the maintenance costs of less desirable materials makes it easier for a home builder to estimate construction expenditures
    D. The most economical procedure in home building is to balance the capital costs of the most permanent materials against the costs of less expensive materials that are cheaper to maintain

25. Personnel selection has been a critical problem for local housing authorities. The pool of qualified workers trained in housing procedures is small, and the colleges and universities have failed to grasp the opportunity for enlarging it. While real estate experience makes a good background for management of a housing project, many real estate men are deplorably lacking in understanding of social and governmental problems. Social workers, on the other hand, are likely to be deficient in business judgment.
On the basis of this statement, it would be MOST accurate to state that:

    A. Colleges and universities have failed to train qualified workers for proficiency in housing procedures
    B. Social workers are deficient in business judgment as related to the management of a housing project
    C. Real estate experience makes a person a good manager of a housing project
    D. Local housing authorities have been critical of present methods of personnel selection

KEY (CORRECT ANSWERS)

1.	B	11.	A
2.	C	12.	D
3.	B	13.	A
4.	B	14.	D
5.	D	15.	A
6.	B	16.	A
7.	B	17.	B
8.	D	18.	C
9.	D	19.	A
10.	D	20.	C

21. B
22. B
23. C
24. B
25. A

PHILOSOPHY, PRINCIPLES, PRACTICES, AND TECHNICS OF SUPERVISION, ADMINISTRATION, MANAGEMENT, AND ORGANIZATION

TABLE OF CONTENTS

	Page
MEANING OF SUPERVISION	1
THE OLD AND THE NEW SUPERVISION	1
THE EIGHT (8) BASIC PRINCIPLES OF THE NEW SUPERVISION	1
I. Principle of Responsibility	1
II. Principle of Authority	2
III. Principle of Self-Growth	2
IV. Principle of Individual Worth	2
V. Principle of Creative Leadership	2
VI. Principle of Success and Failure	2
VII. Principle of Science	3
VIII. Principle of Cooperation	3
WHAT IS ADMINISTRATION?	3
I. Practices Commonly Classed as "Supervisory"	3
II. Practices Commonly Classed as "Administrative"	3
III. Practices Commonly Classed as Both "Supervisory" and "Administrative"	4
RESPONSIBILITIES OF THE SUPERVISOR	4
COMPETENCIES OF THE SUPERVISOR	4
THE PROFESSIONAL SUPERVISOR-EMPLOYEE RELATIONSHIP	4
MINI-TEXT IN SUPERVISION, ADMINISTRATION, MANAGEMENT, AND ORGANIZATION	5
I. Brief Highlights	5
A. Levels of Management	6
B. What the Supervisor Must Learn	6
C. A Definition of Supervision	6
D. Elements of the Team Concept	6
E. Principles of Organization	6
F. The Four Important Parts of Every Job	7
G. Principles of Delegation	7
H. Principles of Effective Communications	7
I. Principles of Work Improvement	7
J. Areas of Job Improvement	7
K. Seven Key Points in Making Improvements	8

	L.	Corrective Techniques for Job Improvement	8
	M.	A Planning Checklist	8
	N.	Five Characteristics of Good Directions	9
	O.	Types of Directions	9
	P.	Controls	9
	Q.	Orienting the New Employee	9
	R.	Checklist for Orienting New Employees	9
	S.	Principles of Learning	10
	T.	Causes of Poor Performance	10
	U.	Four Major Steps in On-the-Job Instructions	10
	V.	Employees Want Five Things	10
	W.	Some Don'ts in Regard to Praise	11
	X.	How to Gain Your Workers' Confidence	11
	Y.	Sources of Employee Problems	11
	Z.	The Supervisor's Key to Discipline	11
	AA.	Five Important Processes of Management	12
	BB.	When the Supervisor Fails to Plan	12
	CC.	Fourteen General Principles of Management	12
	DD.	Change	12
II.	Brief Topical Summaries		13
	A.	Who/What is the Supervisor?	13
	B.	The Sociology of Work	13
	C.	Principles and Practices of Supervision	14
	D.	Dynamic Leadership	14
	E.	Processes for Solving Problems	15
	F.	Training for Results	15
	G.	Health, Safety, and Accident Prevention	16
	H.	Equal Employment Opportunity	16
	I.	Improving Communications	16
	J.	Self-Development	17
	K.	Teaching and Training	17
		1. The Teaching Process	17
		a. Preparation	17
		b. Presentation	18
		c. Summary	18
		d. Application	18
		e. Evaluation	18
		2. Teaching Methods	18
		a. Lecture	18
		b. Discussion	18
		c. Demonstration	19
		d. Performance	19
		e. Which Method to Use	19

PHILOSOPHY, PRINCIPLES, PRACTICES, AND TECHNICS
OF
SUPERVISION, ADMINISTRATION, MANAGEMENT, AND ORGANIZATION

MEANING OF SUPERVISION

The extension of the democratic philosophy has been accompanied by an extension in the scope of supervision. Modern leaders and supervisors no longer think of supervision in the narrow sense of being confined chiefly to visiting employees, supplying materials, or rating the staff. They regard supervision as being intimately related to all the concerned agencies of society, they speak of the supervisor's function in terms of "growth," rather than the "improvement" of employees.

This modern concept of supervision may be defined as follows: Supervision is leadership and the development of leadership within groups which are cooperatively engaged in inspection, research, training, guidance, and evaluation.

THE OLD AND THE NEW SUPERVISION

TRADITIONAL
1. Inspection
2. Focused on the employee
3. Visitation
4. Random and haphazard
5. Imposed and authoritarian
6. One person usually

MODERN
1. Study and analysis
2. Focused on aims, materials, methods, supervisors, employees, environment
3. Demonstrations, intervisitation, workshops, directed reading, bulletins, etc.
4. Definitely organized and planned (scientific)
5. Cooperative and democratic
6. Many persons involved (creative)

THE EIGHT (8) BASIC PRINCIPLES OF THE NEW SUPERVISION

I. Principle of Responsibility
    Authority to act and responsibility for acting must be joined.
    A. If you give responsibility, give authority.
    B. Define employee duties clearly.
    C. Protect employees from criticism by others.
    D. Recognize the rights as well as obligations of employees.
    E. Achieve the aims of a democratic society insofar as it is possible within the area of your work.
    F. Establish a situation favorable to training and learning.
    G. Accept ultimate responsibility for everything done in your section, unit, office, division, department.
    H. Good administration and good supervision are inseparable.

II. Principle of Authority
The success of the supervisor is measured by the extent to which the power of authority is not used.
   A. Exercise simplicity and informality in supervision
   B. Use the simplest machinery of supervision
   C. If it is good for the organization as a whole, it is probably justified.
   D. Seldom be arbitrary or authoritative.
   E. Do not base your work on the power of position or of personality.
   F. Permit and encourage the free expression of opinions.

III. Principle of Self-Growth
The success of the supervisor is measured by the extent to which, and the speed with which, he is no longer needed.
   A. Base criticism on principles, not on specifics.
   B. Point out higher activities to employees.
   C. Train for self-thinking by employees to meet new situations.
   D. Stimulate initiative, self-reliance, and individual responsibility
   E. Concentrate on stimulating the growth of employees rather than on removing defects.

IV. Principle of Individual Worth
Respect for the individual is a paramount consideration in supervision.
   A. Be human and sympathetic in dealing with employees.
   B. Don't nag about things to be done.
   C. Recognize the individual differences among employees and seek opportunities to permit best expression of each personality.

V. Principle of Creative Leadership
The best supervision is that which is not apparent to the employee.
   A. Stimulate, don't drive employees to creative action.
   B. Emphasize doing good things.
   C. Encourage employees to do what they do best.
   D. Do not be too greatly concerned with details of subject or method.
   E. Do not be concerned exclusively with immediate problems and activities.
   F. Reveal higher activities and make them both desired and maximally possible.
   G. Determine procedures in the light of each situation but see that these are derived from a sound basic philosophy.
   H. Aid, inspire, and lead so as to liberate the creative spirit latent in all good employees.

VI. Principle of Success and Failure
There are no unsuccessful employees, only unsuccessful supervisors who have failed to give proper leadership.
   A. Adapt suggestions to the capacities, attitudes, and prejudices of employees.
   B. Be gradual, be progressive, be persistent.
   C. Help the employee find the general principle; have the employee apply his own problem to the general principle.
   D. Give adequate appreciation for good work and honest effort.
   E. Anticipate employee difficulties and help to prevent them.
   F. Encourage employees to do the desirable things they will do anyway.
   G. Judge your supervision by the results it secures.

VII. Principle of Science
Successful supervision is scientific, objective, and experimental. It is based on facts, not on prejudices.
   A. Be cumulative in results.
   B. Never divorce your suggestions from the goals of training.
   C. Don't be impatient of results.
   D. Keep all matters on a professional, not a personal, level.
   E. Do not be concerned exclusively with immediate problems and activities.
   F. Use objective means of determining achievement and rating where possible.

VIII. Principle of Cooperation
Supervision is a cooperative enterprise between supervisor and employee.
   A. Begin with conditions as they are.
   B. Ask opinions of all involved when formulating policies.
   C. Organization is as good as its weakest link.
   D. Let employees help to determine policies and department programs.
   E. Be approachable and accessible—physically and mentally.
   F. Develop pleasant social relationships.

WHAT IS ADMINISTRATION

Administration is concerned with providing the environment, the material facilities, and the operational procedures that will promote the maximum growth and development of supervisors and employees. (Organization is an aspect and a concomitant of administration.)

There is no sharp line of demarcation between supervision and administration; these functions are intimately interrelated and, often, overlapping. They are complementary activities.

I. Practices Commonly Classed as "Supervisory"
   A. Conducting employees' conferences
   B. Visiting sections, units, offices, divisions, departments
   C. Arranging for demonstrations
   D. Examining plans
   E. Suggesting professional reading
   F. Interpreting bulletins
   G. Recommending in-service training courses
   H. Encouraging experimentation
   I. Appraising employee morale
   J. Providing for intervisitation

II. Practices Commonly Classified as "Administrative"
   A. Management of the office
   B. Arrangement of schedules for extra duties
   C. Assignment of rooms or areas
   D. Distribution of supplies
   E. Keeping records and reports
   F. Care of audio-visual materials
   G. Keeping inventory records
   H. Checking record cards and books

I. Programming special activities
   J. Checking on the attendance and punctuality of employees

III. Practices Commonly Classified as Both "Supervisory" and "Administrative"
   A. Program construction
   B. Testing or evaluating outcomes
   C. Personnel accounting
   D. Ordering instructional materials

RESPONSIBILITIES OF THE SUPERVISOR

A person employed in a supervisory capacity must constantly be able to improve his own efficiency and ability. He represent the employer to the employees and only continuous self-examination can make him a capable supervisor.

Leadership and training are the supervisor's responsibility. An efficient working unit is one in which the employees work with the supervisor. It is his job to bring out the best in his employees. He must always be relaxed, courteous, and calm in his association with his employees. Their feelings are important, and a harsh attitude does not develop the most efficient employees.

COMPETENCES OF THE SUPERVISOR

   I. Complete knowledge of the duties and responsibilities of his position.
   II. To be able to organize a job, plan ahead, and carry through.
   III. To have self-confidence and initiative.
   IV. To be able to handle the unexpected situation and make quick decisions.
   V. To be able to properly train subordinates in the positions they are best suited for.
   VI. To be able to keep good human relations among his subordinates.
   VII. To be able to keep good human relations between his subordinates and himself and to earn their respect and trust.

THE PROFESSIONAL SUPERVISOR-EMPLOYEE RELATIONSHIP

There are two kinds of efficiency: one kind is only apparent and is produced in organizations through the exercise of mere discipline; this is but a simulation of the second, or true, efficiency which springs from spontaneous cooperation. If you are a manager, no matter how great or small your responsibility, it is your job, in the final analysis, to create and develop this involuntary cooperation among the people whom you supervise. For, no matter how powerful a combination of money, machines, and materials a company may have, this is a dead and sterile thing without a team of willing, thinking, and articulate people to guide it.

The following 21 points are presented as indicative of the exemplary basic relationship that should exist between supervisor and employee:

1. Each person wants to be liked and respected by his fellow employee and wants to be treated with consideration and respect by his superior.
2. The most competent employee will make an error. However, in a unit where good relations exist between the supervisor and his employees, tenseness and fear do not exist. Thus, errors are not hidden or covered up, and the efficiency of a unit is not impaired.

3. Subordinates resent rules, regulations, or orders that are unreasonable or unexplained.
4. Subordinates are quick to resent unfairness, harshness, injustices, and favoritism.
5. An employee will accept responsibility if he knows that he will be complimented for a job well done, and not too harshly chastised for failure; that his supervisor will check the cause of the failure, and, if it was the supervisor's fault, he will assume the blame therefore. If it was the employee's fault, his supervisor will explain the correct method or means of handling the responsibility.
6. An employee wants to receive credit for a suggestion he has made, that is used. If a suggestion cannot be used, the employee is entitled to an explanation. The supervisor should not say "no" and close the subject.
7. Fear and worry slow up a worker's ability. Poor working environment can impair his physical and mental health. A good supervisor avoids forceful methods, threats, and arguments to get a job done.
8. A forceful supervisor is able to train his employees individually and as a team, and is able to motivate them in the proper channels.
9. A mature supervisor is able to properly evaluate his subordinates and to keep them happy and satisfied.
10. A sensitive supervisor will never patronize his subordinates.
11. A worthy supervisor will respect his employees' confidences.
12. Definite and clear-cut responsibilities should be assigned to each executive.
13. Responsibility should always be coupled with corresponding authority.
14. No change should be made in the scope or responsibilities of a position without a definite understanding to that effect on the part of all persons concerned.
15. No executive or employee, occupying a single position in the organization, should be subject to definite orders from more than one source.
16. Orders should never be given to subordinates over the head of a responsible executive. Rather than do this, the officer in question should be supplanted.
17. Criticisms of subordinates should, whoever possible, be made privately, and in no case should a subordinate be criticized in the presence of executives or employees of equal or lower rank.
18. No dispute or difference between executives or employees as to authority or responsibilities should be considered too trivial for prompt and careful adjudication.
19. Promotions, wage changes, and disciplinary action should always be approved by the executive immediately superior to the one directly responsible.
20. No executive or employee should ever be required, or expected, to be at the same time an assistant to, and critic of, another.
21. Any executive whose work is subject to regular inspection should, wherever practicable, be given the assistance and facilities necessary to enable him to maintain an independent check of the quality of his work.

MINI-TEXT IN SUPERVISION, ADMINISTRATION, MANAGEMENT, AND ORGANIZATION

I. Brief Highlights

Listed concisely and sequentially are major headings and important data in the field for quick recall and review.

A. Levels of Management
Any organization of some size has several levels of management. In terms of a ladder, the levels are:

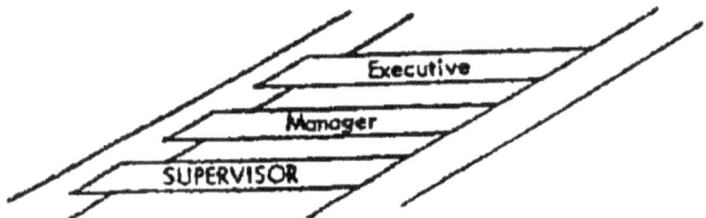

The first level is very important because it is the beginning point of management leadership.

B. What the Supervisor Must Learn
A supervisor must learn to:
1. Deal with people and their differences
2. Get the job done through people
3. Recognize the problems when they exist
4. Overcome obstacles to good performance
5. Evaluate the performance of people
6. Check his own performance in terms of accomplishment

C. A Definition of Supervisor
The term supervisor means any individual having authority, in the interests of the employer, to hire, transfer, suspend, lay-off, recall, promote, discharge, assign, reward, or discipline other employees or responsibility to direct them, or to adjust their grievances, or effectively to recommend such action, if, in connection with the foregoing, exercise of such authority is not of a merely routine or clerical nature but requires the use of independent judgment.

D. Elements of the Team Concept
What is involved in teamwork? The component parts are:
1. Members
2. A leader
3. Goals
4. Plans
5. Cooperation
6. Spirit

E. Principles of Organization
1. A team member must know what his job is.
2. Be sure that the nature and scope of a job are understood.
3. Authority and responsibility should be carefully spelled out.
4. A supervisor should be permitted to make the maximum number of decisions affecting his employees.
5. Employees should report to only one supervisor.
6. A supervisor should direct only as many employees as he can handle effectively.
7. An organization plan should be flexible.

8. Inspection and performance of work should be separate.
9. Organizational problems should receive immediate attention.
10. Assign work in line with ability and experience.

F. The Four Important Parts of Every Job
1. Inherent in every job is the *accountability* for results.
2. A second set of factors in every job is *responsibilities*.
3. Along with duties and responsibilities one must have the *authority* to act within certain limits without obtaining permission to proceed.
4. No job exists in a vacuum. The supervisor is surrounded by key *relationships*.

G. Principles of Delegation
Where work is delegated for the first time, the supervisor should think in terms of these questions:
1. Who is best qualified to do this?
2. Can an employee improve his abilities by doing this?
3. How long should an employee spend on this?
4. Are there any special problems for which he will need guidance?
5. How broad a delegation can I make?

H. Principles of Effective Communications
1. Determine the media.
2. To whom directed?
3. Identification and source authority.
4. Is communication understood?

I. Principles of Work Improvement
1. Most people usually do only the work which is assigned to them.
2. Workers are likely to fit assigned work into the time available to perform it.
3. A good workload usually stimulates output.
4. People usually do their best work when they know that results will be reviewed or inspected.
5. Employees usually feel that someone else is responsible for conditions of work, workplace layout, job methods, type of tools/equipment, and other such factors.
6. Employees are usually defensive about their job security.
7. Employees have natural resistance to change.
8. Employees can support or destroy a supervisor.
9. A supervisor usually earns the respect of his people through his personal example of diligence and efficiency.

J. Areas of Job Improvement
The areas of job improvement are quite numerous, but the most common ones which a supervisor can identify and utilize are:
1. Departmental layout
2. Flow of work
3. Workplace layout
4. Utilization of manpower
5. Work methods
6. Materials handling

7. Utilization
8. Motion economy

K. Seven Key Points in Making Improvements
1. Select the job to be improved
2. Study how it is being done now
3. Question the present method
4. Determine actions to be taken
5. Chart proposed method
6. Get approval and apply
7. Solicit worker participation

l. Corrective Techniques of Job Improvement
Specific Problems
1. Size of workload
2. Inability to meet schedules
3. Strain and fatigue
4. Improper use of men and skills
5. Waste, poor quality, unsafe conditions
6. Bottleneck conditions that hinder output
7. Poor utilization of equipment and machine
8. Efficiency and productivity of labor

General Improvement
1. Departmental layout
2. Flow of work
3. Work plan layout
4. Utilization of manpower
5. Work methods
6. Materials handling
7. Utilization of equipment
8. Motion economy

Corrective Techniques
1. Study with scale model
2. Flow chart study
3. Motion analysis
4. Comparison of units produced to standard allowance
5. Methods analysis
6. Flow chart and equipment study
7. Down time vs. running time
8. Motion analysis

M. A Planning Checklist
1. Objectives
2. Controls
3. Delegations
4. Communications
5. Resources
6. Manpower

7. Equipment
8. Supplies and materials
9. Utilization of time
10. Safety
11. Money
12. Work
13. Timing of improvements

N. Five Characteristics of Good Directions
In order to get results, directions must be:
1. Possible of accomplishment
2. Agreeable with worker interests
3. Related to mission
4. Planned and complete
5. Unmistakably clear

O. Types of Directions
1. Demands or direct orders
2. Requests
3. Suggestion or implication
4. volunteering

P. Controls
A typical listing of the overall areas in which the supervisor should establish controls might be:
1. Manpower
2. Materials
3. Quality of work
4. Quantity of work
5. Time
6. Space
7. Money
8. Methods

Q. Orienting the New Employee
1. Prepare for him
2. Welcome the new employee
3. Orientation for the job
4. Follow-up

R. Checklist for Orienting New Employees   Yes   No
1. Do you appreciate the feelings of new employees
   when they first report for work?   ___   ___
2. Are you aware of the fact that the new employee must
   make a big adjustment to his job?   ___   ___
3. Have you given him good reasons for liking the job and
   the organization?   ___   ___
4. Have you prepared for his first day on the job?   ___   ___
5. Did you welcome him cordially and make him feel needed?   ___   ___

		Yes	No

6. Did you establish rapport with him so that he feels free to talk and discuss matters with you? ___ ___
7. Did you explain his job to him and his relationship to you? ___ ___
8. Does he know that his work will be evaluated periodically on a basis that is fair and objective? ___ ___
9. Did you introduce him to his fellow workers in such a way that they are likely to accept him? ___ ___
10. Does he know what employee benefits he will receive? ___ ___
11. Does he understand the importance of being on the job and what to do if he must leave his duty station? ___ ___
12. Has he been impressed with the importance of accident prevention and safe practice? ___ ___
13. Does he generally know his way around the department? ___ ___
14. Is he under the guidance of a sponsor who will teach the right way of doing things? ___ ___
15. Do you plan to follow-up so that he will continue to adjust successfully to his job? ___ ___

S. Principles of Learning
   1. Motivation
   2. Demonstration or explanation
   3. Practice

T. Causes of Poor Performance
   1. Improper training for job
   2. Wrong tools
   3. Inadequate directions
   4. Lack of supervisory follow-up
   5. Poor communications
   6. Lack of standards of performance
   7. Wrong work habits
   8. Low morale
   9. Other

U. Four Major Steps in On-The-Job Instruction
   1. Prepare the worker
   2. Present the operation
   3. Tryout performance
   4. Follow-up

V. Employees Want Five Things
   1. Security
   2. Opportunity
   3. Recognition
   4. Inclusion
   5. Expression

W. Some Don'ts in Regard to Praise
1. Don't praise a person for something he hasn't done.
2. Don't praise a person unless you can be sincere.
3. Don't be sparing in praise just because your superior withholds it from you.
4. Don't let too much time elapse between good performance and recognition of it

X. How to Gain Your Workers' Confidence
Methods of developing confidence include such things as:
1. Knowing the interests, habits, hobbies of employees
2. Admitting your own inadequacies
3. Sharing and telling of confidence in others
4. Supporting people when they are in trouble
5. Delegating matters that can be well handled
6. Being frank and straightforward about problems and working conditions
7. Encouraging others to bring their problems to you
8. Taking action on problems which impede worker progress

Y. Sources of Employee Problems
On-the-job causes might be such things as:
1. A feeling that favoritism is exercised in assignments
2. Assignment of overtime
3. An undue amount of supervision
4. Changing methods or systems
5. Stealing of ideas or trade secrets
6. Lack of interest in job
7. Threat of reduction in force
8. Ignorance or lack of communications
9. Poor equipment
10. Lack of knowing how supervisor feels toward employee
11. Shift assignments

Off-the-job problems might have to do with:
1. Health
2. Finances
3. Housing
4. Family

Z. The Supervisor's Key to Discipline
There are several key points about discipline which the supervisor should keep in mind:
1. Job discipline is one of the disciplines of life and is directed by the supervisor.
2. It is more important to correct an employee fault than to fix blame for it.
3. Employee performance is affected by problems both on the job and off.
4. Sudden or abrupt changes in behavior can be indications of important employee problems.
5. Problems should be dealt with as soon as possible after they are identified.
6. The attitude of the supervisor may have more to do with solving problems than the techniques of problem solving.
7. Correction of employee behavior should be resorted to only after the supervisor is sure that training or counseling will not be helpful.

8. Be sure to document your disciplinary actions.
9. Make sure that you are disciplining on the basis of facts rather than personal feelings.
10. Take each disciplinary step in order, being careful not to make snap judgments, or decisions based on impatience.

AA. Five Important Processes of Management
1. Planning
2. Organizing
3. Scheduling
4. Controlling
5. Motivating

BB. When the Supervisor Fails to Plan
1. Supervisor creates impression of not knowing his job
2. May lead to excessive overtime
3. Job runs itself—supervisor lacks control
4. Deadlines and appointments missed
5. Parts of the work go undone
6. Work interrupted by emergencies
7. Sets a bad example
8. Uneven workload creates peaks and valleys
9. Too much time on minor details at expense of more important tasks

CC. Fourteen General Principles of Management
1. Division of work
2. Authority and responsibility
3. Discipline
4. Unity of command
5. Unity of direction
6. Subordination of individual interest to general interest
7. Remuneration of personnel
8. Centralization
9. Scalar chain
10. Order
11. Equity
12. Stability of tenure of personnel
13. Initiative
14. Esprit de corps

DD. Change

Bringing about change is perhaps attempted more often, and yet less well understood, than anything else the supervisor does. How do people generally react to change? (People tend to resist change that is imposed upon them by other individuals or circumstances.

Change is characteristic of every situation. It is a part of every real endeavor where the efforts of people are concerned.

1. Why do people resist change?
   People may resist change because of:
   a. Fear of the unknown
   b. Implied criticism
   c. Unpleasant experiences in the past
   d. Fear of loss of status
   e. Threat to the ego
   f. Fear of loss of economic stability

2. How can we best overcome the resistance to change?
   In initiating change, take these steps:
   a. Get ready to sell
   b. Identify sources of help
   c. Anticipate objections
   d. Sell benefits
   e. Listen in depth
   f. Follow up

II. Brief Topical Summaries

   A. Who/What is the Supervisor?
   1. The supervisor is often called the "highest level employee and the lowest level manager."
   2. A supervisor is a member of both management and the work group. He acts as a bridge between the two.
   3. Most problems in supervision are in the area of human relations, or people problems.
   4. Employees expect: Respect, opportunity to learn and to advance, and a sense of belonging, and so forth.
   5. Supervisors are responsible for directing people and organizing work. Planning is of paramount importance.
   6. A position description is a set of duties and responsibilities inherent to a given position.
   7. It is important to keep the position description up-to-date and to provide each employee with his own copy.

   B. The Sociology of Work
   1. People are alike in many ways; however, each individual is unique.
   2. The supervisor is challenged in getting to know employee differences. Acquiring skills in evaluating individuals is an asset.
   3. Maintaining meaningful working relationships in the organization is of great importance.
   4. The supervisor has an obligation to help individuals to develop to their fullest potential.
   5. Job rotation on a planned basis helps to build versatility and to maintain interest and enthusiasm in work groups.
   6. Cross training (job rotation) provides backup skills.

7. The supervisor can help reduce tension by maintaining a sense of humor, providing guidance to employees, and by making reasonable and timely decisions. Employees respond favorably to working under reasonably predictable circumstances.
8. Change is characteristic of all managerial behavior. The supervisor must adjust to changes in procedures, new methods, technological changes, and to a number of new and sometimes challenging situations.
9. To overcome the natural tendency for people to resist change, the supervisor should become more skillful in initiating change.

C. Principles and Practices of Supervision
1. Employees should be required to answer to only one superior.
2. A supervisor can effectively direct only a limited number of employees, depending upon the complexity, variety, and proximity of the jobs involved.
3. The organizational chart presents the organization in graphic form. It reflects lines of authority and responsibility as well as interrelationships of units within the organization.
4. Distribution of work can be improved through an analysis using the "Work Distribution Chart."
5. The "Work Distribution Chart" reflects the division of work within a unit in understandable form.
6. When related tasks are given to an employee, he has a better chance of increasing his skills through training.
7. The individual who is given the responsibility for tasks must also be given the appropriate authority to insure adequate results.
8. The supervisor should delegate repetitive, routine work. Preparation of recurring reports, maintaining leave and attendance records are some examples.
9. Good discipline is essential to good task performance. Discipline is reflected in the actions of employees on the job in the absence of supervision.
10. Disciplinary action may have to be taken when the positive aspects of discipline have failed. Reprimand, warning, and suspension are examples of disciplinary action.
11. If a situation calls for a reprimand, be sure it is deserved and remember it is to be done in private.

D. Dynamic Leadership
1. A style is a personal method or manner of exerting influence.
2. Authoritarian leaders often see themselves as the source of power and authority.
3. The democratic leader often perceives the group as the source of authority and power.
4. Supervisors tend to do better when using the pattern of leadership that is most natural for them.
5. Social scientists suggest that the effective supervisor use the leadership style that best fits the problem or circumstances involved.
6. All four styles—telling, selling, consulting, joining—have their place. Using one does not preclude using the other at another time.

7. The theory X point of view assumes that the average person dislikes work, will avoid it whenever possible, and must be coerced to achieve organizational objectives.
8. The theory Y point of view assumes that the average person considers work to be a natural as play, and, when the individual is committed, he requires little supervision or direction to accomplish desired objectives.
9. The leader's basic assumptions concerning human behavior and human nature affect his actions, decisions, and other managerial practices.
10. Dissatisfaction among employees is often present, but difficult to isolate. The supervisor should seek to weaken dissatisfaction by keeping promises, being sincere and considerate, keeping employees informed, and so forth.
11. Constructive suggestions should be encouraged during the natural progress of the work.

E. Processes for Solving Problems
1. People find their daily tasks more meaningful and satisfying when they can improve them.
2. The causes of problems, or the key factors, are often hidden in the background. Ability to solve problems often involves the ability to isolate them from their backgrounds. There is some substance to the cliché that some persons "can't see the forest for the trees."
3. New procedures are often developed from old ones. Problems should be broken down into manageable parts. New ideas can be adapted from old one.
4. People think differently in problem-solving situations. Using a logical, patterned approach is often useful. One approach found to be useful includes these steps:
   a. Define the problem
   b. Establish objectives
   c. Get the facts
   d. Weigh and decide
   e. Take action
   f. Evaluate action

F. Training for Results
1. Participants respond best when they feel training is important to them.
2. The supervisor has responsibility for the training and development of those who report to him.
3. When training is delegated to others, great care must be exercised to insure the trainer has knowledge, aptitude, and interest for his work as a trainer.
4. Training (learning) of some type goes on continually. The most successful supervisor makes certain the learning contributes in a productive manner to operational goals.
5. New employees are particularly susceptible to training. Older employees facing new job situations require specific training, as well as having need for development and growth opportunities.
6. Training needs require continuous monitoring.
7. The training officer of an agency is a professional with a responsibility to assist supervisors in solving training problems.

8. Many of the self-development steps important to the supervisor's own growth are equally important to the development of peers and subordinates. Knowledge of these is important when the supervisor consults with others on development and growth opportunities.

G. Health, Safety, and Accident Prevention
1. Management-minded supervisors take appropriate measures to assist employees in maintaining health and in assuring safe practices in the work environment.
2. Effective safety training and practices help to avoid injury and accidents.
3. Safety should be a management goal. All infractions of safety which are observed should be corrected without exception.
4. Employees' safety attitude, training and instruction, provision of safe tools and equipment, supervision, and leadership are considered highly important factors which contribute to safety and which can be influenced directly by supervisors.
5. When accidents do occur, they should be investigated promptly for very important reasons, including the fact that information which is gained can be used to prevent accidents in the future.

H. Equal Employment Opportunity
1. The supervisor should endeavor to treat all employees fairly, without regard to religion, race, sex, or national origin.
2. Groups tend to reflect the attitude of the leader. Prejudice can be detected even in very subtle form. Supervisors must strive to create a feeling of mutual respect and confidence in every employee.
3. Complete utilization of all human resources is a national goal. Equitable consideration should be accorded women in the work force, minority-group members, the physically and mentally handicapped, and the older employee. The important question is: "Who can do the job?"
4. Training opportunities, recognition for performance, overtime assignments, promotional opportunities, and all other personnel actions are to be handled on an equitable basis.

I. Improving Communications
1. Communications is achieving understanding between the sender and the receiver of a message. It also means sharing information—the creation of understanding.
2. Communication is basic to all human activity. Words are means of conveying meanings; however, real meanings are in people.
3. There are very practical differences in the effectiveness of one-way, impersonal, and two-way communications. Words spoken face-to-face are better understood. Telephone conversations are effective, but lack the rapport of person-to-person exchanges. The whole person communicates.
4. Cooperation and communication in an organization go hand in hand. When there is a mutual respect between people, spelling out rules and procedures for communicating is unnecessary.
5. There are several barriers to effective communications. These include failure to listen with respect and understanding, lack of skill in feedback, and misinterpreting the meanings of words used by the speaker. It is also common

practice to listen to what we want to hear, and tune out things we do not want to hear.
6. Communication is management's chief problem. The supervisor should accept the challenge to communicate more effectively and to improve interagency and intra-agency communications.
7. The supervisor may often plan for and conduct meetings. The planning phase is critical and may determine the success or the failure of a meeting.
8. Speaking before groups usually requires extra effort. Stage fright may never disappear completely, but it can be controlled.

J. Self-Development
1. Every employee is responsible for his own self-development.
2. Toastmaster and toastmistress clubs offer opportunities to improve skills in oral communications.
3. Planning for one's own self-development is of vital importance. Supervisors know their own strengths and limitations better than anyone else.
4. Many opportunities are open to aid the supervisor in his developmental efforts, including job assignments; training opportunities, both governmental and non-governmental—to include universities and professional conferences and seminars.
5. Programmed instruction offers a means of studying at one's own rate.
6. Where difficulties may arise from a supervisor's being away from his work for training, he may participate in televised home study or correspondence courses to meet his self-development needs.

K. Teaching and Training
1. The Teaching Process
Teaching is encouraging and guiding the learning activities of students toward established goals. In most cases this process consists of five steps: preparation, presentation, summarization, evaluation, and application.

   a. Preparation
   Preparation is two-fold in nature; that of the supervisor and the employee. Preparation by the supervisor is absolutely essential to success. He must know what, when, where, how, and whom he will teach. Some of the factors that should be considered are:
   1) The objectives
   2) The materials needed
   3) The methods to be used
   4) Employee participation
   5) Employee interest
   6) Training aids
   7) Evaluation
   8) Summarization

   Employee preparation consists in preparing the employee to receive the material. Probably the most important single factor in the preparation of the employee is arousing and maintaining his interest. He must know the objectives of the training, why he is there, how the material can be used, and its importance to him.

b. Presentation
In presentation, have a carefully designed plan and follow it. The plan should be accurate and complete, yet flexible enough to meet situations as they arise. The method of presentation will be determined by the particular situation and objectives.

c. Summary
A summary should be made at the end of every training unit and program. In addition, there may be internal summaries depending on the nature of the material being taught. The important thing is that the trainee must always be able to understand how each part of the new material relates to the whole.

d. Application
The supervisor must arrange work so the employee will be given a chance to apply new knowledge or skills while the material is still clear in his mind and interest is high. The trainee does not really know whether he has learned the material until he has been given a chance to apply it. If the material is not applied, it loses most of its value.

e. Evaluation
The purpose of all training is to promote learning. To determine whether the training has been a success or failure, the supervisor must evaluate this learning.
In the broadest sense, evaluation includes all the devices, methods, skills, and techniques used by the supervisor to keep himself and the employees informed as to their progress toward the objectives they are pursuing. The extent to which the employee has mastered the knowledge, skills, and abilities, or changed his attitudes, as determined by the program objectives, is the extent to which instruction has succeeded or failed.
Evaluation should not be confined to the end of the lesson, day, or program but should be used continuously. We shall note later the way this relates to the rest of the teaching process.

2. Teaching Methods
A teaching method is a pattern of identifiable student and instructor activity used in presenting training material.
All supervisors are faced with the problem of deciding which method should be used at a given time.

a. Lecture
The lecture is direct oral presentation of material by the supervisor. The present trend is to place less emphasis on the trainer's activity and more on that of the trainee.

b. Discussion
Teaching by discussion or conference involves using questions and other techniques to arouse interest and focus attention upon certain areas, and by doing so creating a learning situation. This can be one of the most

valuable methods because it gives the employees an opportunity to express their ideas and pool their knowledge.

c. Demonstration
The demonstration is used to teach how something works or how to do something. It can be used to show a principle or what the results of a series of actions will be. A well-staged demonstration is particularly effective because it shows proper methods of performance in a realistic manner.

d. Performance
Performance is one of the most fundamental of all learning techniques or teaching methods. The trainee may be able to tell how a specific operation should be performed but he cannot be sure he knows how to perform the operation until he has done so.
As with all methods, there are certain advantages and disadvantages to each method.

e. Which Method to Use
Moreover, there are other methods and techniques of teaching. It is difficult to use any method without other methods entering into it. In any learning situation, a combination of methods is usually more effective than any one method alone.

Finally, evaluation must be integrated into the other aspects of the teaching-learning process.

It must be used in the motivation of the trainees; it must be used to assist in developing understanding during the training; and it must be related to employee application of the results of training.

This is distinctly the role of the supervisor.

TENANT'S RIGHTS

CONTENTS

INTRODUCTION 1

LEASES
    What Is a Lease? 1
    Renewal Leases. 2
    Month-to-Month Tenants 2

RENT
    Rent Charges 2
    Rent Overcharges 3
    Rent Security Deposits. 3

LEASE SUCCESSION OR TERMINATION
    Subletting or Assigning Leases 4
    Lease Succession Rights 5
    Senior Citizen Lease Terminations. 6
    Lease Terminations for Military Personnel 6
    Eviction 6-7

HABITABILITY AND REPAIRS
    Warranty of Habitability 7
    Landlords' Duty of Repair 8
    Lead Paint 8

SAFETY
    Crime Prevention 8
    Entrance Door Locks and Intercoms 8
    Lobby Attendant Service 8
    Elevator Mirrors 9
    Individual Locks, Peepholes and Mail 9
    Smoke Detectors 9
    Window Guards 9

TENANT'S PERSONAL RIGHTS
    Tenants' Organizations. 9
    Retaliation 10
    Right to Privacy 10
    Discrimination 10
    Harassment 10

UTILITY SERVICES
    Heating Season 11
    Truth in Heating 11
    Continuation of Utility Service 11
    Oil Payments 11

CONTENTS (Continued)

FINDING AN APARTMENT
    Real Estate Brokers 11
    Apartment Information Vendors and Listing Agencies 12

OTHER PROVISIONS
    Apartment Sharing 12
    Pets 12
    Special Types of Housing 12-13

TENANT'S RIGHTS GUIDE

INTRODUCTION

This guide highlights some of the principal rights of residential tenants in this state. These rights are protected by a variety of Federal, State and local laws. In addition, those areas of the State which are subject to rent stabilization, rent control or other rent regulation, may have special rules applicable to certain dwellings. For example, rent stabilization laws apply in New York City and in certain communities in Nassau, Rockland and Westchester counties. Tenants are advised to consult a lawyer regarding particular situations of concern to them.

LEASES

WHAT IS A LEASE?

A lease is a contract between a landlord and tenant which contains the terms and conditions of the rental. It cannot be changed while it is in effect unless both parties agree. Leases for apartments which are not rent stabilized may be oral or written. However, to avoid disputes the parties may wish to enter into a written agreement. An oral lease for more than one year cannot be legally enforced. (General Obligations Law §5-701)

At a minimum, leases should specify the names and addresses of the parties, the amount and due dates of the rent, the duration of the rental, the conditions of occupancy, and the rights and obligations of both parties. Except where the law provides otherwise, a landlord may rent on such terms and conditions as are agreed to by the parties.

Leases must use words with common and everyday meanings and must be clear and coherent. Sections of leases must be appropriately captioned and the print must be large enough to read easily. (General Obligations Law §5-702; C.P.L.R. §4544)

Lease provisions which exempt landlords from liability for injuries to persons or property caused by the landlord's negligence or that of his employees - are null and void. Further, a lease provision that waives the tenant's right to a jury trial in any lawsuit brought by either of the parties against the other for personal injury or property damage is also null and void. (General Obligations Law §5-321; Real Property Law §259-c)

If the court finds a lease or any lease clause to have been unconscionable at the time it was made, the court may refuse to enforce the lease or the clause in question. (Real Property Law §235-c) A lease provision which requires a tenant to pledge his/her household furniture as security for rent is void. (Real Property Law §231)

Tenants protected by rent stabilization have the right to either a one or two year lease when they move into an apartment except under certain circumstances such as, for example, when the apartment is not used as the tenant's primary residence. Rent stabilized tenants must also be given a rent stabilization lease rider, prepared by the New York State Division of Housing and Community Renewal ("DHCR"), which summarizes their rights under the law and provides specific information on how the vacancy rent was calculated. For certain luxury apartments, a landlord may seek DHCR approval to deregulate the rent to be charged.

New York City rent stabilized tenants are entitled to receive from their landlords a fully executed copy of their signed lease within 30 days of the landlord's receipt of the lease signed by the tenant. The lease's beginning and ending dates must be stated. (Rent Stabilization Code ("RSC") §2522.5)

RENEWAL LEASES

Except for rent-regulated apartments, a tenant may only renew the lease with the consent of the landlord. A lease may contain an automatic renewal clause. In such case, the landlord must give the tenant advance notice of the existence of this clause between 15 and 30 days before the tenant is required to notify the landlord of an intention not to renew the lease. (General Obligations Law §5-905)

The renewal leases for rent stabilized tenants must be on the same terms and conditions as the prior lease and rent increases, if any, are limited by law but may provide for a rent increase according to rates permitted by the Rent Guidelines Board. Rent stabilized tenants may choose either a one-year or a two-year renewal lease. For New York City rent-stabilized tenants, the landlord must give written notice to the rent-stabilized tenant of the right to renewal no more than 150 days and not less than 120 days prior to the end of the lease. After the notice of renewal is given, the tenant has 60 days in which to accept. If the tenant does not accept the renewal offer within the prescribed time, the landlord may refuse to renew the lease and seek to evict the tenant through court proceedings.

MONTH-TO-MONTH TENANTS

Tenants who do not have leases and pay rent on a monthly basis are called "month-to-month" tenants. In localities without rent regulations, tenants who stay past the end of a lease are treated as month-to-month tenants if the landlord accepts their rent. (Real Property Law §232-c)

A month-to-month tenancy outside New York City may be terminated by either party by giving at least one month's notice before the expiration of the term. For example, if the rent is due on the first of each month, the landlord must inform the tenant by September 30th before the October rent is due that he wants the tenant to move out by November 1st. The termination notice need not specify why the landlord seeks possession of the apartment. Such notice does not automatically allow the landlord to evict the tenant. A landlord may raise the rent of a month-to-month tenant with the consent of the tenant. If the tenant does not consent, however, the landlord can terminate the tenancy by giving appropriate notice. (Real Property Law §232-b)

In New York City, the landlord must serve the tenant with a written termination giving 30 days notice before the expiration of the term. The notice must state that the landlord elects to terminate the tenancy and that refusal to vacate will lead to eviction proceedings. (Real Property Law §232-a)

RENT

RENT CHARGES

Where an apartment is not subject to rent stabilization or rent control or other rent regulation, a landlord is free to charge any rent agreed upon by the parties. If the apartment is subject to such rent regulation, the rent and subsequent rent increases are set by law. A tenant may challenge the regulated rent with the DHCR. If the challenge is upheld, DHCR will order a refund of any overcharges plus interest and, where appropriate, it may assess penalties.

Landlords of rent stabilized buildings may seek rent increases for certain types of building-wide major capital improvements (MCI), such as the replacement of a boiler, and for new services, new equipment or improvements to an apartment in accordance with the law and regulations. Under certain circumstances, a landlord may also apply for a hardship rent increase.

Landlords must provide tenants with a written receipt when rent is paid in cash, a money order, a cashier's check or in any form other than the personal check of a tenant. Where a tenant pays the rent by personal check, (s)he may request in writing a rent receipt from the landlord. The receipt must state the payment date, the amount, the period for which the rent was paid, and the apartment number. The receipt must be signed by the person receiving the payment and state his or her title. (Real Property Law §235-e)

It is illegal for any person to require a prospective tenant to pay a bonus -commonly called "key money" - above the lawful rent and security deposit - for preference in renting a vacant apartment. (Penal Law 180.55) Key money is not to be confused with fees that may be legally charged by a licensed real estate broker. (See the section below on "Real Estate Brokers")

RENT OVERCHARGES

In New York City and certain communities in Nassau, Rockland and Westchester counties where rent stabilization laws apply, the landlord may not charge more than the legal-regulated rent. Under the housing law, landlords must register each rent-stabilized apartment wit DHCR and provide tenants annually with a copy of the registration statement. Tenants may also get a copy of the rent history for their apartment directly from DHCR. A tenant may only challenge rents and collect any overcharges going back four years from the tenant's filing a complaint. The tenant is also entitled to recover interest, plus reasonable costs and attorney's fees, for the overcharge proceeding.

In addition, if the overcharge is willful, the landlord is liable for a penalty of three times the amount of the overcharge. The penalty includes the amount of the overcharge itself. The landlord has the burden of proving the overcharge is not willful. This treble damages penalty is limited to two years. Contact DHCR if you believe you are being overcharged.

RENT SECURITY DEPOSITS

Virtually all leases require tenants to give their landlords a security deposit. The security deposit is usually one month's rent. The landlord must return the security deposit, less any lawful deduction, to the tenant at the end of the lease or within a reasonable time thereafter. A landlord may use the security deposit: (a) as reimbursement for the reasonable cost of repairs beyond normal wear and tear, if the tenant damages the apartment; or (b) as reimbursement for any unpaid rent.

Landlords, regardless of the number of units in the building, must treat the deposits as trust funds belonging to their tenants and they may not co-mingle deposits with their own money. Landlords of buildings with six or more apartments must put all security deposits in New York bank accounts earning interest at the prevailing rate. Each tenant must be informed in writing of the bank's name and address and the amount of the deposit. Landlords are entitled to annual administrative expenses of 1% of the deposit. All other interest earned on the deposits belongs to the tenants. Tenants must be given the option of having this interest paid to them annually, applied to rent, or paid at the end of the lease term. If the building has fewer than six apartments, a landlord who voluntarily places the security deposits in an interest bearing bank account must also follow these rules. For example: A tenant pays a security deposit of $400. The landlord places the deposit in an interest bearing bank account paying 2.5%. At the end of the year the account will have earned interest of $10.00. The tenant is entitled to $6.00 and the landlord may retain $4.00, 1% of the deposit, as an administrative fee.

If the building is sold, the landlord must transfer all security deposits to the new owner within five days, or return the security deposits to the tenants. Landlords must notify the tenants, by registered or certified mail, of the name and address of the new owner. Purchasers of rent-stabilized buildings are directly responsible to tenants for the return of security deposits and any interest. This responsibility exists whether or not the new owner received the security deposits from the former landlord.

Purchasers of rent-controlled buildings or buildings containing six or more apartments where tenants have written leases are directly responsible to tenants for the return of security deposits and interest in cases where the purchaser has "actual knowledge" of the security deposits. The law defines specifically when a new owner is deemed to have "actual knowledge" of the security deposits.

When problems arise, tenants should first try to resolve them with the landlord before taking other action. If a dispute cannot be resolved, tenants may contact the nearest local office of the Attorney General.

LEASE SUCCESSION OR TERMINATION

SUBLETTING OR ASSIGNING LEASES

Subletting and assignment are methods of transferring the tenant's legal interest in an apartment to another person. A sublet transfers less than the tenant's entire interest while an assignment transfers the entire interest. A tenant's right to assign the lease is much more restricted than the right to sublet.

A tenant may not assign the lease without the landlord's written consent. The landlord may withhold consent without cause. If the landlord reasonably refuses consent, the tenant cannot assign and is not entitled to be released from the lease. If the landlord unreasonably refuses consent, the tenant is entitled to be released from the lease after 30 days notice.

Tenants with leases who live in buildings with four or more apartments have the right to sublet with the landlord's advance consent. The landlord cannot unreasonably withhold consent. If the landlord consents to the sublet, the tenant remains liable to the landlord for the obligations of the lease. If the landlord denies the sublet on reasonable grounds, the tenant cannot sublet and the landlord is not required to release the tenant from the lease. If the landlord denies the sublet on unreasonable grounds, the tenant may sublet. If a lawsuit results, the tenant may recover court costs and attorney's fees if a judge rules that the landlord denied the sublet in bad faith.

These steps must be followed by tenants wishing to sublet:
1. The tenant must send a written request to the landlord by certified mail, return-receipt requested. The request must contain the following information: (a) the length of the sublease; (b) the name, home and business address of the proposed subtenant; (c) the reason for subletting; (d) the tenant's address during the sublet; (e) the written consent of any co-tenant or guarantor; (f) a copy of the proposed sublease together with a copy of the tenant's own lease, if available.
2. Within 10 days after the mailing of this request, the landlord may ask the tenant for additional information to help make a decision. Any request for additional information may not be unduly burdensome.
3. Within 30 days after the mailing of the tenant's request to sublet or the additional information requested by the landlord, whichever is later, the landlord must send

the tenant a notice of consent, or if consent is denied, the reasons for denial. A landlord's failure to send this written notice is considered consent to sublet.
4. A sublet or assignment which does not comply with the law may be grounds for eviction.

In addition to these sublet rules, there are additional requirements limited to rent stabilized tenants. These rules include the following:

- The rent charged to the subtenant cannot exceed the stabilized rent plus a 10% surcharge payable to the tenant for a furnished sublet. Additionally, the stabilized rent payable to the owner, effective upon the date of subletting, may be increased by a "sublet allowance" equal to the vacancy allowance then in effect. A subtenant who is overcharged may file a complaint with DHCR or may sue the prime tenant in court to recover any overcharge plus treble damages, interest, and attorneys' fees (RSC §2525.6(e))
- The prime tenant must establish that at all times he/she has maintained the apartment as a primary residence and intends to reoccupy it at the end of the sublet.
- The prime tenant, not the subtenant, retains the rights to a renewal lease and any rights resulting from a co-op conversion. The term of a sublease may extend beyond the term of the prime tenant's lease. The tenant may not sublet for more than two years within any four-year period. (Real Property Law §226-b, RSC §2525.6)
- Rent stabilized tenants who sublet their apartments should note that the Rent Stabilization Code published on December 20, 2000 created a new subdivision setting forth what constitutes a tenant's primary residence. Section 9: 9 NYCRR §2520.6(u) states in part that a rent stabilized tenant subletting his or her apartment may now permit a landlord to seek possession of the subject premises on the basis of non-primary residence.

LEASE SUCCESSION RIGHTS

Family members living in an apartment not covered by rent control or rent stabilization generally have no right to succeed a tenant who dies or permanently vacates the premises. The rights of a "family member" living in a rent controlled or rent stabilized apartment to succeed a tenant of record who dies or permanently vacates are covered by DHCR Regulations.

Under these regulations, a "family member" is defined as husband, wife, son, daughter, stepson, stepdaughter, father, mother, stepfather, stepmother, brother, sister, grandfather, grandmother, grandson, granddaughter, father-in-law, mother-in-law, son-in-law or daughter-in-law of the tenant; or any other person residing with the tenant in the apartment as a primary resident who can prove emotional and financial commitment, and interdependence between such person and the tenant.

A family member would succeed to the rights of the tenant of record upon the tenant's permanent departure or death, provided the family member lived with such a primary resident either (1) for not less than two years (one year in the case of senior citizens who are 62 years or older, and disabled persons) or (2) from the commencement of the tenancy or the relationship (if the tenancy or relationship were less than two years or one year old, as the case may be). (RSC §2523.5)

Remaining family members living in government involved housing such as a public development; or in an apartment owned by the local municipality; or in an apartment where the prime tenant had some type of Section 8 Rental Assistance; and where the named tenant of record has died or moved out, may also have the right to succeed to that tenant's leasehold and/or rent subsidy. Family members seeking succession rights in these circumstances must ascertain the applicable federal and municipal regulations as well as the local public housing authority rules to determine if they might meet the eligibility requirements. Under federal regulations, persons alleging they are remaining family members of tenant family are entitled to a grievance hearing before eviction if they have a colorable claim to such status.

SENIOR CITIZEN LEASE TERMINATIONS

Tenants or their spouses living with them, who are sixty-two years or older, or who will attain such age during the term of their leases, are entitled to terminate their leases if they relocate to an adult care facility, a residential health care facility, subsidized low-income housing, or other senior citizen housing.

When such tenants give notice of their opportunity to move into one of the above facilities, the landlord must release the tenant from liability to pay rent for the balance of the lease and adjust any payments made in advance.

Senior citizens who wish to avail themselves of this option must do so by written notice to the landlord. The termination date must be effective no earlier than thirty days after the date on which the next rental payment (after the notice is delivered) is due. The notice is deemed delivered five days after mailing. The written notice must include documentation of admission or pending admission to one of the above mentioned facilities. For example, a senior citizen mails a notice to the landlord of his or her intention to terminate the lease on April 5; the notice is deemed received April 10. Since the next rental payment (after April 10) is due May 1, the earliest lease termination date will be effective June 1.

Anyone who interferes with the tenant's or his or her spouse's removal of personal effects, clothing, furniture or other personal property from the premises to be vacated will be guilty of a misdemeanor.

Owners or lessors of a facility of a unit into which a senior citizen is entitled to move after terminating a lease, must advise such tenant, in the admission application form, of the tenant's rights under the law. (Real Property Law §227-a.)

LEASE TERMINATIONS FOR MILITARY PERSONNEL

Individuals entering or called to active duty in the military service may terminate a residential lease if: (1) the lease was executed by the service member before he/she entered active duty; and (2) the leased premises have been occupied by the member or his/her dependents. Any such lease may be terminated by written notice delivered to the landlord at any time following the beginning of military service. Termination of a lease requiring monthly payments is not effective until 30 days after the first date on which the next rent is due. For example, if rent is due on the first day of the month, and notice is mailed on January 1, then rent is next due on the first of February and the effective date of lease termination is the first of March (N.Y. Military Law §309).

EVICTION

Following appropriate notice, a landlord may bring a summary non-payment court proceeding to evict a tenant who fails to pay the agreed rent when due and to recover outstanding rent. A landlord may also bring a summary holdover eviction proceeding if, for example, a tenant significantly violates a substantial obligation under the lease, such as using the premises for illegal purposes, committing or permitting a nuisance, or staying beyond the lease term without permission. (Real Property Actions Proceedings Law ("RPAPL")§711)

You can be legally evicted only after the landlord has brought a court proceeding and obtained a judgement of possession. An eviction notice can be sent to you if: you signed an agreement (stipulation) with the landlord in court granting the landlord a final judgement and you did not fulfill the terms of the agreement; or you had a trial and the judge ruled in the landlord's favor; or you did not appear in court to answer court papers (petition) that the landlord sent you. Only a sheriff, marshal or constable can carry out a court ordered warrant to evict a tenant. (RPAPL §749) A landlord may not take the law into his/her own hands and evict a tenant by use of force or unlawful means. For example, a landlord cannot use threats of violence, remove a tenant's possessions, lock the tenant out of the apartment, or willfully discontinue essential services such as water or heat. (Real Property Law §235) When a tenant is evicted, the landlord may not retain the tenant's personal belongings or furniture.

A tenant who is put out of his/her apartment in a forcible or unlawful manner is entitled to recover triple damages in a legal action against the wrongdoer. Landlords in New York City who use illegal methods to force a tenant to move are also subject to both criminal and civil penalties. Further, the tenant is entitled to be restored to occupancy. (RPAPL §713, §853)

It is wise to consult an attorney to protect your legal rights if your landlord seeks possession of your apartment. Never ignore legal papers.

HABITABILITY AND REPAIRS

WARRANTY OF HABITABILITY

Tenants are entitled to a livable, safe and sanitary apartment. Lease provisions inconsistent with this right are illegal. Failure to provide heat or hot water on a regular basis, or to rid an apartment of insect infestation are examples of a violation of this warranty. Public areas of the building are also covered by the warranty of habitability. The warranty of habitability also applies to cooperative apartments, but not to condominiums. Any uninhabitable condition caused by the tenant or persons under his direction or control does not constitute a breach of the warranty of habitability. In such a case, it is the responsibility of the tenant to remedy the condition. (Real Property Law §235-b)

If a landlord breaches the warranty, the tenant may sue for a rent reduction. The tenant may also withhold rent, but in response, the landlord may sue the tenant for nonpayment of rent. In such a case, the tenant may countersue for breach of the warranty.

Rent reductions may be ordered if a court finds that the landlord violated the warranty of habitability. The reduction is computed by subtracting from the actual rent the estimated value of the apartment without the essential services.

A landlord's liability for damages is limited when the failure to provide services is the result of a union-wide building workers' strike. However, a court may award damages to a tenant equal to a share of the landlord's net savings because of the strike.

Landlords will be liable for lack of services caused by a strike when they have not made a good faith attempt, where practicable, to provide services.

In emergencies, tenants may make necessary repairs and deduct reasonable repair costs from the rent. For example, when a landlord has been notified that a door lock is broken and willfully neglects to repair it, the tenant may hire a locksmith and deduct the cost from the rent. Tenants should keep receipts for such repairs.

LANDLORDS' DUTY OF REPAIR

Landlords of buildings with three or more apartments must keep the apartments and the buildings' public areas in "good repair" and clean and free of vermin, garbage or other offensive material. Landlords are required to maintain electrical, plumbing, sanitary, heating and ventilating systems and appliances landlords install, such as refrigerators and stoves in good and safe working order. Tenants should bring complaints to the attention of their local housing officials. (Multiple Dwelling Law (MDL) 78 and 80; Multiple Residence Law (MRL) §174. The MDL applies to cities with a population of 325,000 or more and the MRL applies to cities with less than 325,000 and to all towns and villages.)

LEAD PAINT

Landlords of apartments in multiple dwellings in New York City where a child 6 years old or younger lives must protect against the possibility that children will be poisoned by peeling of dangerous lead based paint. Landlords must remove or cover apartment walls and other areas where lead based paint was used in the apartment if the building was built prior to January 1, 1960. (NYC Health Code §173.14) Landlords must provide all tenants with a pamphlet prepared by the federal Environmental Protection Agency which warns the tenants of the hazards of lead based paint and a disclosure form advising what the landlord knows about the presence of lead based paint in the apartment and building.

SAFETY

CRIME PREVENTION

Landlords are required to take minimal precautions to protect against foreseeable criminal harm. For example, tenants who are victims of crimes in their building or apartment, and who are able to prove that the criminal was an intruder and took advantage of the fact that the entrance to the building was negligently maintained by the landlord, may be able to recover damages from the landlord.

ENTRANCE DOOR LOCKS AND INTERCOMS

Multiple dwellings which were built or converted to such use after January 1, 1968 must have automatic self-closing and self-locking doors at all entrances. These doors must be kept locked at all times - except when an attendant is on duty.

If this type of building contains eight or more apartments it must also have a two-way voice intercom system from each apartment to the front door and tenants must be able to "buzz" open the entrance door for visitors.

Multiple dwellings built or converted to such use prior to January 1, 1968 also must have self-locking doors and a two-way intercom system if requested by a majority of the tenants. Landlords may recover from tenants the cost of providing this equipment. (Multiple Dwelling Law 50-a)

LOBBY ATTENDANT SERVICE

Tenants of multiple dwellings with eight or more apartments, are entitled to maintain a lobby attendant service for their safety and security, whenever any attendant provided by the landlord is not on duty. (Multiple Dwelling Law §50-c)

ELEVATOR MIRRORS

There must be a mirror in each self-service elevator in multiple dwellings so that people may see - prior to entering - if anyone is already in the elevator. (Multiple Dwelling Law §51-b; NYC Admin. Code §27-2042)

INDIVIDUAL LOCKS, PEEPHOLES AND MAIL

Tenants in multiple dwellings can install and maintain their own locks on their apartment entrance doors in addition to the lock supplied by the landlord. The lock may be no more than three inches in circumference, and tenants must provide their landlord with a duplicate key upon request.

The landlord must provide a peephole in the entrance door of each apartment. Landlords of multiple dwellings in New York City must also install a chain-door guard on the entrance door to each apartment, so as to permit partial opening of the door. (Multiple Dwelling Law §51-c; NYC Admin. Code §27-2043)

United States Postal regulations require landlords of buildings containing three or more apartments to provide secure mail boxes for each apartment unless the management has arranged to distribute the mail to each apartment. Landlords must keep the mail boxes and locks in good repair.

SMOKE DETECTORS

Outside New York City and in Buffalo, each apartment in a multiple dwelling (three or more apartments) must be equipped by the landlord with at least one smoke detector that is clearly audible in any sleeping area. (Multiple Residence Law §15; Buffalo Code Ch. 395)

Landlords of multiple dwellings in New York City must also install one or more approved smoke detectors in each apartment near each room used for sleeping. Tenants may be asked to reimburse the owner up to $10.00 for the cost of purchasing and installing each battery-operated detector. During the first year of use, landlords must repair or replace any broken detector if its malfunction is not the tenant's fault. Tenants should test their detectors frequently to make sure they work properly. (NYC Admin. Code §27-2045, §27-2046)

WINDOW GUARDS

Landlords of multiple dwellings in New York City must install government approved window guards in each window in any apartment where a child ten years old or younger lives. Tenants are required to have such guards installed. In other cases, landlords are required to install window guards provided the tenant requests them. Windows giving access to fire escapes are excluded. Protective guards must also be installed on the windows of all public hallways. Landlords must give tenants an annual notice about their rights to window guards and must provide this information in a lease rider. Rent controlled and stabilized tenants may be charged for these guards. (NYC Health Code §131.15)

TENANT'S PERSONAL RIGHTS

TENANTS' ORGANIZATIONS

Tenants have a legal right to organize. They may form, join, and participate in tenants' organizations for the purpose of protecting their rights. Landlords may not harass or penalize tenants who exercise this right. (Real Property Law §230)

RETALIATION

Landlords are prohibited from harassing or retaliating against tenants who exercise their rights. For example, landlords may not seek to evict tenants solely because tenants (a) make good faith complaints to a government agency about violations of any health or safety laws; or (b) take good faith actions to protect rights under their lease; or (c) participate in tenants' organizations. Tenants may collect damages from landlords who violate this law, which applies to all rentals except owner-occupied dwellings with fewer than four units. (Real Property Law §223-b)

RIGHT TO PRIVACY

Tenants have the right to privacy within their apartments. A landlord, however, may enter a tenant's apartment with reasonable prior notice, and at a reasonable time: (a) to provide necessary or agreed upon repairs or services; or (b) in accordance with the lease; or (c) to show the apartment to prospective purchasers or tenants. In emergencies, such as fires, the landlord may enter the apartment without the tenant's consent. A landlord may not abuse this limited right of entry or use it to harass a tenant. A landlord may not interfere with the installation of cable television facilities. (Public Service Law §228)

DISCRIMINATION

Landlords may not refuse to rent to anyone or renew leases of, or otherwise discriminate against, any person or group of persons because of race, creed, color, national origin, sex, disability, age, marital status or familial status. (Executive Law §296 (5)) In addition, in New York City, tenants are further protected against discrimination with respect to lawful occupation, sexual orientation or immigration status. Aggrieved tenants may complain to the New York City Human Rights Commission. (NYC Admin. Code §8-107(5)(a))

Landlords may not refuse to lease an apartment or discriminate against any person in the terms and conditions of the rental because that person has children living with them. This restriction does not apply to housing units for senior citizens which are subsidized or insured by the federal government or to one- or two-family owner occupied houses or manufactured homes. An aggrieved family may sue for damages against a landlord who violates this law and may recover attorneys fees. (Real Property Law §236)

In addition, a lease may not require that tenants agree to remain childless during their tenancy. (Real Property Law §237)

HARASSMENT

A landlord may not take any action to unlawfully force rent regulated tenants to vacate their apartments or to give up any rights they have under the rent laws. Landlords found guilty of harassment are subject to fines of up to $5,000 for each violation. Tenants may contact DHCR if they believe they are the victims of harassment. Under certain circumstances, harassment can constitute a class E felony. (Penal Law Article §241)

UTILITY SERVICES

HEATING SEASON

Heat must be supplied from October 1 through May 31, to tenants in multiple dwellings if: (a) the outdoor temperature falls below 55 degrees Fahrenheit, between 6 A.M. and 10 P.M., each apartment must be heated to a temperature of at least 68 degrees Fahrenheit; (b) the outdoor temperature falls below 40 degrees Fahrenheit, between the hours of 10 P.M. and 6 A.M., each apartment must be heated to a temperature of at least 55 degrees Fahrenheit. (Multiple Dwelling Law §79)

TRUTH IN HEATING

Before signing a lease requiring payment of individual heating and cooling bills, prospective tenants are entitled to receive from the landlord, a complete set or summary of the past two years' bills. These copies must be provided free upon written request. (Energy Law §17-103)

CONTINUATION OF UTILITY SERVICE

When the landlord of a multiple dwelling is delinquent in paying utility bills, the utility must give advance written notice to tenants and to certain government agencies of its intent to discontinue service. Service may not be discontinued if tenants pay the landlord's current bill directly to the utility company. Tenants can deduct these charges from future rent payments. The Public Service Commission can assist tenants with related problems.

If a landlord of a multiple dwelling fails to pay a utility bill and service is discontinued, tenants can receive payment for damages from the landlord. (Real Property Law §235-a; Public Service Law §33)

OIL PAYMENTS

Tenants in oil heated multiple dwellings may contract with an oil dealer, and pay for oil deliveries to their building, when the landlord fails to ensure a sufficient fuel supply. These payments are deductible from rent. Local housing officials have lists of oil dealers who will make fuel deliveries under these circumstances. (Multiple Dwelling Law §302-c; Multiple Residence Law §305-c)

FINDING AN APARTMENT

REAL ESTATE BROKERS

A consumer may retain a real estate broker to find a suitable apartment. New York State licenses real estate brokers and salespersons. Brokers charge a commission for their services which is usually a stated percentage of the first year's rent. The amount of the commission is not set by law and should be negotiated between the parties. The broker must assist the client in finding and obtaining an apartment before a commission may be charged. The fee should not be paid until the client is offered a lease signed by the landlord. Complaints against real estate brokers may be brought to the attention of the New York Department of State. (Real Property Law, Article 12-A)

APARTMENT INFORMATION VENDORS AND LISTING AGENCIES

Businesses that charge a fee for providing information about the location and availability of rental housing must be licensed by the State. The fees charged by these firms may not exceed one month's rent. When the information provided by the firms does not result in a rental, the entire amount of any pre-paid fee, less $15.00, must be returned to the tenant. Criminal prosecution for violations of this law may be brought by the Attorney General. (Real Property Law, Article 12-C)

OTHER PROVISIONS

APARTMENT SHARING

It is unlawful for a landlord to restrict occupancy of an apartment to the named tenant in the lease or to that tenant and immediate family. When the lease names only one tenant, that tenant may share the apartment with immediate family, one additional occupant and the occupant's dependent children, provided that the tenant or the tenant's spouse occupies the premises as their primary residence.

When the lease names more than one tenant, these tenants may share their apartment with immediate family, and, if one of the tenants named in the lease moves out, that tenant may be replaced with another occupant and the dependent children of the occupant. At least one of the tenants named in the lease or that tenant's spouse must occupy the shared apartment as his or her primary residence.

Tenants must inform their landlords of the name of any occupant within 30 days after the occupant has moved into the apartment or within 30 days of a landlord's request for this information. If the tenant named in the lease moves out, the remaining occupant has no right to continue in occupancy without the landlord's express consent. Landlords may limit the total number of people living in any apartment to comply with legal overcrowding standards. (Real Property Law §235-f)

PETS

Tenants may keep pets in their apartments if their lease permits pets or is silent on the subject. Landlords may be able to evict tenants who violate a lease provision prohibiting pets. In multiple dwellings in New York City and Westchester County, a no-pet lease clause is deemed waived where a tenant "openly and notoriously" kept a pet for at least three months and the owner of the building or his agent had knowledge of this fact. However, this protection does not apply where the animal causes damage, is a nuisance, or substantially interferes with other tenants. (NYC Admin. Code §27-2009.1(b); Westchester County Laws, Chapter 694). Tenants who are blind or deaf are permitted to have guide dogs or service dogs regardless of a no-pet clause in their lease. (Civil Rights Law §47)

SPECIAL TYPES OF HOUSING

The rights, duties and responsibilities of *Manufactured Home Park's* owners and tenants are governed by Real Property Law §233, popularly known as the "Manufactured Home Owners Bill of Rights." The DHCR has the authority to enforce compliance with this law.

The rights, duties and responsibilities of *New York City loft owners and tenants are* governed by Multiple Dwelling Law, Article 7-C. The New York City Loft Board has the authority to enforce this law.

The rights, duties and responsibilities of *New York City residential hotel owners and tenants* are governed by the rent stabilization law. The DHCR has the authority to enforce compliance with this law.

Public housing is a federally authorized and funded program in which state-charted public housing authorities develop, own and manage public housing developments. Public housing in New York State is subject to federal, state, and local laws and regulations. See 42 U.S.C. §1437 et seq.; Public Housing Law (statutes); 24 CFR Parts 912-999; and 9 NYCRR §1627 et seq. (regulations). Generally, tenants in government-involved housing are entitled to due process protections which may constrain any action by the landlord. By and large, tenants can not be evicted from their homes without proof of some "good cause" by the landlord where the government is involved in the housing, whether through direct ownership, subsidy or regulation.

www.ingramcontent.com/pod-product-compliance
Lightning Source LLC
Chambersburg PA
CBHW081802300426
44116CB00014B/2218